Transformation of Poetic Discourse in Rasa and Post-structuralist Poetics

Dedicated to My Lovely Daughter Manhavi

You are the most beautiful girl I have seen in the world.
You are like the sunshine, always giving me the feeling of
warmth, happiness, hope and peace, so proud to be your mother.

Transformation of Poetic Discourse
in
Rasa and Post-structuralist Poetics

Vandana Rajoriya

DK PRINTWORLD
Publishers of Indian Traditions

Cataloging in Publication Data — DK
[Courtesy: D.K. Agencies (P) Ltd. <docinfo@dkagencies.com>]

Rajoriya, Vandana, 1981-
Transformation of poetic discourse in rasa and post-structuralist poetics / Vandana Rajoriya.
p. cm.
Originally presented as the author's thesis (Ph. D.) — Dr. Harisingh Gour University.
Includes bibliographical references (p.).
ISBN 13: 9788124606414

1. Poetics. 2. Rasas. 3. Poststructuralism. 4. Sanskrit poetry — History and criticism. I. Title.

DDC 808.1 23

First published in India, 2012
ISBN 13: 978-81-246-0641-4 ISBN 10: 81-246-0641-2

Published and printed by:
D.K. Printworld (P) Ltd.
Regd. Office: 'Vedaśrī', F-395, Sudarshan Park
(Metro Station: Ramesh Nagar)
New Delhi — 110 015-13
Phones: (011) 2545 3975; 2546 6019 *Fax*: (011) 2546 5926
E-mail: indology@dkprintworld.com
Website: www.dkprintworld.com

Preface

THIS research study aims at providing scholars of literature and literary criticism a unique outlook. Literary criticism and literature constitute the two sides of a coin. Both are co-related, just like breathing is essential to living and the primary matter to a substantial form. *Rasa*, the Indian literary theory and post-structuralism, the western literary theory constitute two of the most important areas of study that no volume of this size can suffice without certain degree of simplification. So I've not attempted to engage in any prolonged consideration of the major critics. As will be clear from the Introduction, I have concentrated not so much on the major literary figures as on *rasa* and post-structuralist theories themselves. The account I offer here is an agenda of critical discussion in the aesthetic world. Application of *rasa* theory, in spite of its dynamic nature, has remained mostly confined to the Indian sub-continent without shedding much light on the international arena, and it is equally true of the post-structuralist theories which have hardly been applied to Indian and other (languages) in general and Sanskrit poetry in particular. So I've attempted to expound *rasa*, and apply this on canonical English poems and epics like Dante's *Divine Comedy*, Milton's *Paradise Lost* and the like, and post- structuralism, the western literary theory to canonical works of Sanskrit Poetry like '*Śṛṅgāraśataka*' of Bhartṛhari, *Mṛcchakaṭikā*' of Śūdraka, *Daśakumāracarita* of Daṇḍin, *Mudrārākṣasa* of Viśākhadatta, *Harṣacarita* of Bāṇabhaṭṭa, *Śiśupālavadha* of Māgha and the like.

The advantages of such an approach are many. First of all an attempt has been made to define *rasa* and post-structuralist theories in clear and graphical terms so as to enable my readers to become aware of such unique literary theories as *rasa* and post-structuralism. Secondly, inter-cultural application of these theories instead of analyses, gradation, evaluation and judgement in a pedagogical manner is a unique contribution.

Literary critics of the 1990s emphasise that the aim of an aesthetic criticism is to describe the artwork and to infer/draw from the art, the aesthetic that may be generated. Description of various situations in the epics and texts of my choice will certainly enable the appreciative readers/viewers to enjoy the aesthetic called the *rasa* experience.

A comparative study of the post-structuralism and *rasa* will indeed unfold the uniqueness of the latter as it dwells on reincarnation of the mystic experience that subsequently follows *śānta rasa*. But artwork here is to infer and enjoy *rasa* and post-structuralist theories. Appropriate description of the situations in the artwork will enable the readers to infer *rasa* and post-structuralist theories and enjoy them, no matter whether it is a tragedy or a comedy.

I hope that the chronological development of this study will help my readers to proceed easily through the natural progression of the study. It aims at bringing the East and West, the North and South closer to each other. Of all the literary theories, modern and ancient, eastern and western, *rasa* stands aloft as a lighthouse that keeps shining and giving out light to a very large area of the ocean guiding the vessels. At the outset, the scope of this study may seem to be of glaring artificiality and high hopes. Indeed, the structure of this study is so planned in a chronological and sequential order that the readers, I hope, will perceive and read through the lines, the things I describe, and enjoy and embrace *rasa*, the Sanskrit literary theory, as a unique literary theory.

Having declared some of the unique characteristics of this study and certain limitations, I would like to state that there are writers, who have extensively dwelt on *rasa* and post-structuralism; for further reference the appendices include bibliographies and an index on all major critics and the works of art.

Acknowledgements

COMPLETION of this thesis is a highly satisfying accolade for me and I find myself rejoicing over this achievement, but credit for this achievement must go to my revered guide Bhavatosh Indra Guru. He is not only an erudite scholar but also a great human being. His ungrudging and invaluable guidance has been instrumental in leading this work to emerge successfully in the present form. It is almost impossible to quantify his help that I received during the last three years. Without his guidance, my thesis would never have been finished in time. Furthermore without his timely help and patience, I could perhaps never have worked on application of post-structuralism on Sanskrit poetry. I extend my profound indebtedness and gratitude to him.

I offer my sincere gratitude to A.K. Awasthi, Head of the Department and Nivedita Maitra, Senior Lecturer in the Department of English and other European Languages, Hari Singh Gour University, Sagar (M.P.) and Nisha Indra Guru, Department of English, Government Girls Degree College, Sagar, for their constant inspiration, cooperation and encouragement.

Of the many libraries, where it had been necessary to spend long hours of fascinating exploration, I owe the greatest debt to the Jawaharlal Nehru Library of Hari Singh Gour University, Sagar (M.P.). I am deeply grateful to the director and staff for all their willing assistance.

The work thus undertaken and accomplished has made

me experience many ups and downs, although I had been putting up with it, but there are some people who have knowingly or unknowingly played a major role in its completion. Here, I acknowledge my indebtedness, from the innermost recess of my heart, to my husband Umakant Rajoriya for having performed various invaluable tasks ranging from the secretarial to the menial. His subtle blend of tolerance and occasional exasperation has been a source of great encouragement as also an ever present warning against the dangers of a consuming interest from becoming an obsession. I am also thankful to my mother-in-law, Sunder Devi Rajoriya, bhabhis Anjani and Rani, Krishnakanti didi and Krishnakant bhaiya for their constant inspiration and moral support rendered by them. It would have been very difficult to finish the task in time had Krishna didi not shouldered the household responsibilities with me. I am grateful to the kids Animesh, Akash, Anshu and Moksha for their love and affection.

My papa, Tulasi Ram Tripathi, plays the role of a guiding spirit behind each and every work that I undertake and accomplish. If I am in this field, it is just because of him. I am extremely thankful to him for being a mentor to me. It is really difficult to find words of gratefulness for my mama, Indira Tripathi, the pillar of my life. How can I express indebtedness to my sisters, Yamini, Meenakshi and Deepika and brother, Ashutosh, who have always been eagerly walking by my side for anything and everything. Yamini's composure always gave me the strength to keep patience for such a long and strenuous task. Meenu's spirit never failed in giving me the zest, the killing instinct required to do some real research work. I would also like to thank her for helping me in proofreading. Although it applies to them all, but I would especially like to thank my youngest sister Deepika (Sona) who always eagerly and gladly took the pain of extending a helping hand to me, no matter when and in which form I asked for. Ashutosh's faith in me and my 100 per cent success rate was, in fact, such a relief in very tough and trying times.

I would like to thank Rameti, who is like an elder daughter to me, for happily taking care not only of my daughter but also me and my family throughout the research work.

I am also thankful to Ratnesh bhaiya for helping me in typing the manuscript.

Finally, the most important thanks here go to my little daughter Manhavi, for giving me the space required to finish the work in time. Although she may not have known what it was about, but she has given me a sense of purpose and nurtured me as only an understanding child can.

Above all I'm grateful to the Almighty whose blessings made the completion of this Thesis possible.

Vandana Rajoriya

List of Illustrations

Figures

Tables

Contents

1

Introduction

THE creation of an artistic situation encompasses a necessity of indicating a suitable preference for logical, rational and structural synthesis. In fact, the range, extent and variety of functional and conjunctive situations arising at the behest of a vast range of concentrated forms of association within the categories like thought, experience, imagination, language, words, letters, syllables and the like would obtain, definitely, a form of consideration in that the events that constitute an artistry, are also those which bring about a compulsory assortment of the whole situation. There are, at least, two important views which settle the argument we have raised here. In the first place, the primordial enrichment of the participating categories evokes, on its own account, an equivalent of universal form and the transfer, communication and comprehensibility of the formed and the received contents would be adequately befitting in relation to the invoked intensity of comprehension. In the second place, the situation of communication of content to the medium and medium to the content, is received and transferred simultaneously, and for this reason, the methodology of an ideal artistic form would always be open to the necessity of valuation and assessment.

In *rasa* and the post-structuralist theoretical systems a due recognition has been made of this situation with confirmed and rationalised differences. In *rasa*, for example, the conduct of the situation has to be appropriately incorporated into the construction of scheme, method, modality, paradigm, and model of the whole situation in such a way that the effect of presentation and the strength of reception of the logic of the content, construct and the categories are nearly the same and also fulfil the necessary interpretative consequence of rationalisation of the categories.

The beginning of a creative situation in *rasa* could be one of the ideal instances of the transmutation of an observation into an object, hence the resolution of an object into event. Accordingly, the principality of the universal realisation is immediately and forthwith established. To this extent, *rasa* deals with the basic necessity of developing concrete universals for the evolution of an experience into a significant experience, language into an ideal language, and because of this, the categories which are involved in the making of *rasa* presuppose a commitment for independent, systematic and coherent sets of transformation to achieve this ideological modelisation. This attitude, to accord an authority and approval to the idea of synthesis, is really very distinct and significant in the creative principles expounded in *rasa*. There can be two distinct and different stages for the completion of the entire process of realisation and exposition of an experience; at the very beginning, the inquisitive models are created through the meditative excellence constituted proportionally in *bhāva* and simultaneously, the greater and richer part of the experience is relocated in the *sthāyī bhāva* and the condition of relocation is functionally idealised by an act of homogeneous distribution of the contents. The next stage, that comes realistically as a consequence, is the transfer of concentrated experience into reversible forms of mutation, and, for the purpose, *vibhāva* and *anubhāva* could be simultaneously the standards of achievement proposed and obtained. Accordingly, further systematisation and idealisation is approved by introducing an indiscrete rationalisation of the infinite contents from the beginning and till the end. This process is designated as the phase of *sañcārī bhāva*s and the most realistic, realised and realisable form of experience thus obtained is to be called *rasa*. What is important to learn and note is the way in which creation, composition, comprehension and exposition of the entire categorical apparatus (*bhāva, sthāyī bhāva, vibhāva, anubhāva, sañcārī bhāva, śabda, pada* and *vākya*) is formatively conceived. The priority of strength built around the specific categories like *bhāva* and others is an instance of the point that random functioning of the categories is concretely marginalised, and, for that matter, only the absolute and concrete universals are observed. The correspondence of the functional categories to figural forms is another important occasion to create the highest concentration of denoted objects. The act of correspondence between a formal function and aberrated figures approves a methodology of inter-functional transformation. Strength of a category in *bhāva* is located primarily and meaningfully in the universal feature that it could develop around itself. In fact, it would be better to say that an artistic experience is inverted proportionally in *rasa,* and therefore, the measure of direction, proportion is equal to the length of growth and expansion of the whole experiential notation. In *rasa,* the distinction of distribution of content is homogenised while the function of transformation is to mark, identify and heterogenise the entire form of creation.

II

It is now possible to understand how the creation of an ideal artistic situation is comprehended in accordance with the nature of transformation involved in each, for example, at the beginning, we could understand that experience is inducted and approved through the credit of strength observed in the functional part of the category; hence *bhāva* begins the process of creation by inventing the recognised, recognisable, known, knowable, comprehended, comprehensible forms of attitudes, perception, thought, judgement, imagination and experience. It certainly confirms the larger strength to the extent of purity and upholds a valid presentation of an experiential system or code or the effect of such a graduation is only remarkable inasmuch as the extent, the priority, emphasis and inclination are revived in the most extraordinary generative form. This is, in a way, a primordial facility that is accorded as an act of reconstitution, and, in *bhāva*, the principle of synthesis holds the merit. This manner of imitation of an experience is really very remarkable and exceptional inasmuch as it could cover every possible situation of the organic attitude, for example, it could be as various as *rati, hāsa, śoka, krodha, utsāha, bhaya, jugupsā, vismaya, nirveda*. The inception so generated becomes manifest through the condition of certainty and confirmation of evidences generated. In the second stage of exposition, the exposed and invented terms of the categories, for example, *karuṇa* in *śoka*, *utsāha* in *vīra* and *nirveda* in *śānta* are appropriately redistributed till the time exceptional value variants are defined through rediscovered coordinates of the artistic forms. Here we could find that symmetry, similarity, coherence, suitability and homogeneity of figural and formal contents are obtained and the strength of the function is approved in the second important universal known by the name *sthāyī bhāva*. The necessity of conjunction and the manner of inquisition, both are directly proportional to each other inasmuch as *sthāyī bhāva*s locate and distribute a function of the category in accordance with the privacy of cognitive universality that is immense and infinite till the beginning and up to the end. The presentative excellence of the situation is now exposed to the evolutionary sequence of communication generated as a rule in the third stage of exposition in the form and content.

III

The act of evolution is received and appropriated through two vertical codes of inter-substitutional communication, namely, *vibhāva* and *anubhāva*. Here in this stage, the complete reorganisation of the total strength of function attributed to the participating categories (*bhāva, sthāyī bhāva, vibhāva, anubhāva, sañcārī bhāva, śabda, pada* and *vākya*) is listed and indexed and cyclically mutated till the time the function of structure is rationalised as the function of form, and hence, the formation of absolutes in the artistic situation appear to be nearing the end of completion. The principality or the conceptual motives, plans and organisation conceive a general reaffirmation through projective synthesis obtained now as a role and the model that none the less comes to obtain this projection of strength is called as *sañcārī bhāvas*. The models of application which are conscious and homogenous, unconscious or heterogeneous, both are brought to a large-scale conviction or commitment, hence a genuine and an ideal artistic formation now emerges. Now, in accordance with the principles established in the foregoing and the account that has been taken, furnishes a general scheme of representation of *rasa* as a reinvention of cognitive universals with regard to the application of concentrated models, synthesised contents, and cohesive medium and the function of *rasa* is to concretise and rationalise the whole artistic formation in such a way that emergence of an ideal universal within an ideal artistic situation is possible.

The conduct of the categories (*bhāva, sthāyī bhāva, vibhāva, anubhāva, sañcārī bhāva, śabda, pada* and *vākya*) in *rasa*, primarily puts forth an imposive necessity with regard to the constitution and creation of an authoritative meaning with implied assertion and large-scale conceptual manifestations. One of the earliest situations recorded in the simulacrum of considered effects of *rasa* upon the artistic situations is that it turns the distributive necessities of the contents into coherence of purity, and, following this, indivisibility, trans-impersonality, wonder, surprise, extraordinary rationalisation emerge as the confirmed objects of knowledge. In each, there is a merit involved inasmuch as the reception of the contents and presentation of the medium both are regulated through the scale of effect they constitute. It is because of this that *rasa* is necessarily a grand principle of constitution, composition, creation and comprehension of the artistic form and the significance of the situation has been thoroughly explained in the foregoing.

IV

In the post-structuralist theories, specially those advanced and suggested by Derrida, Lacan and Foucault, one can understand how the independence of a category, say, for example, language or experience could produce infinite multiples without its own entering into any correspondence whatsoever with the generated multiples. For this reason post-structuralism is one such situation in which inadequacy of systematic correspondence and interrelationship between meaning and language is created, developed and perpetuated right from the beginning and till the end. One of the reasons why the situation tends to be like this may be that the evolution growth and mutation of the artistry involved in the content of language and the meaning is reverted and hence turned into semi-cyclical or half-cyclical inversions, therefore, the significance of interpretation is never adequately sustained. This may have one of the principal errors of progression, since evolution of language has a credit inasmuch as it could revive and re-invent nearly all the primordial forms, and when it undergoes a change, it must strengthen the necessary structures which will include both the orthodox and the recent ones. While looking at the substance of discoursal representation made by Derrida,

Lacan and Foucault, an opportunity is provided to find out why exactly the situation like the above comes into existence.

The form of language and the nature of meaning do not have the suitability of a place-specific or time-specific reorientation, for this reason, language is primarily a scheme of uncertain interrelationship in which the models and constructs like the letters, syllables, words and the sentences have an indefinite figural and formal situation and every form of the concept only proves the point that there is nothing in terms of the content motive of the language that may build up an associative or conjunctive interrelationship with the corresponding, preceding and succeeding models of the contents. For this reason, basically, the configuration of the contents is largely half-cyclical and subsequently it cannot approach any conjunction whatsoever with the forthcoming, upcoming and lapsed formations. Similar account seems to be valid and complete for the formative terms in the meaning if one could believe what Derrida, Foucault and Lacan have to say. One would definitely understand the instability of grossly inadequate generative contents in the meaning. For Lacan and others, meaning isn't the reception and exposition of a length of value, it is rather only the lengthening of value in such a way that commitment to interact and interpret either object or event within it turns out to be ineffectual.

The progress of an event or an object always underscores the fact that preceding content is formatively united and engaged, yet however, the receptive material continues to build up a scheme of classification having known outward or inward turn of the significance. This characteristic of post-structuralism poses one of the great problems in understanding as to how and why even within the progression, a category in itself, could suggest the resolution. In Foucault, for example, the creation, perpetuation, prolongation and establishment of a discourse doesn't find any meaning, whatsoever, in relation to the external formations, therefore, the ideational history of institutions like society, culture, religion, literature and to an extent history itself is rendered incoherent inasmuch as the basic unity that may invent corollary for participating models is never really evident. In Lacan, on the other hand, the growth of linguistic form from the unconscious and appearance of value as a model in the conscious is obstructed by a condition of comprehension, therefore, a child could understand and create a meaning when and only when he could repose a form in himself. Similarly, an adult could comprehend the necessity of situation in language when and only when he could revive the role, function and privacy of primitive unconscious forms into his conscious. While we work out an application of Lacanian situation in literary discourse, we can only understand that the creation of a category in the unconscious and re-inventions of the same construct in the conscious, the observer will need a concentrated commitment and an attitude of conviction till the time the process of evolution is accomplished and complete. One of the points that must be observed in this is that evolution of a category is never proposed or interpreted as an idealisation of meaning in the manner of an assured or confirmed commitment, rather it is only an explanatory motive invented for the sake of classification. Such an exposition only strengthens the potential and possibility of aberration inasmuch as the observer may or may not dislocate the possibility of invention or reinvention, accordingly, the interpretation of the situation would remain by and large incomplete.

In Derrida, on the still other hand, the presentation of language as a category undergoes a systematic degeneration just for the reason that the primitive form of language and the orthodox conceptualisation of the language and recent re-invention of a possibility of modelisation are logically invalidated. Language doesn't stay as a form of categorical classification because of the fact that every unit found in it is in a constant state of mutation and the process of mutation doesn't have any strength in generation. Subsequently, the definition of language undergoes a great change in Derridean Scheme. He believes that language is inadequate as a comprehensive term because the units (letters) are not arranged and organised in accordance with the method of correlation. No preceding and no succeeding event, discharges the functionality through the possibility of a meaning that should have been the instrument of effect. It appears as if the separation of resolution from the event, object from the subject (say, for example, a syllable from the word and word from the syllables) is only lengthened rather than being conjunct with each other. Such a necessity becomes functional and operative since the inception of language has any vehicle or form of organisation. The intended effects are not procured nor are even brought to any recognition while the motion of the contents is always progressing. This may have a preliminary foundation and general application in the deviance of language as an assured motive for the formation of the contents and the situation that Derrida is developing seems to be derived from the epistemic uncertainty of the native experiences. What actually happens is that the originary strength of an experience is assuredly random and when the situation is introduced to the external space or the universe at large, the receptive position of the categories is both at odds and at variance with the initial projection; consequently, we can well understand how and why every form of concept is essentially inclined towards a prejudicial motive and for the similar reasons no meaningful situation could be provided for the creation of a concept as organisation. This view of experiential indifference certainly helps us in opting for a position and viewpoint in Derridean interpretation of the linguistic and emotive categories. If language is exclusive to the extent that it obtains its progression only for the length of exclusion, the relevance of the effect so created must find its explanation and interpretation through the random functioning of native experiences. The philosophical system of inquiry built in Europe after Descartes, force the presumptions and assurances to be normally projected by a sequence of regression, accordingly, the function of an ideology in the same regard would obviously be wanting and lacking and the resultant experience would continue to be consequential and effective only in so far as it got off from the random system. The condition of experience found to be created in either the intellect or in the imaginative situation there would always be a motive for inclination, and inclination is assuredly the presupposition of an infinite interaction. In post-structuralist conditionalities, the form of function attending the language and experience could be held to be opposed through the effects, accents, unities and emphases, hence, Derrida or Lacan or Foucault — each has to put up a necessity of finding a form of meaning in language or experience in such a way that the result of the situation could be brought about. One of the essential features of this situation is that it categorises the unity of form and unity of content through an independent assortment and similarity that the prospect of concept formation isn't very much regulated through association or conjunction, rather it is built around a system of aberration in which only the visual part of the category performs a function and the inward content, context or the medium do not respond to the crisis raised invariably through such an account.

V

The ideological perceptions conceived in *rasa* and post-structuralist theories invent a rather distinct form of transformational configuration of the categories like language, thought, experience, imagination, *bhāva*, *sthāyī bhāva*, *vibhāva*, *anubhāva*, *sañcārī bhāva*, *śabda*, *pada* and *vākya* to opt for an actual strength in artistic formation. In *rasa*, for example, the basic nature of resolution of an object into event is presented by a series of pure, harmonious, refined, idealised and canonised forms of the enrichment of the categories. The nature of change as suggested in *rasa* of form into content or content into form is primarily what is built around the creation of independent assortment in the first place of language and experience and thereafter the multiple division of both the language and experience into committed and concrete universals, and this process continues till the time the categories are idealised and universalised. For this reason, we must think that *rasa* brings forth creation, interpretation in the first place, of the participating models in the artistic situation, and, in the second place, it suggests an organised system of comprehension of the created experience through the discharge of pre-disposed, post-disposed and proto-disposed situations. It would mean that the constitution of an experience is not nearly an event of existence in the text or beyond the text, it rather recovers and constitutes a series of functions for its perpetuation in the temporal as well as timeless formulations recorded in the generative events. With this particular situation in hand, the conduct of transformation must be obtained by including the principal effects of cognition in and around the denotative and suggestive facts, consequently, every experience will have a strength in inter-reversibility as a part of continuation of the movement and motion of the artistic contents. Such a fact necessitates a further inquiry by finding the concern for denotation as a method in comprehending the larger aspects of resolution. As has been suggested *rasa* could give rise to varieties of denotative facts and figures in such a way that each situation would tend to achieve the state of complete indivisibility and even to an extent the absolute purities. It must be understood that the event of suggestion, in *rasa*, is invariably inherent in the enrichment of *bhāva* as a mode of cognition. Similarly, the consequent effects of *bhāva* would propose the creation of both external and internal systems of reversibility of manner and method of suggestion. The intensity of denotation and suggestion is effective from the beginning of the artistic formation till the end of the situation and the intermediate stages are completed and occupied by the cyclical coordinates of synthesis and convergence. For this reason, *bhāva* is implicated at length by the *sthāyī bhāva* and the upward and downward suggestibility is always approved by the rotation, mutation and the variation brought about into the system by the same situation. The necessity of understanding the qualitative nature of transformation is not, in any way, brought about by the obvious predetermination of the valid conceptualisation of the content. In fact, the primordial strengthening exposes the contents to form specific and independent states of universality, and for this reason, *rasa* is practically as well as theoretically the most effective construction to handle the whole artistic idealisation. In post-structuralism the preliminary groundwork of transformation of object into event is suggested by reduction, regression, divergence and deviance of the contents within and outside the specified categories. In fact, the time at which either the language or experience purports to interact a situation conducive for the growth or expansion, the situated contents open up themselves only for the sake of stationary motives inasmuch as each fall of a movement begets only a functioning of denotation. The reversibility of the whole form is stopped and the motion cannot continue beyond a specified limit. For example, in Derridean scheme of the arrangement of the categories, the strength of formative part is not directly proportional to the realistic generation of the contents and cleavage within the categories is primarily very meaningful and remarkable. Similarly, in Lacan and Foucault, the magnitude of presentation of a category is equal to the expanded version of the intended and desirable proportion, and because of this language and experience, both function in accordance with the achieved unity within the system, yet however, the normative part of an experience is once again only half-cyclical and half-proportional. In fact, the projection of expansion within language and experience by identifying the strengthened unit, for example, strengthened syllable or concrete experience, conscious or unconscious, will be the part of a reduced denotation operating at the behest of a prejudicial, instinctual urgency and in turn is guided by the conscious or unconscious form of reality. In Foucault especially, the event of resolution is exceptionally suggested by a specific interrelationship within the acquired thought and intended idealisation of the thought in relation to the purported institutionalisation of the primitive terms. The event of rationalisation does not meaningfully incorporate every formal content presented in coherence or the order, and, for this reason, there cannot be successfully a description of, let us say, history, religion or culture, or any form whatsoever. In approved and accepted literary discourses the separation of object from the subject and event from the object would once again present an unrealistic formative notion with regard to each. On the whole, transformation as an event, object or institution doesn't have qualitative categorisation as it is obtained in the case of *rasa*.

VI

The circumstance and necessity of finding out a meaning or significance of text as a generative condition procured and obtained on account of the idealisation of artistic situation has a manner, mode, nature and authority of interpretation in *rasa* and post-structuralist situation. In *rasa*, the text is coherent, absolute, pure, and indivisible, and, precisely, the most concentrated aspect of the evolution of language into experience, and for this reason, the intensity of valuation and composition always falls within the purview of cognition, correlation, conjunction, injunction, modelisation and the like. It would be an aspect of inquisition to mould the system of inquiry by saying that the condition of textuality in *rasa* is in direct proportion to the observance of supra-rationalisation of the language and experience. The length, the boundary, the margin and the dimension are both inclusive and exclusive just for the reason that the movement of the content from content to the medium is acquired by a direct union and correspondence with the internal form and external space. It is because of this that, in *rasa*, the formation of text is realistically valid from the beginning and till the end. And it is also an important aspect to note that the function of text is both communication and presentative in view of the situation that the cognised model and correlated proportion of functional, inter-functional, denotative, inter-denotative, suggestive, inter-suggestive, substitutional and inter-substitutional variants always reciprocate the spatial, linear and cyclical motion of the linguistic and emotive categories. In post-structuralism, however, the condition of text is logically intended through the deviation of legitimate and approved cognitive strength, and therefore, the movement and language of experience is thoroughly disproportional to the length that it desires to achieve. In fact, it is absolutely significant in the scheme of organisation of the categories of language and experience that the intention of the content is not homogeneous to the limit of expansion and consequently no geometrical arrangement of the situation could be observed, achieved, found or exposed. Accordingly, the chief determinants of textuality like event, context, medium, object and the observer are lengthened and disproportionately interacted for the sake of an achievement of the extremity of rationalisation. In the wake of such a consequence, we can only observe that the textual condition is approved not through direct synthesis but by a margin and proportion of uncertain and reduced scheme of resolution.

VII

Discussions on the foregoing observations would suggest long, distinct, defined and discreet figures of explanation, valuation, assessment and revaluation of the system of the creation, comprehension, communication and exposition of the categories participating in the creation of an ideal artistic situation with differential version and differential notes of assertion in *rasa* and post-structuralist theoretical frameworks, and, in the forthcoming discussions, we have evaluated the situation with an equal generosity of intention.

2

Formative Principles

RASA is a principle of creation, construction and universalisation of those forms of artistic methods and situations which are normally idealised in the nearest possible instance, and therefore, the beginning of a valid definition of *rasa*[1] must begin with the presentation of *rasa* as a form of genuine, ideal and absolute situation. For that matter, *rasa* is conceived as an instrument and apparatus to present the best possible form of human consciousness to the interpretation of both the medium and the content. In the generation of a model of conscious the underlying categories specified as a part of both verbal and non-verbal models, the merit is immediately understood. *Rasa* begins as the highest expression by composing both similarity and the difference between received and expressed contents. In receiving a content of formation it always transmutes every single situation to the process of standardisation. This effect could be considered as an elementary and native principle that generates the most authentic expressions.

---

1. The idea of *rasa* is primarily a notion to advance the argument that the artistic situation could be grown and developed to the extent of universality in such a way that truth, precision and absolute are recurrent and basic to the achievement of such a situation. See for example *Sāhityadarpaṇa* of Viśvanātha Kavirāja:

   धर्मार्थकाममोक्षेषु वैचक्षण्यं कलासु च ।
   करोति कीर्तिं प्रीतिं च साधुकाव्यनिषेवणम् ।।

   — *Sāhityadarpaṇa* of Viśvanātha Kavirāja with *Vimalā* (Hindī commentary) by Śrī Śālgrāmśāstrī, 1956, Motilal Banarsidass, p. 10

The structure of an experience that continues the form of ideal expression generates wide-ranging possibilities with regard to the formation of the meaning both within and outside the artistic environments. In *rasa,* there is a model bearing condition that upholds the merit of complete and perfect content formation. It must be understood that both as a principle and as a rule in an artistic situation, the strength of a category must be based on the range of possibilities and extent of transformations that can be accomplished within a single idealised content of a participating formation.

In understanding this definition of *rasa* it is necessary that one should focus one's attention on the empirical and the rational form that induct and obtain the division of an artistic situation into number of independent variables and hence, continues the process of optimum selection by the virtue of immediate as well as permanent denotation. In this regard, it might be a term of understanding that *rasa* is so necessary a part of both behaviour consciousness and experience that in an artistic creation, its utility and presence is simultaneously conceived and established.

The method of understanding *rasa* doesn't have any limitations whatsoever on the grounds of its elevation, its supposed height and its possible universalisation. In either of the situations, it remains part and parcel of the native experience, native location and extraordinary transmutation into native centre from which experience can be seen to be forming it and presenting itself for the sake of comprehension and interpretation. It now appears worth the while to say that the *rasa* is an extensive process of realisation of the total and absolute forms of experience by (specific) arrangement of the content and medium within and outside the artistic situation.

Conception of Categories in Rasa Theory

It could be seen from our discussion in the foregoing that *rasa* is a manner of interpreting every known and possible category that appears before the consciousness, experience, perception, imagination, thought and language and there can be no difficulty in accommodating ourselves to the presentation of the conceptions by introducing the whole notion through the following figural form:

RASA

⇓

Conception
(Structure)

⇓

Synthesis

⇓

Exposition

⇓

Application

fig. **1.1**: Scheme of understanding the *rasa* theory.

This is quite obvious in explaining the scheme of understanding and the situation that is generated in a historical tradition of *rasa* in the Indian tradition.

Bharatamuni, at a rather uncertain time, approximately 6,000 to 8,000 years ago, came out with a theory, which he called *rasa,* and since then this concept or theory has become a part of artistic interpretation, comprehension, evaluation and realisation. It is also quite interesting to note the fact that the debate initiated by Bharatamuni on the ways to acquire a validity for concrete experience and an acknowledgement for the presence of same experience in the object or event that is being attended to, brought in a remarkably large number of commentators and interpreters. Of the most important of the commentators/interpreters were Bhaṭṭa Nāyaka, Bhaṭṭa Lollaṭa, Śrī Śaṅkuka, Abhinavagupta, Paṇḍit Rāj Jagannāth, Mahimabhaṭṭa and Kṣemendra. In each of these commentators the concept of *rasa* underwent a new meaning and new interpretation. In these 6,000 or 7,000 years the argumentative function of *rasa* and the receptive effect of *rasa* created a sound base for the projection of a theory and because of this the ideational features involved in *rasa*, are merited through a process of interaction between the object and the subject and the medium and the content.

In the beginning, it appears worth our while to consider how Bharatamuni proposes significance for content as well as medium construction for an otherwise ideal artistic situation. He observes:

> विभावानुभावव्यभिचारिसंयोगाद्रसनिष्पत्तिः।[2]
> *vibhavānubhāva-vyabhicārī-saṁyogāt rasa-niṣpattiḥ*।
> — *Nāṭyaśāstra*, VI.1

> In understanding the idea of *rasa* one has to consider the fact that precision and eminence of *rasa* is brought about through the canonisation of categories like *bhāva*, *sthāyī bhāva*, *vibhāva*, *anubhāva*, *sañcārī bhāva*, *śabda*, *pada* and *vākya*.

In this observation there is a method to explain and interpret how meaning, content, medium, and the object constituting the core of an artistic situation are created and subsequently how they build up a concrete framework for their own functions and structure. Accordingly, any ideal formation in artistry shall have to begin with the presentation of *bhāva* or universal disposition and for this *bhāva* we will have the creation of *vibhāva*, *anubhāva* and *sañcārī bhāvas* simultaneously

2. *Gaṅgānāthajhā-Granthamālā* (vol. 14), Nāṭyaśāstra of Bharatamuni (part 2) with *Abhinavabhāratī by Abhinavaguptācārya* & *Manoramā* (Hindi commentary) by Pārasanātha Dvivedī, 1996, ed. Dr. Pārasanātha Dvivedī, Sampurnanand Sanskrit University, Varanasi p. 34.

and separately. This would suggest that the realisable experience always enters into a correlation with sub-ordinate categories, hence, the highest function of this structure is to identify and define the inter-association between two immediate categories like *vibhāva* and *anubhāva* (external and internal objects of expression) are brought to a conjunction through the transformation of values underlying them.

Bharatamuni says that the development of *bhāva* as an assorted and concentrated effect is, in fact, the first value principle that could bring every other minor situation and turn them into wholesome aggregates. With this point in mind, we can think of dividing the absolute part of experience into three important segments, first inter, second intra and third intermediate forms of meaning generation. In the inter-phase of meaning formation, the contents of *bhāva* are homogeneous throughout the different coordinates of an artistic situation and the effect of distribution is combined in network of conjunctions through which the transfer of an ideal and a concrete universal takes place. For example, in an artistic creation the poet willing to suggest a method for construction of an experience and transferring an experience shall have to accord a necessary commitment to this issue of homogeneous distribution of the contents of experience. It is also quite necessary to suggest that the experience, where it moves from one universal to the other and other to yet another and another to still another, it dislocates the denotative form of the content or category and Bharatamuni, because of this, speaks of *saṁyoga*[3] as a necessary conjunction to find out the medium for inter-association, and in the present circumstance, we can understand that the earliest denotative significance occurring

3. The formation of an ideal artistic situation while the process of expression and reception of the contents in *rasa* is underway is borne out of an idea that emotive and verbal facts are so adequately transferred through correlatives to the text that their release from the text becomes imminent. See Ānandavardhana in *Dhvanyāloka*.

within the category is of most important comprehensive type because from this and this only the effect of inter-formation could take place. There can be no doubt as to why Bharatamuni begins with *vibhāva* and closes the terms on *saṁyoga* with an inclusion of *anubhāva* and *sañcārī bhāva*s. The answer to this question is very simple. One has to understand only the fact that concentrated universal beginning with the first term *vibhāva* revolved and rotated both horizontally and vertically through the effect of ideal function created at the instance of this movement.

In the inter-stage of association, the form and function of the categories are very exclusive in nature and because of this it becomes possible to correlate and combine the primary and secondary scales of relational effect, and in the present case, one has to find out that *vibhāva* is only primarily a scale of effect while *sañcārī* is a secondary mutation of the whole situation and the action of this evolution from primary notation to secondary denotation is just to merit the synchronisation of synthesis by both the real and empirical actions. The conception of motion acquired from the external space has an optimum validity in the remarks put forth by Bharatamuni and for that matter the universe that contains the arrangement of particles at random is, in fact, a model conception for the transfer of primary term into the recognisable space, and quite naturally, the extent of observation made by Bharata bears upon the expansion of perception beyond the limits imposed on the human consciousness. On the other hand, the realisation of the primary and the secondary terms through a range of affordable perceptions could always commit itself to the meaningful interpretation.

The method of constructing a basis of association so far as the primary categories introduced by Bharatamuni is concerned, we can rely on the fact that *bhāva* has a length of expansion and also stretch for the sake of measurement and for that matter where it is issued right at the creation of an intensity of realisation of an external event, the observer is necessarily in a position to conduct nearly all the cohesive forms of perception. In this regard it would be necessary to examine the possibility of having an ability of denotation so far as *bhāva* as an object of expression as well as model of reception is concerned. The appearance of *bhāva* could be a logical re-structuring of external and internal sources of generation of artistic contents and when the perception is motivated, it activates a continuous series of displacements and from this the second important aspect of Bharata's, i.e. *vibhāva*, the intermediate form and by all means a cohesive unit reduces the figural margins obtained in other categories like *anubhāva* and *sañcārī bhāva*, hence quite affirmatively, brings about the various acts of association and conjunction. This could be understood to be as the beginning of wholeness inasmuch as *vibhāva* could easily dislocate a primary term of significance through both inception and reception. This is to prove the point that in an artistic situation the continuity of refinement is recorded and comprehended as a process of addition, and for this reason, Bharatamuni could easily conceive the situation to be primarily the matter of a succession of additions in which comprehensibility is established as a reliable and valid basis.

The activity of synthesis in which reception, inception and inversion and to an extent mutation of the transformation is apprehended, must be the greatest idea to deal with immediate as well as permanent forms of an artistic situation.[4] The style

4. One of the important evidences of the fact that *rasa* opts for a total and complete enrichment is based on the reversibility principle created by an exceptional movement of the categories from the point of beginning to the point of end in such a way that both are capable of being created in each. See *Abhinavbhāratī* of Abhinavagupta.

of composition by obtaining the worth of artistic value within a category is thereby mitigated by a sequence of changes in such a way that concrete universals are obtained, must be the important event associated with the whole theoretical framework. In the continuation of the sequence of injunction we can arrive at the third important possibility and that is the intermediate addition of the categories mentioned by Bharatamuni. In this, the content orientation and content formation, both are dislocated at the point of junction and through it an intersection is established and the absolute part of the experience is conceived.[5]

To understand the manner of comprehending the effective position of Bharatamuni's observation it seems worth our while to look at the following utterances in Rimbaud's *Fetes de la faim*:

> Feasts of Hunger. My hunger Anne, Anne, run away on your donkey. If I have any taste, it is for hardly anything but earth's soil and stones. Dinn! dinn! dinn! dinn! I feed on air, rock, soil, iron. Turn round and round, hungers, graze the meadows of sound! Then the nice vibrant venom of the morning glories; the stones a poor man breaks, the old slabs of churches, the beach, pebbles, children of deluge, bread, loves lying in the gray valleys! My hungers, they are crumbs of black air; the azure bell-ringer; its my stomach that aches. It's unhappiness. Loves have come out on earth! I am going to the flesh of overripe fruit, from the heart of the furrow I pick lambs lettuce and the violet. My hunger, Anne, Anne! run away on your donkey.[6]
>
> — Cited in Culler's *The Pursuit of Signs* p. 93

5. While there is a formation of direct correlation between communicable experience and received experience, the manner of synthesis of the categorical events in *rasa* is by cognition and displacement, the effect of each is situated on an exact scale of enrichment. See for further discussion on the subject *Rasagaṅgādhara* of Gaṅgānātha.

6. Rimbaud's, "fetes de la faim" cited in Jonathan Culler's "The Pursuit of Signs", *Routledge Classics* 2001, London EC_4p_4EE, p. 93.

In these verses the configuration of principle *bhāva* is extraordinary and remarkable. The poet opens the description with a consideration of mockery, denial, reception and award and thereby creates two different centres of argument. In the one, we have those who have the privilege of everything right from the excellent food to the other bounties of the world and, on the other hand, there are those who do not have any privilege or position, and therefore, they always run short of eating. Between these two formations, there is always an opposition of presumption, imagination, fantasies and possible resolution of the crisis.

The speaker who speaks, laughs at the destiny of hunger given to him by the god and the same laughter in a moment is turned into a fantasy for a possible ride with a lady as a sheer release (donkey) through a mockery added to the humiliation and suffering. At the very beginning the speaker laments through *karuṇa* about the "feasts of hunger" compounded by a multiplication of *karuṇa* by "my hunger". The genitive formation includes a new variant for this narrative of pathos presented through both laughter and lamentation. The resolution of *karuṇa* into an absolute form of comedy carries the divisive medium and the content and in that way the expressions "On your Donkey", "Dinn! dinn! dinn! dinn!" the stylistic figuration presents still important facets of a composite *bhāva* that keeps moving around the changing and shifting and always displacing mood. For example, the speaker conveys the sense of *karuṇa* (hunger) and then proceeds to understand god's mockery on his face by a projected fun at this that: "I feed on air, rock, soil, iron. Turn round and round, hungers, graze the meadows of sound! Then the nice vibrant venom of the morning glories; the stones a poor man breaks." This evolution evidently suggests that even within *karuṇa* and *hāsa* the attendant mood is greatly changing. The speaker considers all the possibilities like, for example, "the poor man working", "god residing inside the temple", "the vast ocean flowing uninterruptedly" and at the end of creation the *mahāpralaya* (deluge) abandoning everything except for the children of god with a piece of bread in their hand. The range of *sañcārī bhāva*s from certainty to uncertainty and uncertainty to infinity and from infinity to reality could be immediately considered to be the magnificence of the poet. In this we can understand the *vibhāva* in food and *anubhāva* presented through the stone, the slab, the deluge, black air, the violet so and so forth, bring up exactly the tenor of the movement of the verses and the finer resolution reached by the poet in making hunger a primary facet of his destiny appears to be very well handled. It would mean that "hunger" the thing of lamentation and "Donkey" an object of mockery created by the fate, whose sole guardian is the god, create two distinct conceptual systems in the poem, yet the synthesis that has been variously and independently achieved through the presentation of a realistic form of observation is really befitting for the sake of the observation whose principal concern is to speak of a situation that could conduct the principal categories of "*vibhāva*, *anubhāva* and *sañcārī bhāva* into an exemplary concrete universal in *rasa*". There can be a method in suggesting the fact that the creation of *rasa* is primarily significant for a situation and for a composition in which the forms of content and the extent of medium projection have entered into a possible state of intersection, meaning thereby, that the observable and perceptible sequence of the content is such that each could be independently assorted into a scheme of universalisation.

If we could understand the scale of graduation presented by the poet in this poem we will have better insight into the proposition established by Bharatamuni. The title of the poem could speak of a resolution yet within it the implications of fate and fame with prospective reception and denial of being blessed with any fate and fame. And, in the context, hunger is the expression of both on a parallel level. We can understand that the value that is equal to the fact is also the value that is both the reality and necessity of the life and the living. In our conceptual form it would further mean that the title has been exposed to an extraordinarily vast range of *bhāvas* in which *karuṇa* and the *hāsa* appear to be the most important. And the speaker, on the other hand, proceeds to resolve the situation by dividing the genitive circumstances and therefore he obtains a friend in the form of Anne and himself so that he could speak out before his friend hence relieve his heart. The scale of lamentation has a systematic and gradual explication and division into powerful yet smaller variants. The hunger that was the principal object has now become equal to compulsive coordinates in donkey, air, rock, soil, iron and the like. The whole scheme could be graphically contained in the following formulation:

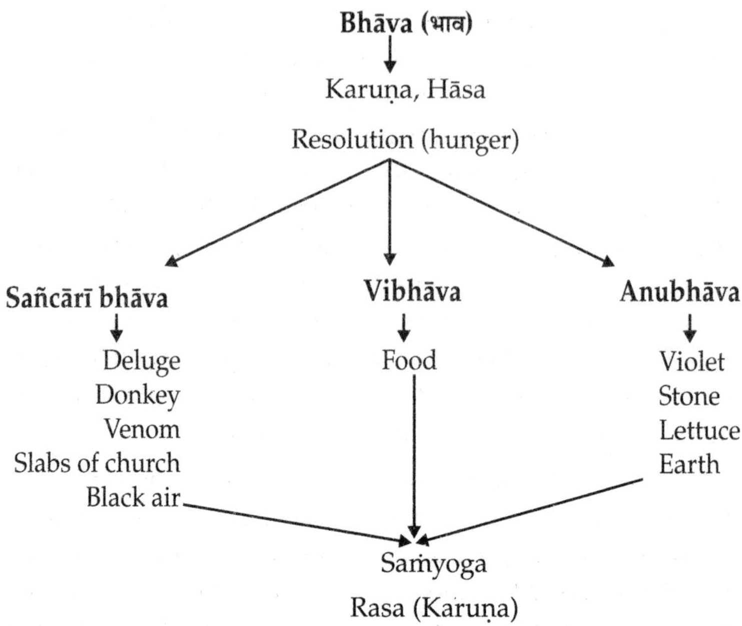

fig. 1.2: ***Karuṇa rasa* in Rimbaud's, *Fetes de la faim***

The approach that tends to define the nature of *rasa* is also evident in a rather heterogeneous formulation. For example, in John Donne's *The Relique* one could understand that the whole artistic situation presents a conceived model of synthesis through division and union. The following utterances are remarkable in this context:

When my grave is broke up againe
Some second ghest to entertaine,
(For graves have learn'd that woman-head
To be to more then one a Bed)
And he that digs it, spies
A bracelet of bright haire about the bone,
Will he not let'us alone,
And thinke that there a loving couple lies,
Who thought that this device might be some way
To make their soules, at the last busie day,
Meet at this grave, and make a little stay?[7]

— John Donne (1572-1631), p. 1633

The artistic situation identifies both the object and the subject as creators of an experience that is mounted on a feeling of goodness, completeness and totality. The speaker is situationally disposed to bring about the possibilities of change in the whole situation and therefore he proceeds to opt for a choice and hence exercises the choice inasmuch as he desires a union with someone even at the instance of death. It would mean that the experience is sustained as an object of transformation in such a way that reality and infinity both become one and the all. The poet maintains the point that the quest for beauty and perception of the beauty have an orientation towards the creation of infinity, for that matter observation, realisation, and perception of beauty tend to be very eternal in nature, and therefore, the speaker in this poem is willing to move from fullness to fullness and even at the

7. John Donne (1572-1631), 1633, http:/www.portablepoetry.com/poems/john_donne/the_extasie1.html

thought of the death there isn't much that is to be lost, and hence, the assertion that even in the grave there is a possibility to find a bracelet, a bright hair about the bone. In other words, the position of both the object and the subject is continuously compounded by the fact of addition and for that matter the grave turns out to be an object of beauty, and in turn, becomes fulfilment and infinite fulfilment in the last place what mortal man, on this earth, could think of.

By all standards, the whole idea is contained in *śṛṅgāra* in which perfect, composite and ideal feeling of goodness about oneself and also about the other self has been distinctly conceived and in this the *vibhāva* obtained in the woman is fairly sustained through *anubhāva*s in bracelet, bright hair and the bone. Simultaneously, the poet intends an association through consistently changing states of experience, for example, inside the grave the poet thinks of something that is really very beautiful and intends a union and from union he proceeds to the perfection that alone can understand the effect of *sañcārī bhāva*s inasmuch as the death as a state of being in the grave is turned into a pleasure principle through the hypothetical presence of the woman.

It appears as if commitment towards *śṛṅgāra* has an equal and perfect division into independent yet composite situations in the form of *vibhāva, anubhāva* and *sañcārī bhāva* and for each we have the ideal value equivalents.

The whole scheme could be presented through a term of description that would obtain the following graphical design:

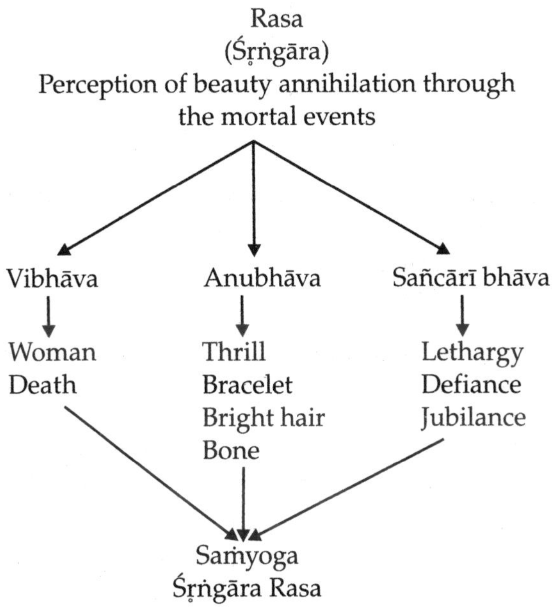

fig. 1.3: *Śṛṅgāra rasa* in John Donne's *The Relique*

Scheme of Conceptualisation in Rasa: The Principal Constituents

The idea of *rasa* has an extensive plan and scheme of conceptualisation and for that matter when the categories are intended for the sake of idealisation, the intensity of synthesis within the contents is absolutely so powerful that it gives rise immediately to the following large and independent variables. Hence an ideal description of *rasa* must commit itself to the following system of figural conceptualisation:[8]

---

8. The figural forms and formal configuration created by various transformational events in *rasa* must be stated to be appropriately changed into one another so that difference is not obtained to suggest any lack on the part of the enrichment of the categories. *Daśarūpa* of Dhanañjaya.

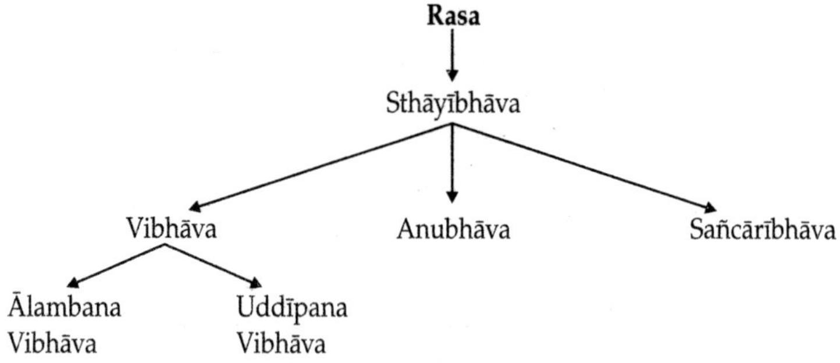

fig. 1.4: **Figural conceptualisation of system of *rasa* description**

The creative principle embodied in conceptual figuration of the *rasa* is methodically oriented for the sake of a valid definition of every possible content, construct and category obtained in an artistic situation. The view of artistry is founded not on the local or occasional or even situational circumstances, it is rather viewed perceptibly through comprehension of an extent of variation, opposition, similarity and difference within the categories, and in this regard, we can understand that the preliminary enquiry with regard to the making of an artistic situation is always considered to be carrying exceptional and ideational opportunities. The first important requirement for the projection of *rasa* as a necessary method for the sake of reception and expression and a concrete universal placed within either the observer or the reader is to understand the evolutionary assortment of primary and secondary universals and the determinants, which go a long way to shape the form and manner of the principles. For example, look at the following lines from Baudelaire's *Spleen*:

> Pluvius, annoyed at the whole city, pours torrents of dark cold out of his urn down onto the pale tenants of the cemetery next door, torrents of mortality over the foggy suburbs. On the filing, my cat is looking for a litter to bed down on; he shifts his thin mangy body about restlessly. The soul of an

> old poet wanders through the rainspot with the sad voice of a chilly ghost. The great bell is lamenting and the smoke-blackened log, in falsetto, accompanies the wheezy clock, the while, in a deck of cards filled with foul perfumes — fatal bequest of a dropsical old fiag — the handsome knave of hearts and the queen of spades talk of their dead ones sinisterly.[9]

The consideration of the verses has been a model for interpretation and is, of course, based on the idea that the expansion of an artistic situation cannot only be merited through the presentation of an experience via resolute and realistic groundwork rather at every stage of the presentation about the object and subject must be exactly brought forth. For this reason Baudelaire's *Spleen* becomes exactly an exceptional case that befits the merit of *rasa*. It is definitely possible to look at the atmosphere created on account of *bhaya,* in that in a rather stationary and stagnant formation, changes are being introduced. The city that was quiet, now bears the wrath of the god accordingly, the handiwork of destruction is being carried on. From this rather grand opening, the poet proceeds to the benefit that he could acquire by the remarkable lack of human forms to come to terms with this destruction and only a cat is left to brood upon this. Here, the transformation of *bhaya* into *utsāha* could be understood in so far as man is standing in opposition to the fear of the god and even in the midst of these drastic changes, a man like animal is standing in opposition to the fear of the god, without any fear and with all courage. Yet the uncertainty about the possibility of life and being continues unabatedly and in this darkness the appearance of the poet is remarkable and the situation now becomes a third stage of transmutation of *bhāva* from *bhaya* to *utsāha* and from *utsāha* to *āścarya*. The poet could proceed and write down the history of this description while

9. Cited in Jonathan Culler's "The Pursuit of Signs", *Routledge Classics* 2001, London EC_4p_4EE, p. 97.

himself being a part of this curse and destruction and with this the last stage of transmutation of *bhāva* into quietitude or *śānta* is completed. We can understand that the poet who is born to write doesn't know how to take refuge in this, rather he proceeds to write down the whole mystery of the great catastrophe spelt upon the earth by the god. Even the poet could understand the irony and says that the fate that the poet carries doesn't allow him to fall short of writing and on this occasion he writes of "the handsome knave of hearts and the queen of spades talking of their dead ones sinisterly".

The occasion and the instance of comprehending the form of *rasa* bears the notice of an excellence that is created or performed upon an artistic situation and in Baudelaire's *Spleen* one has the possibility to look into the principle circumstances (*bhaya*) misery, lamentation of existence and the associated conditions like the surprise over the doom, acceptance of the destiny, meditation upon the destiny and fears and defined observation to record the committed circumstances as in "the handsome knave of hearts and the queen of spades talk of their dead ones sinisterly". There cannot be any question with regard to the sincerity of the application because *bhāva* undergoes divisions and sub-divisions through *vibhāva*, *anubhāva* and *sañcārī bhāva* and finally a universal form of *rasa* appears before us. The mention of a term of application,[10] of necessity, includes a definition of all the constituents of *rasa*, and for that matter, it is worth the while to begin with *bhāva* as being the principal constituent of *rasa*.

Bhāva

Bhāva is a functional situation, hence, it systematises both the

10. The most exclusive condition that puts up a truthful perspective of *rasa* is the concept of independent assortment of the categories hence before being transferred to the canonical art the strength of a category is almost complete in every respect. *Kāvyaprakāśa* of Mammaṭa.

active, non-active and interactive shades of the disposition. In an environment in which artistic situation is being comprehended and conceived the division of a situation into three cohesive orders in the form of active, non-active and interactive forms is quite obvious. The perception of an external event is open both to the prospect of synthesis and disintegration and when the event is synthesised it is purely based on a resolution of an object into event performed by the various contents of the disposition, and in that way, it must be stated with clarity and conviction that the beginning of an acquisition of *bhāva* is primarily based on the fact that the observer who is performing an activity conducive to the artistry is simultaneously encoding both the figural as well as non-figural dimension, hence it opens up an infinite possibility of arriving at an intercepted meaning within and outside the given category. The motivation of an external sensation is required to be graduated into a sequence which would lead to the creation of independent *bhāva*s capable of effecting the considerate forms of an artistic situation.

The apprehension of a *bhāva* confirms the process of the largest expansion and stretch of the content-based and medium-oriented figures, hence *bhāva* is the first principle and merit of calling it the first principle assuredly lies in the fact that it is the beginning and also for that matter middle and end. Bharatamuni could understand that the *bhāva* shall be applicable to the typologies within the situation hence a *bhāva* at any point of time, with the changes in external sensation, perception and realisation, changes in nature, form and function, accordingly, we can have *sthāyī bhāva*s, *sāttvika bhāva*s and *sañcārī bhāva*s and each in turn will bear the differentiation and classification in the following manner:

Bhāva

Sthāyī bhāva

1. Rati or love,
2. Hāsa or mirth,
3. Śoka or grief,
4. Krodha or anger,
5. Utsāha or enthusiasm,
6. Bhaya or fear,
7. Jugupsā or disgust,
8. Vismaya or surprise,
9. Sama or placidity

Sattvika bhāva

1. Sveda or perspiration,
2. Stambha or torpidity,
3. Romāñca or horripilation,
4. Svarabhaṅga or change in tone,
5. Vepathu or trembling,
6. Vaivarṇya or discoloration,
7. Aśru or tears,
8. Pralaya or swoon

Sañcārī bhāva

1. Nirveda or aversion,
2. Glāni or depression,
3. Śaṅkā or doubt,
4. Asūyā or envy,
5. Mada or intoxication,
6. Śrama or weariness,
7. Ālasya or indolence,
8. Dainya or piteousness,
9. Cintā or sorrow,
10. Moha or passion,
11. Smṛti or recollection,
12. Dhṛti or courage,
13. Vriḍa or shame,
14. Capalatā or waywardness,
15. Harṣa or joy,
16. Avega or agitation,
17. Jaḍatā or stupor,
18. Garva or arrogance,
19. Viṣāda or despair,
20. Autsukya or inquisitiveness,
21. Nidrā or sleep,
22. Apasmāra or epilepsy,
23. Spuṭa or dream,
24. Vibodha or awakening,
25. Amarṣa or indignation,
26. Avahitta or concealment,
27. Ugratā or ferocity,
28. Mati or knowledge,
29. Vyādhi or sickness,
30. Unmāda or insanity,
31. Maraṇa or death,
32. Trāsa or fright, and
33. Vitarka or deliberation.

fig.* 1.5: Classification of the *sthāyī bhāvas, sāttvika bhāvas* and *sañcārī bhāvas

[Source: Gaṅgānāthajhā-Granthamālā [Vol. 14], **Nāṭya Śāstra of Śrī Bharatamuni** [Part Two] with Abhinavabhāratī by Śrī Abhinavaguptācārya & Manoramī (Hindi Commentary) by Dr. Pārasanatha Dvivedī, 1996, ed. Dr. Pārasanatha Dvivedī, Sampurnanand Sanskrit University, Varanasi-221002][11]

In this scheme of classification of *bhāva*, the exceptional form of generation and comprehension of the meaning is at once brought to the notice. The length of perception and extent of sensation both coordinate the assertive formation inside the *bhāva* and therefore when comprehensibility is motivated through extraordinary rational circumstances, it is simultaneously adopted for the sake of content formation in an artistic situation. Evidently, the construction of an external and internal environment for the sake of cause and effect association[12] could generate the alignment of the whole situation and in that way completes the formation of *bhāva* in a given situation.

Thus *bhāva* associates the content and medium with functionality, synthesis and synchronisation, for example, in the following verses, from Blake's *London*, there is a certainty of understanding how the creation and application of the *bhāva* is meant and conceived:

I wander thro' each charter'd street
Near where the charter'd Thames does flow,
And mark in every face I meet
Marks of weakness, marks of woe.
In every cry of every Man,
In every infant's cry of fear,
In every voice, in every ban,

11. *Gaṅgānāthajhā-Granthamālā* (vol. 14), p. 131.

12. The objects of knowledge which emerge on account of realisation of *rasa* are in a way most authentic occasions of committing a truthful function for the sake of effect brought about by *rasa*. In an object of knowledge cause and effect are the simultaneous occasions See *Sāhityadarpaṇa* of Viśvanātha Kavirāja.

The mind-forg'd manacles I hear.
How the chimney-sweeper's cry
Every black'ning church appalls;
And the hapless Soldier's sigh
Runs in blood down Palace walls.
But most thro' midnight streets I hear
How the youthful Harlot's curse
Blasts the new born Infant's tear
And blights with plague the Marriage hearse[13]
— Cited in Culler's *The Pursuit of Signs*, p. 75

In this poem by William Blake, there is a sequence of qualitative perception that is denoted in such a way that the position of the poet, situation of the subject and placement of the object fall into the one single unity. The beginning of the poem has been laid in a rather oppositional framework and for that matter the determinate and indeterminate both are brought successfully together. The movement of "I" shows definite and determinate instance of time yet "wander" is absolutely an indetermination and precisely because of this the configuration of pathos appears to have been infused into the whole situation. For that matter we can say that object cannot be successfully resolved into the subject, hence binary opposition is methodologically a fact of observation.

Right from the beginning and till the end the observations of the poet are mounted on this principle of opposition between street and wander, charter and Thames, mark and woe, cry and man, infant and fear, voice and ban, soldier and sigh, church and blackening, blood and wall, blast and infant, plague and marriage. With these compulsive handiworks, the poet is displaced from place to place, event to event and situation to situation, as he is appalled by the massive force of repulsion from those places were he thought he could have found some stay. It becomes immediately perceptible that

13. Cited in Jonathan Culler's "The Pursuit of Signs", *Routledge Classics* 2001, London EC_4p_4EE, p. 75.

process of denotation is successfully at work inasmuch as there is no entry of the poet in any of the situations mentioned by him. He proceeds to lament and goes on agonising, weeping, shedding tears on different situations he comes across yet he could not find any substantial term for his final reason or resolution.

The coordinates that he has drawn for expression and reception of the expressions take a path that is absolutely turbulent in nature. Beginning with a street is impressive, yet wandering on the street in such a way, that the street is merging into a river as big as the Thames, hence presenting him with both weakness and woe is definitely not a habit healthy for the poet. The crisis for a sequence of suggestions becomes remarkably obvious in the second stanza in which the poet proceeds to determine and locate the exact instance of the meaning of lamentation he has been searching for, and therefore, the indefinite pronouns in the manner of repeated employment of "every" in the accompanying verses could only be a loss of poetic strength and perception.

The style of interpreting denotation has been very unsuccessful, because on each of the occasions where the poet could think he could stand, he really finds himself to be generally displaced and the process of presenting denotative figures becomes uncertain and indefinite, for example, the agony of a working boy on the chimney could only add to a multiplied version of crisis in the poem and at that the church is blackening and the palaces are ruined. Even till the end the poet does not seem to be in a position to complete his search for suggestive formula that could have completed the process of his entrance into the genuine part of the artistic situation created by him. Every object in the poem deflects the motive and intention of the poet and the reception of an experience in equally unsuitable for a thematic perception like this. As a matter of fact, the denotative figure in cry (agony or pathos) should have been compounded with a series of suggestive marks so as to carry on the thinking part still further.

The poet introduces a number of conjunctions and through each conjunction he intends an absolute transformation and through each transformation he would like to come out with a full-scale meaning. For example, wander and street are approximately nearer but cry and man, ban and voice, church and blackening, sigh and soldier, curse and harlot, are supposedly at two distinct ends and in that way the crises of denotation are never resolved.

For this interpretation, forms of *rasa* could well have an application. The beginning introduces us to the pathos of the speaker who is undergoing the heat of agony and through that agony into confusion leading to the darkness in the ban. The birth of darkness through the curse of cry envelops all the visible and invisible forms of the earth and in that way *karuṇa* is the principal *bhāva* identifiable with the variants in *vibhāva, anubhāva* and *sañcārī bhāva* and the like. The linguistic form adds to the reinforcement and reinvention of *karuṇa*. For example, I wander, nearby, mark in every cry, in every voice, how the chimney-sweeper's cry, every blackening and runs in, but the most through, blasts the new born infant's tear and blights with plague the marriage hearse' could only commute them together to present the state of observer in splendid confusion about being pathetic and being agonised.

Bhāva is principally, if the account of the poem is correct, a suitability approved and adopted in understanding the structure of both the language and experience, for example, in the above poem the opening verses "I wander thro" each charter'd street/near where the charter'd Thames does flow, one can immediately pursue the feeling of *karuṇa* inherent in both I and wander, through and each and charter'd, because the functionality of an experience within these linguistic scripts is lengthened, expanded and prolonged hence the time taken to displace the poet from I to wander, from thorough to each, from near to where and from charter'd to Thames, is considerably increased, thus the resolution is becoming more and more indefinite. The employment of indeterminate verbs in flow, wander and woe could only explicate an infinite resolution.

For this *karuṇa* with its sense of prolonged and lengthened mark of woe and sigh befits the situation which can very well be brought out through the following graphical presentation:

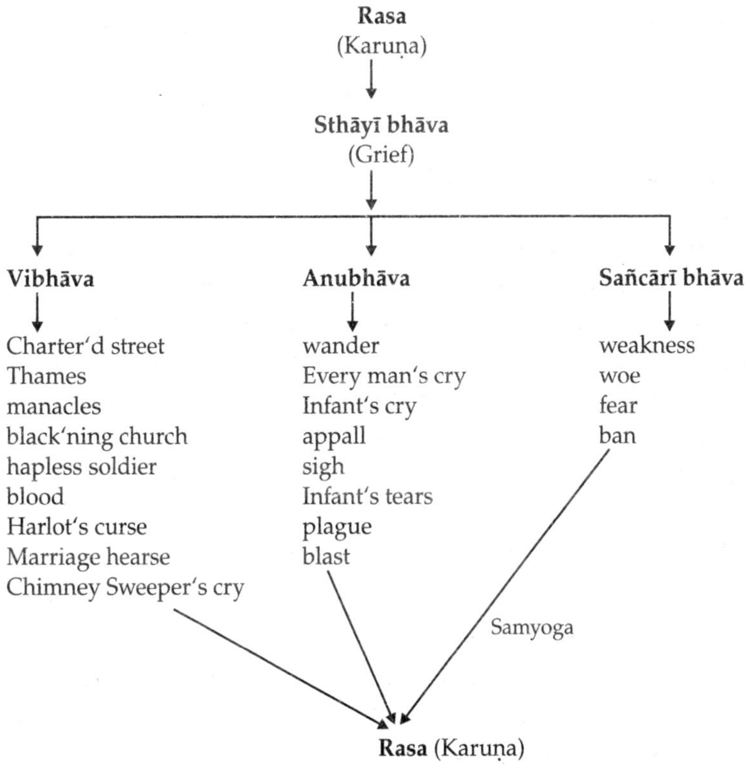

fig. **1.6:** ***Karuṇa*** **in William Blake's** ***London***

There cannot be any doubt with regard to the application and invention of *bhāva* as a methodological perspective. In fact, the creation of *bhāva*, is in itself, a broad guideline for the insistence of comprehensibility in the artistic situation.

As a principle of functional performance of the disposition in an ideal artistic set-up the range and variety of qualitative composition may not invent further conceptional interactions and for that matter the position and status of *bhāva* would be by and large enhanced and expanded. To consider this *bhāva* as a key-effect in the determination of real, supplementary and relative consciousness commonly ideational part of *bhāva* comes for a greater and wider recognition. Normally, *bhāva* categorises, classifies yet re-invents the synthesis at the extremity of functionality and therefore each division could be considered to be functionally independent and having concrete universality in it. The perception of interposing a series of creative conceptions for each of the independent *vibhāva*s has its presupposition in the manner in which the work of consciousness and the effect of intellection together unify the presentation of an art form or an artistic habit by this side of the logical and essentially determined commitment to build up a synthesis in an artistic formation the approximate range of *bhāva* is revealed and created supposedly at the following three different levels, and as one can understand, the aggregation of human disposition (conscious and unconscious) are revealed and affected in the pursuance of both the canon and ideal for the value of an expositional intensity:

I. Conformity to the association of independent variables forming the contents and constructs.

II. As an instrument in transforming the variables into the perceptible suitability for any coherent and committed artistic form.

III. Relocation and distribution of homogeneous and heterogeneous masses of the categories (words, letters, syllables, experience and the like).

Bharatamuni examines the effect of this conditionality in rather concrete terms and says with affirmation:

> *Bhāva* is the instrumental cause of dramatic performance.[14]
>
> — *Nāṭyaśāstra*, chapter I

It would necessarily mean that at any point of time *bhāva* has an authoritative application through a realistic, received, perceived and expressed version of an artistic situation. The idealised habits created on account of primary observation would surely befall the intellectual pursuit of an observer and thereby would promote him to measure the similarities and differences between indicated and denoted versions of experience, thereby, he shall have to bring forth the most real and the most ideal form of linguistic or emotive categories on their own account of the contents in the given categories. The presentation part of the argument is based on the fact that sequential formation and evolutionary rendering of the whole situation in which segments are created and inter-divisions are absolutely prefixed, is for the sake of a better organisation and a better construction of an artistic form. If the beginning or the concentration of organised principles is equated realistically, the merits of an artistic situation would be immediately indicated. This is the reason why there is a considerable relocation of the content tending to be realistic and empirical. In an event in which functional scale of *bhāva* is imminent, the significance is to look at the observer who happens to imbibe an observation from an external source and in consequence of which he would sustain the perception of a necessary logical form and the *bhāva* with its segmental graduations will definitely enter into the makings of the codes preferentially obtained by the observer. The term for such figuration may be absolutely varying and differential yet the resolution is always near at the hand. It is in this way that

14. *Gaṅgānāthajhā-Granthamālā* (vol. 14), p. 19.

three elementary conjunctions would be seen to be at work in this connection:

I. Formation of an object,

II. Creation on an event, and

III. The resolution of an object into event.

The effort to offer an inscribed form of this logical expansion of the perception the notation of *bhāva* normally builds up concentrated centres of generated meaning. For example, the effect of goodness must be observed in the adequate perception of beauty and would only be in addition to the already existing form and manner of content distribution within and outside the medium. Observer's ability to perceive the beauty is by all means the facility created by the dominant *bhāva* of *śṛṅgāra* in him, hence the necessity of principal function is assumed and accordingly, *bhāva* is fundamentally established now. In an act of consciousness *bhāva* is the primordial necessity and its consequence in an artistic formation is its total and complete validity in obtaining a method and procedure for conceptualisation.

Sthāyī bhāvas

The effect of permanence as a suitable and valid measurement of the worth of an artistic situation could be compulsorily comprehended through yet another perceptible category that is associated with recovery of content-wise and medium-wise function in a formation. This category is the second important attributive excellence designated as *sthāyī bhāva*. In *sthāyī bhāva*, the scale of perception and observation and for that matter consciousness is fixed to a never-changing scale of graduation and evolution accordingly we can have as many *sthāyī bhāva*s as *bhāva*s:[15]

15. *Sthāyī bhāva* is a natural event finding its worth in the permanence of functionality and accordingly we have nine *sthāyī bhāva*s porporting to define the idealised form of functional situation. See for example the following:

→

1. *Rati*
2. *Hāsa*
3. *Śoka*
4. *Krodha*
5. *Utsāha*
6. *Bhaya*
7. *Jugupsā*
8. *Vismaya*
9. *Nirveda*

If we can understand the schematic implication, the empirical necessity is at once clear. *Sthāyī bhāva* is absolute, predefined, rationalised and homogeneously concrete in all the known instances of function of an event of experience. In the space for this reason, the strength of *sthāyī bhāvas* are realistically associated with the emergence of a structural form bearing a functional composition. In this regard two things are to be understood. First, the strength of permanence relegated to the artistic form, and second, the composite value of permanence devolved on an artistic form bears the same commitment in being raised and elevated by the *sthāyī bhāvas*. As an object of structure, the *sthāyī bhāvas* have evenly and homogeneously distributed length of the contents, and, for this, the artistry has to undergo multiple divisions.

This division is compounded through a necessary change in the logical structure of the realistic perception and consciousness and for that matter the reduction of abstract

→ रतिहसिश्च शोकश्च क्रोधोत्साहौ भयं तथा।
जुगुप्सा विस्मयश्च्वेजेजतनबजनतंसपेज ति स्थायिभावा: प्रकीर्तिता:।।3।।
निर्वेदस्थायिभावोस्ति शान्तोपि नवमो रस:।।

Mahamāhopādhyāya Sir Ganganatha Jha: *Kāvyaprakāśa* of Mammaṭa with English translation (revised), 1996, Bharatiya Vidya Prakashan, Varanasi, pp. 68-70.

and addition of the concrete goes into the functional parts of the whole situation. In this context the linear arrangement of the contents in the specified length of an observation is rotated through the cyclical reversion and in that way a qualitative idealisation of the parts is established. In this, two situations appear to be very important. Firstly, the construction of an ideal value of an experience is brought about by reinventing the figures and characteristic form of the predisposition of the organised consciousness, hence, any value arrangement that corresponds to the experience as a part of symmetrical or asymmetrical formation, could be inscribed to be the permanent and universal formation. The periodic index that puts up its effect through the recognition of the value inherent upon an experience puts up all the contextual parts together and makes out the validity of organisation by, as we have stated earlier, reduction and expansion. Reduction in this context would mean the reversion of the contents from cyclical into linear and expansion would be a correlation of the homogeneous and heterogeneous contents of the experience. It must be clear at this point of time that *sthāyī bhāva*, because of its terms of effects on the construction of organised value forms of an experience, becomes essentially noteworthy and primary in the given context. Second important formative notion, related to these *bhāva*s is that they suggest nearly all the important variants of the experience, hence, could bring forth a series of comprehensible construction of the same experience. Viśvanātha understands exactly the method involved in the interpretive consequence and accordingly proposes a definition for *sthāyī bhāva* in the following manner:

अविरुद्धा विरुद्धा वा यं तिरोधातुमक्षमाः।
आस्वादादङ्कुरकन्दोऽसौ भावः स्थायीति संमतः।।174।।[16]

---

16. *Sāhityadarpaṇa* of Viśvanātha Kavirāja with Vimalā (Hindi commentary) by Śrī Śālgrāmśāstrī, 1956, Motilal Banarsidass, pp. 104-05.

aviruddhā viruddhā vā yaṁ tirodhātumakṣamāḥ ।
āsvādādāṭandarakando'sau bhāvaḥ sthāyīti saṁmataḥ ॥174॥
— *Sāhitya Darpaṇa*, pp. 104-05

That which is not to be changed by positive and negative assertions is called *sthāyī bhāva.*

Obviously, Viśvanātha is insisting on an origin of an experience earlier than the primordial times and consequence of the same beyond the posterior times. For that matter, the eternal or permanently inscribed forms of the *sthāyī bhāva* are abundantly clear. The progress of content formation through *sthāyī bhāva*s is lengthened beyond the resolution at the beginning and the end and all the necessary correlatives are evidently constituted in between this beginning and the end. Effect of performance of *sthāyī bhāva*s could be the manner of suggesting how configuration of an artistic situation should correspond to the necessity of resolution of the object into the event.

For example, the actual merit of the whole conjunction established to interpret the permanence of these primordial forms could well be established through the following utterances from Baudelaire's *Un Voyage à Cythère*:

Cen'était pas un temple aux ombres bocagéres,
Oùlajeune prêtresse, amoureuse des fleurs,
Allait, le corps brûlé de secrétes chaleurs,
EntrebaŚllant sa robe aux brises passagères.

It was not a temple with bosky shades
Where the young priestess, in love with flowers,
Passed, her body consumed by secret flames,
Her robe blowing open in the fleeting breezes.[17]
— Cited in Culler's *The Pursuit of Signs*, pp. 127-28

In this, the idea is being sustained that actual experience or the truth inherent upon the reality brings forth the larger

17. Jonathan Culler's "The Pursuit of Signs", *Routledge Classics* 2001, London EC_4p_4EE, pp. 127-28.

shades of realisation and therefore what was a sight of love is now only an occasion of disgust and sorrow. In other words, the beauty embodied in the figural form occasions a crisis in the perception of the same formation and therefore the appearance of beautiful results into a commitment for sorrow. In equivalent terms, it can be said that the *rati* or *śṛṅgāra* evident, at least, in the opening lines gets transformed into *karuṇa* just for the fact that empirical reality and the necessity for the perception of such a reality could be immediately felt and actually necessitated. Observer's preparation, in this regard, are diametrically opposed in that he could perceive the truth of the young priestess with flowers yet this truth is inverted and denoted forthrightly with the reversion of received sequence of the truth. For an observer, truth is not an instance of time, rather it is an inherence that has to be accepted. The display of *karuṇa* in the closing verses is the strength of artistic materials gathered in this connection. The measurement of expanding and closing attitudes could be understood in the appearance of the maiden and her entrance into the receding medium where the love reduces down to no love, and therefore, the introduction of the object in the manner of a grand opening invites a sedentary manifestation in not being able either to receive or present the love that was given. Hence, the opposition between ecstasy of love and the sorrow in no love could be obviously the intention of the poet. In the equivalent terms, we can propose to interpret the situation by saying that the beginning through suggestive forms like flowers, shades, temple and closing denotative figures in secret flames, robe blowing open and fleeting breezes, invariably dispose the whole matter through the effect of *karuṇa* felt obviously by the beloved in union and separation. Intensity of separation proceeds remarkably with the agents who denote only the expansion of sorrow or unhappiness. If the context provided by the poet is right, the meaning generation possibilities appear to be very rich inasmuch as the progress of *karuṇa* through *vipralambha* and *viyoga* realistically add the beloved to both the contexts. For this reason, the experience of happiness is further intensified in the conjunctions provided by the body gestures, the ornaments of the body and the lengthened forms of consummation:

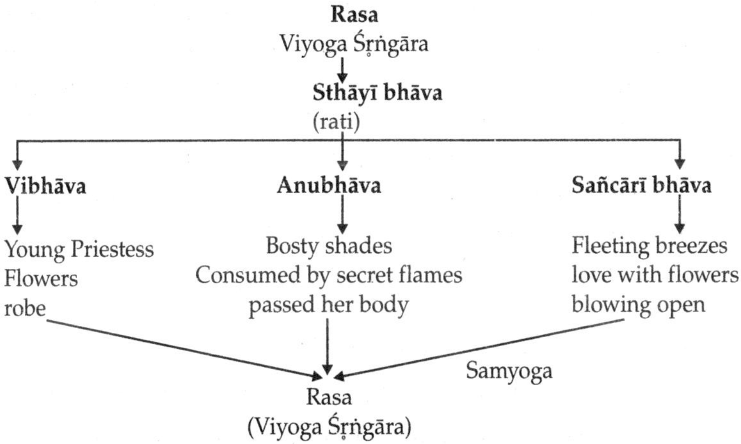

fig.* 1.7: *Viyoga śṛṅgāra* in Baudelaire's *Un Voyage à Cythère

Sthāyī bhāvas interpret the various forms of exclusion and inclusion of an experience and for that matter the extent of perception caused and created by *sthāyī bhāvas* appears to be very wide and large. For example, in a situation in which we come across the expression of indignation or irritation or disgust, the significance of *sthāyī bhāvas* will have to exclude the object and include the subject by posing a question with regard to the constitution of the experience involved.

Vibhāva

The constitutive principles combining a connected focus on an artistic form discover the necessity of division and reorganisation through repeated formation and assessment of a denotative function generated in cognition and rationalisation. On this account, one has to understand that in *rasa*, the terms of the categories are absolutely the manner in which succeeding and preceding evolution must take place, hence, *vibhāva* as a third principle category obtained right at the significance of *bhāva* becomes important. In *vibhāva* the communication of external objects, situations, events, forms and manner is invented as well as comprehended. It would mean that *vibhāva*s are precisely the genuine receptors of those experiential forms which are logically and realistically defined by the *sthāyī bhāva*s. In fact, for a *sthāyī bhāva*, we can say that the next appropriate and receiving objects would be the *vibhāva*s only. In *vibhāva*s the actual assortment of various communicable forms underlying the universal disposition takes place and in each one the composite functionality appears to have been formatively introduced. The whole preposition could be understood in the following four important ways:

I. Identification of the aspect of communication.

II. The interpretation of the method of communication.

III. Resolution of communication.

IV. Distribution of the length of communication.

It is certainly an aspect of understanding both, the external and internal configuration of an artistic situation, and accordingly, presenting the contents for the enrichment of the medium. In *vibhāva* the constructs which are to interpret a particular *sthāyī bhāva* are exposed in the form of contents precisely on account of the best and the highest suitability determined by the performance and function. Once this stage is carried out the figurative reception is done by the medium participating in a conceived situation. It is, therefore, the segmentation of the whole artistry into the fixed principles and as it can be understood that the *vibhāva*s become the primary instruments in accepting the principle of communication for certain formative preparations made and accorded to the artistic event. The entire scheme can be denoted through the following notations specifying the figural as well as the graphical design and performance:

Table 1.1: *Sthāyī bhāvas* and corresponding *vibhāvas*[18]

Sthāyībhāva	Vibhāvas
Rati	seasons, garlands, aromatics, jewellery, company of the dear ones, music, palaces, paintings, aquatic games, gardens, imitating the lofty, etc.
Hāsa	hearing about or looking at improper costumes and jewellery, impudence, indulgence, tickling, the disability, un-warranted fear, uncalled-for action, etc.
Śoka	affliction under curse, separation from the near ones, loss of wealth, killing, bondage, extradition, suffering and death due to fire, etc.
Krodha	battle, anger, threat, insult, abuse, lies, injury, harsh words, cheating, jealousy, etc.
Utsāha	presence of mind, perseverance, strength, valour, power, excitement, etc.
Bhaya	hideous noises, devils, reflex actions, vacant buildings, forests, capture and death of near ones, etc.
Jugupsā	seeing, hearing or discussing about, distasteful, impropitious, unpleasant, disagreeable and contaminated objects, bad odours, harsh sounds, etc.
Vismaya	seeing celestials, attainment of desired objectives, entry into temples, palaces and like, witnessing magic, illusion, etc.
Śama/Nirveda	philosophic outlook, placidity, purity of thought, etc.

18. A monograph on Bharata's *Nāṭyaśāstra* (Indian Dramatology), tr. in English by P.S.R. Appa Rao and P. Sri Rama Sastry, Naatya Maalaa Publishers, 1967, Hyderabad, Appendix B.

In fact, the possibility of communication beyond the actual subjective motivation and the acquisition of higher impersonal variants becomes the important characteristic that must be associated with the *vibhāvas*.

It can be understood that the act of communication, in fact, rationalises the different objects and events which become appropriately fit for being changed into their secondary form. The purpose of presentation of an object or event is completely situated on the configuration of the structure of event that has to be presented and for this reason the *vibhāvas* could be manifested through a distance between the object and the subject; for example, in *karuṇa* the configurable necessity due upon the *vibhāvas* would be to create the pity, involvement, and sympathy, hence, to bring about remorse and sorrow for the situation and in this it would be but natural that the object must have a separation from the subject inasmuch as the projection of the context and the synthesis of the context are supposed to be resolved and do different yet equidistant situations. For example, the effect of *vibhāvas* could be verbally and stylistically composed around the following situation occurring in Aeschylus' *Agamemnon*:

> To care for that duty is no concern of yours. By your hands down he fell, down to death, and down below shall we bury him — but not with wailings from his household. No! Iphigenia, his daughter, as is due, shall meet her father lovingly at the swift-flowing ford of sorrows, and shall fling her arms around him and kiss him.[19]
>
> — tr. H.W. Smyth, Lines 1551 to 1559

The intensity of the artistic situation brings forth the idea that the character in the present circumstance is conceiving *jugupsā* (disgust) and hatred (*ghr̥ṇā*) for the external event and for

19. Aeschylus, Agamemnon 2, Agamemnon Cont., tr. H.W. Smyth, Lines 1551 to 1559, www.theoi.com/Text/Aeschylus Agamemnon2.html

that matter she could be close to the concept of *bībhatsa*. The composition of the situation has two primary merits. In the first place, Clytemnestra suggests death of Agamemnon by mutilation of his body hence it is accompanied by *bībhatsa* and in the second place, she could think of none waiting the loss. The possible motive of examining the objective for prospective communication obtaining them merely on verbal account, for example, anybody who reads "by our hands down he fell, down to death, and down below shall we bury him". The conception of death with obvious expression through the loss of bodily organs on account of being beheaded or stabbed and that too with merciless and pitiless eyes would enable Clytemnestra to find out appropriate *vibhāva*s in red blood and the coagulation of the same blood. The effect is really extraordinary in that the reader pursuing the utterances could immediately think of *bhaya, bībhatsa* and *jugupsā* to completely explain the situation.

The prospects of functionality are remarkably concrete in the case of *vibhāva*s. They not only explain the actual and exact configuration of the given artistry but they also manifest the terms through exposition. In this nativity, the distinction in the *vibhāva*s is generally brought about by changes in the context and situation and they are recreated into the following two objectives:

1. Stimulus (*ālambana*)
2. Stimulant (*uddīpana*)

In the sensory formation in which the whole effect is felt through the bodily constitution, we have these two variants *ālambana* and *uddīpana*, as the two measure-constituting factors. It would be a part examination to show as to how *ālambana* and *uddīpana* go on to make out primary sensory responses. For example, look at the following:

Thou still unravished bride of quietness
Thou foster-child of silence and slow time,[20]
— *Poetical Works of John Keats*, 1895

In this the situation conducts a formal necessity of entering upon the infinity and eternity as the valuated principle of life. It is in this regard that the idea of urn is associated with time without any beginning or an end, or in other words, we can say that the textual inscription inscribed on a page shall have an endurable significance inasmuch as for a mark or a figure or a design or a composition there can be no beginning or the end. Hence, it is precisely the graphical sketch, a mark, a sign or contours or linear or cyclical coordinates that become inconceivably the ethos of totality and completeness. By this standard, the expression is complete and the *vibhāva*s of meditation and comprehension become at once evident. This situation has a perfectly felt interpretation in our curriculum of examination and interpretation and we will say that the *vibhāva*s are the necessary conjunction to associate, to express the external event of the given *sthāyī bhāva*s.

Anubhāva

The condition of communication substantiates the measure of an event by constructing an internal form of reception in *anubhāva*. In fact, it is precisely better to say that the *anubhāva*s are the internal situations, aspects or events which, through various gestures, postures and the like, manifest the reception *vibhāva* to the external world and in that way they not only functionalise but also homogenise the whole artistic situation. It is finally at the instance of *anubhāva* that we can understand that the value of external artistry is equal to the value of internal artistic formation, nevertheless, the figurative resolution might otherwise be homogeneous or heterogeneous

20. *Poetical Works of John Keats*, 1895, ed. Buxton Forman Crowell Publication.

depending upon the nature of content, medium and the context. The *anubhāvas* could be classified according to the magnitude of their resolution that they propose to bring about in any given artistic situation. Accordingly, there can be two forms — first purely synthesising and second purely convulsive. In each of these, as we can understand, the proposition is nearly synchronous by accommodating and assimilating the combination and selection-oriented formations.

In our consideration of the *anubhāva* we could easily establish the point that proper, effective, systematic and rational and realisable communication of the whole experiential state is based on the fact that the realistic, coherent, and well-organised *anubhāvas* have been created and on that account the functionality of the whole artistic situation is not only increased but enlarged as well. The entire scheme of configuration of *anubhāvas* could well be explained through the following graphics:

Table 1.2: The nine *rasas* and corresponding *anubhāvas*[21]

Rasas	Anubhāvas (Consequents)
Śṛṅgāra (amorous)	Union: delicate movements of eyebrows, glances, pleasant words, soft and delicate movements of the limbs, etc. Separation: aversion, depression, doubt, envy, weariness, sorrow, passion inquisitiveness, sleep, dream, awakening, sickness, insanity, epilepsy, stupor, etc.
Hāsya (humorous)	Quick movements of the cheeks and the nostrils, narrow or wide looks, sweat, change of colour of the face, holding the sides.
Karuṇa (pathetic)	Lamentation, dryness of mouth, shedding of tears, discolouration of body, loose limbs, rapid breath forgetfulness, etc.

21. A monograph on Bharata's *Nāṭyaśāstra* (Indian Dramatology), tr. in English by P.S.R. Appa Rao and P. Sri Rama Sastry, Naatya Maalaa Publishers, Hyderabad, 1967, Appendix B.

Raudra (furious)	Breaking, pounding, cutting, beating, taking up and use of arms, bloodshot eyes, perspiration, knitting of eyebrows, grinding the teeth, biting the nether lip, rubbing palms, etc.
Vīra (valorous)	Steadiness, courage, valour, sacrifice, knowledge, ability, etc.
Bhayānaka (horrific)	Blank looks, loose limbs, dry mouth, palpitation of heart, horripilation, change in voice, face and glances, etc. Infectious horror, the action should be delicate.
Bībhatsa (repugnant)	Convulsive contraction of the body, narrow face, vomiting, spitting, closing the nostril, disgustful movement of the teeth.
Adbhuta (wondrous)	Wide eyes, fixed gaze, horripilation, tears of joy, sweat, exhilaration, approbation, generosity, exclamation, movement of hands.
Śānta (quietude)	Self-control, devotion to duty, meditation, worship, self-realisation, compassion, placidity.

Sañcārī Bhāvas

As a matter of fact *sañcārī bhāva*s appear to be the last great and the perfect model of the reception of continuous transformation, inasmuch as they suggest an equal and equivalent fixation of different functional states of experience under different content, different medium and different texts. In this regard, it would be worth our while to understand that the scale of functionality proved and activated by having marginal yet constant shift in the artistic situation is always synthesised through the reception of a deviant sensory attitude that has both perceptivity and imperceptibility. Bharatamuni makes mention of 33 *sañcārī bhāva*s which could be enumerated in the following manner:

Table 1.3: The thirty-three *sañcārī bhāvas*[22]

Sañcārī bhāvas	
1. *Nirveda* or aversion	18. *Garva* or arrogance
2. *Glāni* or depression	19. *Viṣāda* or despair
3. *Śaṅkā* or doubt	20. *Autsukya* or inquisitiveness
4. *Asūyā* or envy	21. *Nidrā* or sleep
5. *Mada* or intoxication	22. *Apasmāra* or epilepsy
6. *Śrama* or weariness	23. *Sputa* or dream
7. *Ālasya* or indolence	24. *Vibodha* or awakening
8. *Dainya* or piteousness	25. *Amarṣa* or indignation
9. *Cintā* or sorrow	26. *Avahita* or concealment
10. *Moha* or passion	27. *Ugratā* or ferocity
11. *Smṛti* or recollection	28. *Mati* or knowledge
12. *Dhṛti* or courage	29. *Vyādhi* or sickness
13. Vrīḍa or shame	30 *Unmāda* or insanity
14. *Capalatā* or waywardness	31. *Maraṇa* or death
15. *Harṣa* or joy	32. *Trāsa* or fright
16. *Āvega* or agitation	33. *Vitarka* or deliberation
17. *Jaḍatā* or stupor	

The principle of organisation composes the method of classification through various means, as we have seen earlier, the creation of *rasa* bears upon the evolution through *bhāva, sthāyī bhāva, vibhāva, anubhāva* and the *sañcārī bhāvas*. The term of resolution of these categories into coherent harmonious

22. A monograph on Bharata's *Nāṭyaśāstra* (Indian Dramatology), tr. in English by P.S.R. Appa Rao and P. Sri Rama Sastry, Naatya Maalaa Publishers, Hyderabad, 1967, Appendix B.

and synthesised forms obviously leads to designated and noteworthy concretisation of the universals so as to explicate and illustrate every possible range of human experience. Bharatamuni stated these experiences to be universal, absolute and complete forms of realisable situations and being eight in number, while Abhinavagupta made it to be nine, adding one more important formation to it. The following figure will show how the comprehensibility of artistry could be as various, as rich and as universal as it should require to be:

Table 1.4: The nine *rasas* and *sthāyī bhāvas*, *vibhāvas*, *anubhāvas* and *sañcārī bhāvas* corresponding to them.[23]

Rasas and Sthāyī bhāvas	Vibhāvas	Anubhāvas	Sañcārī bhāvas
Śṛṅgāra (amorous) *Rati*	Seasons, garlands, aromatics, jewellery, company of dear ones, music, palaces, paintings, acquatic games, gardens, imitating the lofty, etc.	Union: delicate movements of eyebrows, glances, pleasant words, soft and delicate movements of the limbs, etc. Separation: aversion, depression, doubt, envy, weariness, sorrow, passion inquisitiveness, sleep, dream, awakening, sickness, insanity, epilepsy, stupor, etc.	All the emotions with the exception of indolence, fero city and repugnance.
Hāsya (humorous) *Hāsa*	Hearing about looking at improper costumes and jewellery, impudence, indulgence, tickling, prattle, the disabled, unwarranted fear, uncalled-for action, etc.	Quick movements of the cheeks and the nostrils, narrow or wide looks, sweat, change of colour of the face, holding the sides.	Envy, waywardness, dream, sleep, concealment, awakening, etc.

23. A monograph on Bharata's *Nāṭyaśāstra* (Indian Dramatology), tr. in English by P.S.R. Appa Rao and P. Sri Rama Sastry, Naatya Maalaa Publishers, Hyderabad, 1967, Appendix B.

Karuṇa (Pathetic) *Śoka*	Affliction under curse, separation from near ones, loss of wealth, killing, bondage, extradition, suffering and death due to fire, etc.	Lamentation, dryness of mouth, shedding of tears, discolouration of body, loose limbs, rapid breath forgetfulness, etc.	Aversion, depression, sorrow, inquisitiveness, agitation, passion, weariness, fear, despair, piteousness, sickness, stupor, insanity, epilepsy, death, torpidity, trembling, discolouration, tears, change in tone, etc.
Raudra (furious) *Krodha*	Battle, anger, threat, insult, abuse, lies, injury, harsh words, cheating, jealousy, etc.	Breaking, pounding, cutting beating, taking up and use of arms, bloodshot eyes, perspiration, knitting of eyebrows, grinding the teeth, biting the nether lip, rubbing palms etc.	Arrogance, envy, intoxication, waywardness, ferocity, passion, change in tone, horripilation, etc.
Vīra (valorous) *Utsāha*	Presence of mind, perseverance, strength, valour, power, excitement, etc.	Steadiness, courage, valour, sacrifice, knowledege, ability etc.	Courage, knowledge, arrogance ferocity, indignation, recollection, horripilation, awakening etc.
Bhayānaka (horrific) *Bhaya*	Hideous, noises, devils, reflex actions, vacant buildings, forests, capture and death of near ones, etc.	Blank looks, loose limbs, dry mouth, palpitation of heart, horripilation change in voice, face and glances, etc. Infectious horror, the action should be delicate	Torpidity, perspiration, trembling, change in tone and colour, doubt, passion, piteousness, agitation, waywardness, stupor, fright, epilepsy, death, etc.
Bībhatsa (repugnant) *Jugupsā*	Seeing, hearing or discussing about distasteful, unpropitious, unpleaseant, disagreeable and contaminated objects, bad odours, harsh sounds etc.	Convulsive contraction of the body, narrow face, vomiting, spitting, closing the nostril, disgustful movement of the teeth	Epilepsy, insanity, despair, intoxication, death, sickness, fear, etc.

Adbhuta (wondrous) *Vismaya*	Seeing celestials, attainments of desired objective, entry into temples, palaces and the like, witnessing magic, illusion etc.	Wide eyes, fixed gaze, horripilation tears of joy, sweat, exhilaration, approbation, generosity, exclamation, movement of hands.	Torpidity, perspiration, horripilation, change in tone, agitation, joy, waywardness, exuberance, epilepsy, courage, stupor, swoon, etc.
Śānta (blissful) *Śama*	Philosophic outlook, placidity, purity of thought, etc.	Self-control, devotion to duty, meditation, worship, self-realisation, compassion, placidity	Aversion, recollection, courage, torpidity, cleanliness, horripilation, etc.

The performance of a situation attending on any of these absolute forms would depend upon the comprehension of equivalent content, context and the medium. In fact, it is quite appropriate at this stage to remark that *rasa* has an effective meaningfulness both in terms of reception and communication of the absolute inasmuch as the contents which create the *rasa*s are at the same time, also those which communicate the *rasa* to the external world. For this reason *rasa* presupposes the creation of absolute on both of the sides as an object and also as a subject. This remarkable and exceptional circumstance in which we understand the function of a term at the level of reception as well as on the side of communication is a situation in which the realisation of truth becomes equal to the figuration of reality along with the structure of the object.

The precision of methodology and excellence of theoretical framework contained in the idea of *rasa* have proved to be real, truthful, commonplace, practical and very effective in understanding the organisation, construction, configuration and the function of an artistic situation. For that matter the merit of building up a constructive and functional methodology for *rasa* is of great significance and the point must be remembered that the situations expressed or contained in *rasa*, deal with the reception as well as communication of both the formal and non-formal figures contained within it. The strength of any genuine and ideal artistry could successfully respond to the effects produced in *rasa*, by the virtue of the following perceptible formation. First, the creation of synthesis in an artistic formation is absolute and based on the totality that could be arrived at in any context, construct or category. For example, there could be an achievement of an interpretative standard for Baudelaire's utterances recorded in the following manner:

> *Désormais tu n'es plus, O matieère vivante,*
> *Qu'un granit entouré d'une vague épouvante*
>
> Henceforth, O living matter, you are no more
> Than a piece of granite shrouded in vague horror[24]
> —Cited in Culler's *The Pursuit of Signs,* p. 156

We will have to locate the sequence of perception in the strength of organisation provided by *rasa*. Anybody could understand that the given verses are the pure effects of *jugupsā* yet it opts for a transformation into *śānta*. If a situation is understood through that sequence, it would be clearly possible to suggest that the variants involved in the act of creation of *jugupsā* and *śānta* in the form of dislike, disregard, rejection, meditation and purity, perfection, absolute, totality would enable a complete understanding of the wholesome situation that is always there. The extent of this enquiry would further enlist the following methodological form, and hence could invariably complete the understanding.

Transformation of the Categories in Rasa

The intensity of transformation of the categories at the beginning, in the middle or at the end of the situation happens to be a necessary conjunction for the effective creation of *rasa* and for this reason, the position and stability of the entire

24. Jonathan Culler's "The Pursuit of Signs", p. 156.

categories, configuration assumes greater recognition in his particular theoretical system. Bharata's position in this regard (*vibhāvānubhava*) has come for interpretation as reorganisation in the succeeding traditions of theoretical enquiry. For example, Abhinavagupta has examined the wholesome functionality and actual configuration of *bhāva*, *vibhāva*, *anubhāva* and *sañcārī bhāva* and admits the fact that the universals established by this tend to be the concrete universals. It would definitely mean that when universal experience is created on account of an artistic formation, its transfer to the reader bears on the necessity of gradual refinement and on that account the whole sequence is re-established, ratified, re-synthesised and reinvented, hence at the beginning *bhāva* and at the end *sañcārī bhāva* will define the object of reception and the object of communication in such a way that both, the reception and communication, become one and all. The acquisition of a sensation in this regard would invariably mean that the correlatives are already found and achieved, and accordingly, the sequence of modification has been duly established simply for the reason that *bhāva* must achieve the length and functionality of *sthāyī bhāva* and *sthāyī bhāva* must enhance the content synthesis and content projection in *vibhāva* and *anubhāva* and finally the correlated and reassessed preposition will have to be received on equal terms by a *sañcārī bhāva*. From this point on there will be a reverse of evolution and it would continue till the finest of the concrete universal has been established and created. Abhinavagupta's understanding of the situation brings us to the situation in which we have the transformation of the categories and reinvented transformation assuring a total, complex and absolute refinement of the entire artistic formation. This appears to be rather a unique and new development in the terms of application proposed by Bharatamuni. In fact, it would be better to say that Abhinavagupta finds out a new conceptual scheme for the creation, realisation of *rasa* through an alliance with figurative medium and formal contents.

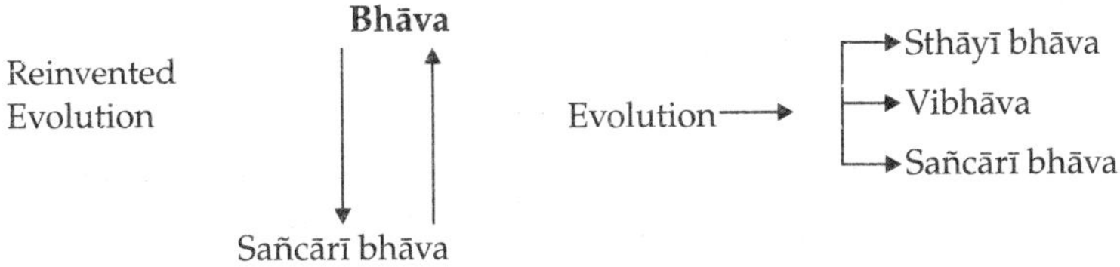

fig. **1.8: Conceptual scheme of *rasa* realisation**[25]

The illustrative significance lies almost entirely in the realisation of the fact that *bhāva*, of necessity, initiates the evocation of *sthāyī bhāva* and all the succeeding contents in other forms are quite naturally intertransmuted and intertransformed till the cyclical evolution reverses the concrete universal severally and in each.

It is obvious from this that the end product of evolution and the reinvented evolution would be *rasa* with an absolutely trans-impersonal figure and will have value equivalents and the addition of the contents even before the beginning and beyond the end of an artistic form. This marks out clearly how the categories involved are brought to depersonalisation

25. The movement of the categories in *rasa* has a merit of advancing a sense of displacement in such a way that it is immediately and forthwith replaced by another rich content. It is in this way that we have exchange property as committed function in *rasa*:

    सा च रसना न प्रमाणव्यापारो न कारकव्यापारः। स्वयं तु नाप्रामाणिकः, स्वसंवेदनसिद्धत्वात्। रसना च बोधरूपैव। किन्तु बोधान्तरेभ्यो लौकिकेभ्यो विलक्षणैव। उपायानां विभावादीनां लौकिकवैलक्षण्यात्। तेन विभावादिसंयोगाद्रसना यतो निष्पद्यतेऽतस्तथाविधरसनागोचरो लोकोत्तरोऽर्थो रस इति तात्पर्यं सूत्रस्य।

    — *Gaṅgānāthajhā-Granthamālā* (vol. 14), p. 76.

by effective and outstanding refinement in which every categorical perception is brought closer to reader's motivation. Hence *rasa* is something that endures even before the logical projection of the contents and also when the meaning is realistically established.

It is now possible to state with conviction that *rasa* is an appropriate theoretical and applicable model of comprehension and assessment of the configuration of the content, constructs, and of the categories involved in the resolution of an object into the event or an event into the universal form of significant organisation; and for this reason, the suitability and applicability of *rasa*, are of necessity, be accepted and approved inasmuch as an artistic situation survives only through the idealisation of adequate reception and authentic communication and to this extent *rasa* invariably is the best principle[26] of both the reception and communication.

Conception of Categories in Post-structuralism

Post-structuralism stands for a situation in which there is no commitment for the exposition, creation, invention, comprehension and reassertion of the truth or of the various objects of knowledge like thought, experience, imagination and the language. The condition of creating the truth by obtaining the means of knowledge, both enter into a process of devolution in which context, medium and the content are brought into an alliance with random fixation of the whole situation. It would mean that the human experience as such doesn't interpret and therefore correlates itself in the content of the emerging and rising intensity of the experience. There can't be a way to find out how and why experience is stopped

26. Style of interpretation that can be brought about by forming coherent and exact ideals of truth is noteworthy in *rasa*. See for further discussion:

    Gaṅgānāthajhā-Granthamālā (vol. 14), p. 19.

just short of a presentation through the possible mediums. Yet, however, we must agree on the fact that the object of experience, like language and imagination, could have a meaning throughout the term that they undergo to refine themselves in the external space system and any provision that tries to deviate the object from its linear position is liable to be questioned and examined. In all fairness, the post-structuralist situation disallows and disapproves the transitory nature of linear and cyclical perception; consequently, language and experience can't be interrelated, correlated or interacted and subsequently there cannot be any inter-transformation[27] as such. Yet, it must be stated with complete conviction that language and experience have their full length structure and formation, and accordingly they are required to be understood.

Language in Post-structuralist Tradition

Language in the post-structuralist tradition stands for a fact of denotation in such a way that range, power, length and magnitude of its denotation comes to be reduced, appreciably and greatly and in that context language[28] is an extraordinarily disembodied version of representation through which only one possible instance of awareness and reorganisation could emerge. In this manner of understanding, the implications involved in denoting the language, the structure and conception of the formal situation must be elaborated with an uncertain finality and it would appear worth the while to say that,

27. In post-structuralism the ability to retain language and experience in their primitive form is not directly possible because of the fact that the creation of meaning is very illusory in nature. Foucault.

28. The configuration of language in Derrida's sense of term is one that views language as a part of dissociative perception inasmuch as there is no prescribed hierarchy to modify the relevance of units and parts in the linguistic system. For example, we cannot find as to how a particular word stands to create value for a particular situation. Derrida.

language, when it stands as an equivalent model to conduct a positive communicative urgency, it shall have to resolve only into remote, distinct and unrealistic value concerns. Precisely, this definition of language suggests the fact that the letters, syllables, words and the sentences which constitute the linguistic content of the language and thought, experience and imagination, which compose an emotive structure of the language, could only associate themselves through the distance caused and created by the margin only. In this situation the creation of content in language, say, for example, a letter will have to disengage a sequence of random perception and in that way could obtain only an abstract value for the whole situation. It appears as if the constitutive situation inherent in the language projection[29] is based on complete reduction through a scale on which only devolution takes place. The whole situation can be given or would befit the following schematic formulation:

$$S = \mathbf{A} — \mathbf{A}^n$$

In this equation, obviously, the range of association between the two formal segments would be unrealistically continued till the fine complete reduction is finally obtained. Here the existence of a letter would be established till the time **A** is completely reduced to the power of **A** which in turn is raised to the power of $\mathbf{A}^n$. The significance of the equation suggests the idea that there can't be prefixing or suffixing of the conceptual structure. Nothing could be stated to be taking its origin from the beginning or reducing itself to the end. The actual circumstances diametrically resolve the situation into endless

29. In post-structuralist tradition the configuration of language is uncertain because of the fact that the displacement of the content is continuous and is consequently never revived even otherwise there has been no attempt to determine the content of language in respect of its form. Derrida, Foucault and Lacan have presented the language as if it is only a manner and variety of division of object into object and subject into subject.

figures and the language for that matter is devoid or bereft of further conjunction and association. There can't be merit involved in the logic of negating a growth situation to the language and reviving the extreme margins for the sake of a hold on the content. This view of language in post-structuralist theories creates a vacancy for the sake of separation and a gap or space for the sake of non-addition of **A** and **B**. If we could suppose the existence of the terms, we cannot straightaway make out an act of addition unless and until the abstract values of both **A** and **B** are defined and determined. From this idea the legitimacy of constituting a medium and an apparatus for linguistic form is forthwith born. It involves a regular and constant interactive and intra-active separation from the object and the subject, hence, from the primary models and the primary categories. The act of conceiving an instrument for language would be almost like finding a worth for intermediated movement of the former linguistic code. For example, determination of **A** in normal circumstances would be based on the subsequent fixation of all the minus **A**s hence, the whole exercise amounts to be forming a methodology and a rule for the extra-determination of the magnitude, characteristic, property and co-relationship of the letter occurring at any instance of the time. While we look at the whole situation in this framework we can be in a position to find a rather preliminary illustrative significance in the situation in the following verses from Kālidāsa's *Abhijñānaśākuntala*:

> ग्रीवाभङ्गाभिरामं मुहुरनुपतति स्यन्दने बद्धदृष्टिः
> पश्चार्धेन प्रविष्टः षरपतनभयाद्भूयसा पूर्वकायम्।
> दर्भैरर्धावलीढैः श्रमविवष्टतमुखभ्रंशिभिः कीर्णवर्त्मा
> पश्योदग्रप्लुतत्वाद्वियति बहुतरं स्तोकमुर्व्यां प्रयाति॥7॥
> (सविस्मयम्!) कथमनुपतत एव मे प्रयत्नप्रेक्षणीयः संवृत्तः।[30]

30. A.B. Gajendragadkar, *The Abhijñānaśākuntala of Kālidāsa*, 7th edn. 1962, The Popular Book Store, Surat, p. 6.

grīvābhaṅgābhirāmaṁ muhuranupatati syandane baddhadṛṣṭiḥ paścārdhene praviṣṭaḥ ṣarapatanabhayādbhūyasā pūrvakāyam ।
darbhairardhāvalīdhaiḥ śramavivaṣṭa mukha bhraṁṣihibhiḥ kīrṇavartmā paśyodagraplutatvādviyati bahutaram stokamurvyo prayāti ॥7॥
(savismayam!) kathamanupatata eva me prayatnaprekṣaṇīyaḥ saṁvṛttaḥ ।

> With graceful curving of his neck,
> He gazes on the chasing car,
> And, to escape the falling dart,
> Contracts his frame with shrinking dread,
> His path is strewn with half-chewed grass
> That drips from his wide-gaping mouth.
> Look, by his bouding, in the air
> Far more than on the earth he flies! (Amazed).
> What now! Though I follow closely I hardly
> can see the antelope.[31]

In this extraordinary suggestion we can understand that the movement of object (king) towards the subject (deer/fawn) enter into a proposition of infinite reduction inasmuch as, king, although, he can apprehend the movement of the deer but can't exactly locate the deer simply because of the fact that the chariot is moving very fast and a great amount of dust is being raised, to the height of the king, sitting on the chariot; yet indetermination, non-location and over-determination of the terms and concepts are logically standing in opposition to the earliest utterance proclaiming the sight of the animal "ग्रीवाभङ्गाभिरामं (*grīvābhaṅgābhirāmam*)" and immediately denying the reception of the concept by saying that "स्यन्दने बद्धदृष्टि: (*syandanebaddhadṛṣtiḥ*)" and for that matter the logic of sound manifested in magnificence and grandeur gets reflected out of the immediate source of perception and in that way

31. *Shakuntala or the Recovered Ring*, Six Sanskrit Plays in English trans, ed. Henry W. Wells, Asia Publishing House, New York, 1964, p. 201.

dislocated from the authority of the subject and has returned to the infinity. And one understands very well that infinity can't be combined with formal order of the things — the composition of truth in the background and context of something that is non-truth. The present manner of versification from *Abhijñānaśākuntala* carries out the exposition of nearly a preliminary ground of explanation and interpretation, and that is exactly how, one has to understand the continuity of linguistic object and the infinity of meaning whereby objects could be sustained and obtained.

The language is one of the primordial necessities to generate the object of communication and the subject of comprehension and to this extent the division of an object of language into letters, syllables, words and sentences and on the equivalent side into thought, imagination, experience would obviously suggest that the process of evolution of a syllable into sentence and the sentence into one of the terms of experience is something that would call for a remarkable understanding of the entire structural situation.

Ferdinand de Saussure could understand that structure of language is something that derives from both the writing and speech and therefore it has a further sub-division into the langue and parole with attendant object manifested in sign, signifier and signified. It means that the creation of language through homogeneous or heterogeneous concentration of the speech or writing, events would obviously be in a position to create equivalent values in whatever manner or form it comes to occupy its place in equivalent scheme of event formation. For example, the production of letter **A** must evoke an equivalent sound formation through a vowel like amplitude for the letter **A** or, in other words, we can say that the written form must have a cyclical correlation with the corresponding spoken form. To this extent the written **A** has to evolve into spoken **A** so that the value could be generated for the situation.

From this standpoint the dichotomy between writing and speaking as one of the necessary standards is established and it also leads to the situation in which the elementary forms in the language derive from the homogeneity in the given context and the principle is established that the equivalence must proceed from equivalence, like must create the like, yet under some exceptional circumstances, the production of the sound and the production of the letter do not keep up the necessary harmony, hence, they are subjected to the correlation in which the validity of value doesn't seem to establish a necessary connection between the phonological form and the semantic situation. This attitude to language is essentially the great foundation of the structuralist tradition and it could be simply stated to be forming a whole in the following manner:

$$A = a + b + c + d \text{ ....} z.$$

From the ground of observation thus substantiated in the above scheme, we could understand now the connection, inter-connection, correlation, inter-correlation and significance and inter-significance are necessarily brought about as and when the event of meaning is due to be forthcoming, and out of necessity, it conducts the significance of the process of evolution that started with the earliest inception of the syllable and the latest generation of the sentence that is expected to perform the last notation of the entire scheme; from this elementary field of observation, the methodology of understanding language receives a remarkable change in post-structuralist view of the situation.

From the post-structuralist perspective an idea or thought is incapable of convening the attendance of a host of contents only because of the fact that it came to be formed in consequence of some mental activity or intellection conceived a pragmatic conception for the whole situation likewise, feeling is more without authority of generation and reasons are more or less nearly the same. The formal fact, let us say, sensibility that consists of a system of equivalent feeling is in itself without a valid orientation through realisable contents and consequently in the temporal scheme the entire ideational feature seems to have been lost. For Derrida, the act of composition of a meaning always carries the misunderstanding of the whole constitution, function of the observer, reference, referred and the determinant. The actual situation or position of each of these is nevertheless never clear and always presupposes less than a concrete meaning for themselves. For example, look at the following opening verses of the *Kādambarī*:

> अस्ति सकलत्रिभुवनललामभूता, प्रसवभूमिरिव कृतयुगस्य, आत्मनिवासोचिता भगवता महाकालाभिधानेन भुवनत्रयसर्गस्थितिसंहारकारिणा प्रमथनाथेनापरेव पृथिवी समुत्पादिता, द्वितीयपृथिवीशङ्कया च जलनिधिनेव रसातलगम्भीरेणजलपरिखावलयेन परिवृता, पशुपतिनिवासप्रीत्या गगनपरिसरोल्लेखिशिखरमालेन कैलासगिरिणेव सुधासितेन प्राकारमण्डलेन परिगता, प्रकटशङ्खशुक्तिमुक्ताप्रवालमरकतमणिराषिभिश्चामीकरचूर्णवालुका निकरनिचितैरायामिभिरगस्त्यपरिपीतसलिलैः .... विकचकुवलयकान्तैरुत्फुल्लकमलवलोदरैरनिमिषदर्शनरमणीयैराखण्डल-लोचनैरिव सहस्रसंख्यैरुद्भासिता सरोभिः, अविरलकदलीवनकलिता-भिरमृतफेनपुञ्जपाण्डुराभिर्दिशि दिशि दन्तवलभिकाभिर्धवलीकृता, यौवनमदमत्तमालवीकुचकलषलुलितसलिलया भगवतो महाकालस्य शिरसि सुरसरितमालोक्य समुपजातेर्ष्ययेव सततसमाबद्ध-तरंगभ्रुकुटिलेखया खमिव क्षालयन्त्या सिप्रया परिक्षिप्ता, सकलभुवनख्यातयशसा हरजटाचन्द्रेणेव कोटिसारेण मैनाकेनेवाविदितपक्षपातेन . . .।[32]
>
> — *Sanskrit Kāvyadhārā*, pp. 586-90

There is, in the country of Avantī, a city called Ujjayinī, which excels in splendour, the world of the gods, and is the ornament of all the three worlds. It is (so holy that it is) as if

32. Bāṇa's *Kādambarī* (Pūrvabhāga complete), ed. Late M.R. Kale, Motilal Banarsidass, Delhi, 1968, pp. 64-66.

> it were the birthplace of the Kṛta age. It is as if it were a second Earth created, suitable for his residence, by the divine Śiva, the lord of the Pramantas, who (Śiva) is called (there) by the name of Mahākāla, and who brings about the creation, the maintenance, and the destruction of the three worlds. It is surrounded by an encircling ditch full of water, so deep as to reach the bottom of the Earth, as though by an ocean mistaking it for another Earth. It is surrounded by a circular rampart which is whitened with *cūnam*-paint, and whose rows of turrets kiss the surface of the sky, (thus) appearing as if it were the mountain Kailāsa (which is white like *cūnam* and whose rows of peaks touch the surface of the sky), surrounding it out of its affection for it as a dwelling-place of Śiva. It is bedecked with long, big market-roads, which look as if they were the oceans (left bare) when their waters were drunk up by (the sage) Agastya, since they (the roads) have on them, exposed (for sale), heaps of conches, oyster-shells, pearls, corals, and emerald gems, and since they are stacked with gold-dust and gravel-heaps. It is bedecked with picture-galleries which are full of (the paintings of) gods, demons, *siddhas*, *gandharvas*, *vidyādharas*, and *nāgas* and which (therefore) look as if they were a fleet of serial cars from heaven, descended there from the sky on account of an eager desire to see the fair ladies engaged in the constant festivities (held in the city). Its squares are bedecked with sacred shrines, which look glossy like the Mandāra mountain when it was whitened with the milk tossed up during the churning (of the ocean), which bear on their tops resplendent jars made of gold, and which, having their white banners fluttering high in the wind, look like the peaks of the Himalaya mountain upon which is falling (from above) the (milk white) stream of the celestial Ganges.[33]

In this unusual and extraordinary presentation of universal motive, reason, cause and effect of truth and reality, one could

33. Bāṇa's *Kādambarī* (Pūrvabhāga complete), ed. Late M.R. Kale, Motilal Banarsidass, Delhi, 1968, pp. 67-68.

understand that the manner of constructing the evidence of appearance and terms of reality are precisely made by the reversible movement of the content and context. The beginning of the passage marks the reality inherent upon the time and in that way it becomes (अस्ति *asti*) and from this the actual commencement of the structures of signification could be noted. In other words, time (अस्ति *asti*) as a reality, could, at the same time, rise to the merger of the material into immaterial hence the place Ujjayinī is both heaven (त्रिभुवन *tribhuvana*), and (भगवत *bhagavata*) and the earth (प्रसवभूमिरिव *prasavabhūmiriva*), the extent of constitution of a formless substance and formal result could be understood on the basis of the fact that the configuration of the object has initiated and evolved a response for the sake of the underlying concept of that form. In the background of such a concrete situation we can only understand that the significant earth is being largely symbolical of material function and the heaven suggesting timeless meanings could hardly be combined and correlated, yet the only combination that is to be intended is one that can be based on the transformation of being into non-being. Derridian equation of loss of significance for the primary forms of content with equally primary forms of concepts, is to an extent, justified in the whole passage. The adequacy of time yields an apparatus for the understanding of the timeless situation none the less in the context, of its assertion in the infinity of the situation. Time could be timeless or for that matter अस्ति *asti* could be महाकाल *Mahākāla* and भगवत *bhagavata* when and only when the truth is so well rendered, precise and meaningful, that it is received into the formal function of the infinity. Because of this, one has to make it a point that the establishment of sign as a necessary process of relegation of the concept to the background requires the worth of eternal motives to be brought in the form of truth and reality.

The exact position of the word and the letters in a sentence occasions a meaningful debate from the various segments of post-structuralist inquisition. For example, Derrida considers the possibility of expansion and extension in relation to the language:

> It is, therefore, as if what we call language could have been in its origin and in its end only a moment, an essential but determined mode, a phenomenon, an aspect, a species of writing. And as if it had succeeded in making us forget this, and *in willfully misleading us*, only in the course of an adventure: as that adventure itself. All in all a short enough adventure. It merges with the history that has associated technics and Logocentric metaphysics for nearly three millennia. . . . All appearances to the contrary, this death of the book undoubtedly announces (and in a certain sense always has announced) nothing but a death of speech. . . . "Death of Speech" is of course a metaphor here: before we speak of disappearance, we must think of a new situation for speech, of its subordination within a structure of which it will no longer be the archon.[34]
>
> — *Of Grammatology*, p. 8

The idea of finding a meaning and definition for language couldn't but be an exercise of establishing language through the words and the letters so as to arrive at a meaningful notation. In contrast to this, Derrida views the problem in a supposedly larger context in which the possibility of exposing and interpreting the form and appearance of the motive and projection of the units of sentence or units of language could be named (seriously disturbed), for example, when we write a word "elephant" then the possible location of the word within the strength forming conceptual system won't invest much of opportunity and exercise, rather it will deform the process by bringing about all the necessary manners of

34. Jacques Derrida, *Of Grammatology*, 1976, tr. Gayatri Chakravorty Spivak, The John Hopkins University Press, Baltimore and London, p.8

deviance in that the appearance of the word elephant is both logically, graphically, semiotically and semantically just and even only and at that is an accidental incident. When the word is written and meant, it is merely by the virtue of strength of appearance that we could say that word has value in such and such object and the life of appearance is logically very unrealistic in that it is always prone to disappearance. It cannot, obviously, enter into the unique necessity of meaning formation, just for the reason that's by the time it is written down, the appearance has already disappeared, so loss of appearance in the first place and reality in the second and truth in the third place together render the whole formative situation and conception very meaningless. It remains to be understood as to how the form of an appearance through a letter or syllable or word could determine the possibility of engaging in an activity through meaning and meaningfulness. When one proceeds to gather the significance through the random motion of the contents involved in the words or letters or even syllables which appear on the surface of an object, one is always led away by the contrasting relations and distinctions and the effort to decipher meaning is precisely lost in the wonderful music of the situation of the whole linguistic framework. A word, for example, can't sustain a methodological necessity to become a fact of coherence that is derived from the content precisely because the conjunctions and other native forms of association would be fairly wanting. In Derrida's term of understanding, appearance or presentation of a word to the context cannot either determine its centrality or the relative efficiency, for this, the origin of word in a multiple context could only be questioned. Similarly, the proportions which are otherwise very distinct and non-locative in nature evoke similar critical response from their placement either within the whole system or slightly outside the projected system. As a matter of fact, any valid term of reference combining both the object and the subject relationship could only guarantee and determine the precise length of the formative principle. In Derrida's consideration language is only an act of intention and intention cannot be a method to discover the configuration of suggestion. To this account the manner of viewing the presentation of idea of the language doesn't appear to be very wrong. Rather the action and primary models through primary categories to build up an object of motion and movement of the creative principles has its structure in the legitimate exposition of the meaning. In these contrasting principles the worth of language could only be understood and appreciated through an understanding of inquisitive principle controlling the movement of minor and major variants of the given structure.

In these interpretative formulations, at least two exceptional issues became very remarkable. In the first place, it has to be understood that language as a consequence of inscribed models does not conduct any unique methodological interpretation of any theoretical inquisition brought before it. Accordingly, the entry of a word or a letter or a syllable into the consequence of resolution cannot be immediately included.

This point of view offers a host of constructive problems and for which their can be no answers. The first of such issues would be the methods to construct an effective arrangement of the various timeless and temporal situations prescribed by Derrida and in the second place, it would amount to finding out the intensity of a reception that a word could initiate either in the action that has been completed or the events which are to follow, yet, in no circumstances does word deny the models of background and foreground. The specific nature of the events underlying in this new conception of language would yield a better appreciation of the terms through the following verse:

> भवन्ति गेहे बन्धक्यः कितवानां युधिष्ठर ।
> न ताभिरुत दीव्यन्ति दया चैवास्ति तास्वपि ॥

bhavanti gehe bandhakyaḥ kitavānāṁ yudhiṣṭhira ।
na tābhiruta dīvyanti dayā caivāsti tāsvapi ॥
— *Mahābhārata*, Sabhā Parva[35]

O Yudhiṣṭhira, slaves are there in the houses of gamblers,
They too are not gambled on. They too are shown mercy — *Sanskrit Kāvyadhārā*, p.118

The interrelationship of the intensity of originary words, consequent words, preceding words and succeeding words could be understood here with regard to the fact that the constitution of proposition has been set in the background of an infinite determination, extra-determination and over-determination of the terms of resolution. For that matter "भवन्ति गेहे (*bhavanti gehe*)" would suggest how the strength of perception logically yields to an imperception, or in other words, the realistic time immediately gets transmuted into illusory time. Hence the nativity of the word and sound both are lost. Even the apostrophised model of utterance that generates a signification for a canonical individual does not yield to the necessity of actual resolution inasmuch as strength has been demolished by not intending a communicative figuration for the principle of truth and the last statement "ताभिरुत दीव्यन्ति दया चैवास्ति तास्वपि (*tābhiruta dīvyanti dayā caivāsti tāsvapi*)" could only suggest that the beginning of a perception in a recorded event has been lost in the imperceptible sequence of resolution, inasmuch as युधिष्ठिर (Yudhiṣṭhira) as a model of truth and time and timelessness, does not exactly explain the consequence of effect proposed for the resolve or realisation, and for this reason, in "भवन्ति (*bhavanti*)","दीव्यन्ति दया चैवास्ति तास्वपि (*dīvyanti dayā caivāsti tāsvapi*)" one has to have the necessity of understanding the fact that truth is infinite, individual is infinite, sequence is infinite and the resolution

35. Rahul Sankrityayan, *Sanskrit Kāvyadhārā*, Kitab Mahal, Sammelan Mudralaya, Prayag, Allahabad, 1957, p. 118.

accordingly is infinite because infinity conceives the methods of illusion.

In the entire system of finding a concept of language in the post-structuralist tradition Derrida primarily relies on three important situations. In the first place, he makes the whole apparatus of language to be necessarily incapable of yielding the equivalents inasmuch as the models of the language have changing status and positions and therefore, there cannot be any certainty with regard to the prospective situation purporting to hold a term for value for the previous situation. Secondly, the associative principle, claiming to associate a particular word with a particular value, is also very unrealistic because of the fact that synchronic and diachronic antecedents both disprove the merit of association, and more particularly, the synchrony of the linguistic form and association rather abruptly disjoint the word's capacity to prove the worth of its merit to generate the phonetic background and the scriptive appearance both do not sum up an authority of significance for the acquired terms and prospective meanings and on that account there is a great deal of dissociation between the words that are created, the sounds that are produced and the letters that are being written. The effect of disharmony is issued naturally in anything that it could give rise to and for that matter Derrida's objections to the situations are thoroughly justified. Yet we can understand that, Derrida, although in a very abrupt manner, develops a thematic side of the language with an indefinite structure. For example, he could state that speech forms and written forms both are infinite and indefinite, hence the structures, which claim to create these two forms must be indefinite, consequently the entry of a letter or syllable or word or even sentence into the written system would prolong and expand the entire system till an uncertain time. In other words, there would be a constant division or addition or subtraction or multiplication to arrive at the endless form. In this way, any realistic structure would be endlessly conjugated in the expanding or reducing formation regardless of the fact whether it has yielded a result or not. And this appears to be one of the great merits of Derridian conception of the language and the experience that is generated by the situation. The total structural form could be understood in the following manner:

$$S=A\times A=A+A=A/A\text{-}A^{n}\times A^{-n}$$

The predominant function of implicating the terms of concept in an equative formation is to make it clear that the intended value and proposed concept both are absolutely uncertain, yet, there is a possibility that the two linguistic structures will either multiply and subtract, divide each other so as to yield a term specific to multiplication although without any merit in advancing the cause of final result. This therefore, becomes in some ways a method to understand the conceptual form of the situation.

Experience in Post-structuralist Tradition

The formation of experience and presentation of an experience under the limitations of deformation and representation is a problem of comprehension and understanding in the post-structuralist system.[36] The experiential category is approached for a formulation in relation to its extreme opposite that is the non-experience or even supra-experience and in this regard Derrida proceeds with the idea of the determination of non-experience. According to him the sensations one apprehends, are, by and large, the products of a continuous transference of perception to attitude, and attitude to will, and will to the

36. The commitment of categories for a participation in artistic situation definitely does not become a motive rather it is only realised in the disintegration of the contents. This appears to be one of the fundamental parts of the theoretical conception intended in post-structuralism.

idea. In this scheme of presentation the entire methodology that purports to work out a situation of possible structures wherein the will or idea or even the attitude is itself subjected to multiple transpositions. Accordingly, the apprehended sensation is not authoritatively received in the purported object and for that matter the prospective equivalence is disrupted. It would mean that the creational sensation and production of context to equal the sensation couldn't be very meaningfully brought to the condition of systematic positioning of one against the other and other against the another. This linear arrangement that comes to be developed within the sensation and the content does not lead to the harmony of convergence at a single point rather multiple foci are created to destroy and disrupt the arrangement of the content. It is precisely because of this that Derrida defines an experience not as a reception of the perceptive sensation but rather as the arrangement of non-perceptible and non-linear sensation that have their meaning and significance only in a random environment. For this the conjunction of perception to find in normal human sensory formation could not be a worthy object of comprehension and understanding, rather it would only be a rarefied, indiscreet and infinite medium that could generate the linear and irreversible flow of irreversible motion of the contents and become a suitable object of interpretation for the situation. In the whole composition, the concept of experience is to be divided into an understanding of the following primary categories:

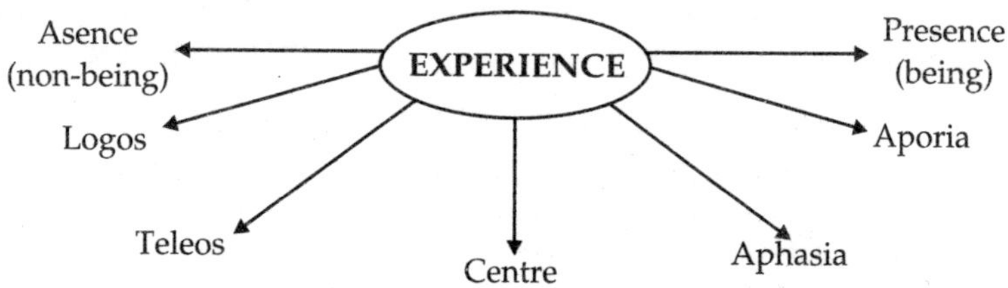

***fig.* 1.9: Nature of experience according to Derrida.**

In this scheme of representation, the view of experience is marked by an indeterminate formation just for the reason that beginning of a sensation and the end of a sensation do not carry the reality of origin and end. It cannot be precisely determined as to how, why, when and where sensation came up and at what particular point of time it would come off inasmuch as the apprehension of a sensory intensity is randomly distributed throughout the course of the progress of the motion and movement of the content and content in a medium that has generated it or precisely and fairly illustrated it and for this single reason their cannot be any certainty in associating any perceived figure with a proposed form. This leads Derrida to view the matter by segregating the presentation of a sensation and reception of the same sensation at an almost infinite distance, and normally the base of projection for such an infinity could only be the supra-mediums, non-mediums and rarefied contents. In this regard, he could generate the following irreversible terms of which the idea of teleos and logos seems to be the most important one. In the Western philosophical tradition the matter has always been viewed with regard to the immediate sensation that it could give rise to, for that matter the object and subject must enter into a correlative proposition so that the subject could perceive and object could transmute the perception. This would suggest that the placement and position of object on the one hand, and content on the other hand should have a decided and a clear end in view to be understood in the present contents as logocentric or teleocentric. Such an extraordinary disruption would obviously lead to the emergence of similar concepts in which there cannot be any commitment or guarantee with regard to the projection and formulation of the idea of perception and generation of the content. The terms aporia (the production of an illusion about the possibility of a great artistic intensity), aphasia (disruption of the intensity of artistry and its relegation to the next illusion) absence (indetermination) (non-being) signify the realisation of indetermination.

The motive and purpose of Derridian interpretation of an experience would obviously lead one to find out difficulties in generating suitable terms for comprehension in that each category obviously does not bring about the normal strength of coherence and commitment. It may be possible to explore the situation by motivating the comprehension just at the beginning of rarefaction. For example, consider this:

> At the centre, the permutation or the transformation of elements (which may of course be structures enclosed within a structure) is forbidden. At least this permutation has always remained *interdicted* (and I am using this word deliberately). Thus it has always been thought that the centre, which is by definition unique, constituted that very theme within a structure which while governing the structure, escapes structurality. This is why classical thought concerning structure could say that the centre is paradoxically, within the structure and outside it. The centre is at the centre of totality (knowledge) yet since the centre does not belong to the totality (is not part of the totality) the totality has its centre elsewhere.[37]
>
> — *Writing and Difference*, p. 352

The terms that Derrida has expounded are worthy of predating the situation with a noteworthy accuracy. Centrality and totality are the two key terms that enter into the discussion, are precisely knowledge and meaning created on account of the perception of the situation, and accordingly, when either the medium or the content is not appropriate to receive the perception, derangement ensures and we can say that centrality

37. Jacques Derrida, *Writing and Difference*, 2001, tr. Alan Bass, translation of: 'L'écriture et la différence', Paris : Éditions du Seuil, 1967, Routledge Classics, London EC_4p_4EE, p. 352.

and totality are not in correspondence with each other. The construction of the content would be well approached by obtaining relevance in the literary/artistic formation in the Western tradition. Look at the following:

> वसन्तसेना - अथ किंनिमित्तमेष रोदिति ?
> रदनिका - एतेन प्रातिवेशिकगृहपतिदारकस्य ।।
> सुवर्णशकटिकया क्रीडितम्। तेन च सा नीता।
> ततः पुनस्तां याचतो मयेयं मृत्तिकाशकटिका कृत्वा दत्ता ।
> ततो भणति - "रदनिके, किं ममैतया मृत्तिकाशकटिकया ?
> तामेव सौवर्णशकटिकां देहि" इति।[38]
>
> — *Sanskrit Kāvyadhārā*, p. 366

> Vasantasenā: Then, for whom do you cry?
>
> Radanikā: This boy used to play with neighbour's son's toy-cart of gold. He has taken that back. He asked me again for it, then I made a toy-cart of clay and gave it to him. On that he says "Radanikā, what have I to do with this toy-cart of clay? Give me that toy-cart of gold".

In this artistic presentation from Śūdraka's *Mṛcchakaṭikā* the exceptional brilliance has been cultivated by conjugation of experience and perception in the first place and by demotivating perception in the second place. For the purpose, the discourse generated by वसन्तसेना (Vasantasenā) and रदनिका (Radanikā) correlates and destroys the content and idea both simultaneously and variously. The first important situation that we can understand in the following episode that the toy-vehicle that used to be the play-toy for a baby has now been taken away. It used to be of gold and although now it has been replaced by one that is made of clay yet the baby is crying and is really very vexed. It would mean that the subject of the situation, the toy of the baby, creates an illusory perception or sensation mounted on the immediate thrill or

38. Rahul Sankrityayan, *Sanskrit Kāvyadhārā*, p. 366.

short-lived pleasure on account of assessing the play-toy of gold. Yet the created perception is rather unrealistic inasmuch as there cannot be any guarantee with regard to the permanence of the experience generated, and moreover, the toy though replaced the baby is still vexed and perplexed and keeps crying. There can be two ways to find a deconstruction model in the given situation. In the first place, the play-toy made of gold defers the purity of experience in the baby and therefore he has become indefinitely indisposed to create any concrete form of experience in it; for the similar reasons he is still crying, making meaning and knowledge both to be infinitely located on the indefinite origins. The utterance "रदनिके, किं ममैतया मृत्तिकाशकटिकया? तामेव सौवर्णशकटिकां देहि (*radanike, kiṁ mamaitaya mr̥ttikāśakaṭikayā? tāmeva sauvarṇaśakaṭikāṁ dehi*)" forms a rather unusual separation between the object and the subject of the whole discoursal situation.

The qualitative configuration of sensory perception has a manifest denial in the opposition between the formation of knowledge and presentation of knowledge through logical contents and perceptible medium and, for this reason, the idea of having a fixed structure rarely stands to terms with the requirement of the wholesome situation. The figural form in sensation rarely evokes a perception that is intended to resolve the object rather it begets heterogeneous dispersion of the models. To explain the situation, let us think of a complete structure intending to put forth a figure for the sake of the reception of contents. No sooner than the contents are supposed to be carried forward with the random and spatial motion, the receiving medium gets both horizontal and vertical breaks, and for that matter, the entire event is disintegrated into the minor forms and each form relegates itself to the linear dimension and hence becomes a part of the infinity. Derrida understands this term, and therefore, just could not believe in the association of the knowledge and the content, and for that matter, being and non-being. Accordingly if there is no harmony between knowledge and content or no exclusive concentration of knowledge into content, the whole idea of having a central function (rupture) for this would be nearly a forgone conclusion. The question now arises as to how and why the creation of knowledge and formation of the contents for the knowledge on the one hand, and reception and communication of the knowledge on the other are diversified through heterogeneous mediums. Derrida's answers to the question are primarily rooted in what he calls expansion of the sign and reduction of the sign. Sign is supposed to convey the value for a concept yet signs are always changing and in this mutability of the signs one can only understand that the creation of fixed value for a concept would be an illegitimate account of the whole situation. For example, the diverse credentials for value generated and created through this would be almost at random inasmuch as every observer will not merit the situation through similar functionalities hence, at every instance, instead of concept variants would be brought about in the following manner:

$A\,{}^{1}B$ ® $A^{I}+A^{II}+A^{III} \ldots An$

The terms which are employed by Derrida to illustrate the situation are precisely decentring, dislocating, reduction bricoleur (fiddle, tinker) totalisation, scandalisation and the like, and in one of the important observations he could make mention of, he explains the situation in the following manner:

> If totalisation no longer has any meaning, it is not because the infiniteness of a field cannot be covered by a finite glance or a finite discourse, but because the nature of the field — that is language and a finite language — excludes totalisation. This field is in effect that of *play*, that is to say, a field of infinite substitutions only because it is finite, that is to say, because instead of being an inexhaustible field, as in the classical hypothesis, instead of being too large, there

> is something missing from it: a centre which arrests and grounds the play of substitutions. One could say — rigorously using that word whose scandalous signification is always obliterated in French — that this movement of play, permitted by the lack or absence of a centre or origin, is the movement of *supplementarity*. One cannot determine the centre and exhaust totalisation because the sign which replaces the centre, which supplements it, taking the centre's place in its absence — the sign is added, occurs as a surplus, as a *supplement*.[39]
>
> — Victor E. Taylor, *Post Modernism: Critical Concepts*, p. 515

The primary emphasis lies mainly on the fact that the extension of a comprehensible knowledge to the realisable contents doesn't have an authentic recognition both in the medium and the contents. We cannot think of a complete situation to be emerging before us and in this regard it has to be taken for granted that significance of a term either at the beginning or at the end would be almost impossible to be achieved because of the reasons we have mentioned in the foregoing. It is now perhaps possible to formulate the entire situation through an idealistic formulation obtained in *Mudrārākṣasa* of Viśākhadatta:

> (प्रत्यक्षवद् लक्ष्यं बद्धवा) राक्षस, राक्षस, विरम्यतां अस्माद् दुर्व्यवसितात्।
> उत्सिक्तः कुसचिवदृष्टराज्यतन्त्रो,
> नन्दोऽसौ न भवति चन्द्रगुप्त एषः।
> चाणक्यस्त्वमपि च नैव केवलं ते,
> साधाम्र्य मदनुकृतेः प्रधनवैरम् ॥12॥[40]
>
> — *Sanskrit Kāvyadhārā*, p. 442

(Fixing the gaze in vacancy) Rākṣasa: refrain from this behaviour.
Overflowing with pride this is no Nanda,

39. Victor E. Taylor, Charles E. Winquist, *Post-Modernism: Critical Concepts*, 1998, Taylor & Francis Publication, p. 515.
40. Rahul Sankrityayan, *Sanskrit Kāvyadhārā*, p. 442.

The onerous duties of whose empire
Where, by evil ministers, supervised,
It is Candragupta;
Nor are you, by any means, Cāṇakya;
The only similarity in your imitation of me,
Is the hostility to the principal personage.[41]

The situation, in this utterance has a propositional variance between object and the subject and puts up an antithesis of opposition between object and the subject; therefore, the reality (चाणक्य *cāṇakya*) is being imminently denied by the unreality (राक्षस *rakṣasa*). Hence there is an infinite expansion and extension of the both structures of signification. There can be yet another way in which we may understand the whole situation. The supposed creation of the knowledge in the universal form of चाणक्य (*cāṇakya*) is being opposed by forming an equivalent idea of strength and power by राक्षस (*rākṣasa*) in himself and therefore राक्षस *rākṣasa* says "साधर्म्य मदनुकृते: प्रधानवैरम् (*sādharmya madanukṛteḥ pradhānavairam*)". This proves the point that when medium and the content are excessively preoccupied with oppositional systematisation, the rendering of the content of sensation and language, are displaced with greater speed and therefore relegated to the infinity in such a way that there cannot be any inter-transformation whatsoever.

The experience, as a category in Derrida's view of the matter, does not form any wholesome perception rather it is an effect of distribution of sensory embodiments to the remarkable diverse orientation of the contents and for that matter each sensation has a free and independent assortment, suggesting a deviance and regression from the completeness of a structure, yet the motion and movement being carried on by the structure is something that one has to take into consideration for understanding the brief and temporary production of synthesis in the terms proposed by Derrida.

41. Viśākhadatta, *Mudrārākṣasa* or *The Singet Ring*, tr. Ranjit Sitaram Pandit, Bombay New Book Company, p. 61.

Function of Language and Experience in Post-structuralism

In post-structuralism the function of language and experience has been a matter of attention and consideration and for that matter these categories have received interpretation both as a conscious manifestation of the situation and as an unconscious expression of the whole event. Three important post-structuralist theorists Derrida, Lacan and Foucault have examined the situation of conscious and unconscious expression of language and experience by introducing typical conceptual structures for the entire framework. Lacan, for example, believes that the mind in unconsciousness creates an apparatus of language, hence it also gives rise to certain definite equative situations without formally being received as an instrument of change, modification and transformation.

The functioning of mind in unconscious state is precisely the creation of two methodical terms of perception. First, there is a silent, hidden and exact formation of impression as a matter of symbolical reconstitution and in that way idea is created by the virtue of an excellent reception of hidden material by the careful functioning of the mental states. The position of the object and the centrality of the subject are at variance with one another for that matter the unconscious mind doesn't have a fixed locus to sustain the creation of an idea. For example, let us consider the case of a child who in the early years learns everything by virtue of its companionship with the mother and at a later stage undergoes the authoritarian rule of the father. Between these two states of perception, the movement of concept is extraordinarily remarkable inasmuch as the consciousness of experience generates an incoherence in the unstable authority of perception. This would suggest that under the circumstances in which the position of subject tends to acquire a relative function in either the generation of value or the production of concept, the corresponding object-function or object-authority would always disinherit the embodied perception. In Lacan's consideration the language is proportionally disembodied since the effect of structure is nowhere to be found. To this end he observes:

> To say that this mortal meaning reveals in speech a centre exterior to language is more than a metaphor; it manifests a structure. This structure is different from the spatialisation of the circumference or of the sphere in which some people like to schematise the limits of the living being and his milieu: it corresponds rather to the relational group that symbolic logic designates topologically as an annulus.[42]
>
> — *Écritis: A Selection*, p. 115

In this observation, Lacan considers the necessity and requirement of obtaining the coherence of structure to sustain the creation of an idea in the given circumstances. For that matter he would say that the fixed, stable and definite forms are rarely of any substantial motivation inasmuch as the division of meaning by value or concept leads to the creation of imperceptible sequence of contents. For example, the idea of colour black and associated value event in sorrow or death would only be an approximate venture simply for the reason that the unconscious source from which the object and subject would tend to derive themselves would be an act of requirement based on the familiarity with the unconscious element and in that way the entire framework would be only an effect of illusion. The motive of perception so recorded can acquire or could afford to acquire a shape or size, form or figure through prospective division of the signifier into the signified or image into the concept, yet both of these situations are only approximately revealed to act in the process of acquisition of experience or perception from rather uncertain and approximate ends. An observer, who proceeds to look

42. Jacques Lacan, *Écritis: A Selection*, tr. Alan Sheridan, 1989, Routledge Classics, London E_{C4p4}EE, p. 115.

at, let us say, a letter or syllable or even a word for the sake of an idea-oriented value, the entire effort is just thwarted by a search for valid signified and the reason that one would like to advance for this would be by saying that the ideal symbols or metaphors haven't been exactly derived from the sources in unstable unconscious. Lacan's conception of language could be understood by making the entire system divided into an intention only in functional terms whose foundations essentially lie in the understanding of unconscious, sub-conscious and conscious. Unconscious, as the term is advanced and propagated, stands for process of relational or relative transformation. Therefore there is no effect of the illustrated meaning. Rather than being an inclusion of perception it becomes an exclusion of imperception and the movement of the figure in the situation is primarily obtained in under effective and sub-effective sensation. On the other hand, the determinants of morphological framework like, for example, "grammar" of the situation would enter into a correlation with indefinite times since transformations are so abrupt and so rapid that inclusive events are rarely formed and rarely created. In a situation like this it may be possible to think of a formal structure of language as being embodied in :

(A) Interactive syllables,

(B) Non-active and un-acted figures of grammar,

(C) Supra-active words and sentences, and

(D) Irrational mental attitude.

These four situations, taken together, constitute fundamental principles in Lacan's ideas on language. For example, he could merit the entire scheme by the following preposition:

By "letter" I designate that material support that concrete discourse borrows from language.

> This simple definition assumes that language is not to be confused with the various psychical and somatic functions that serve it in the speaking subject — primarily because language and its structure enlist prior to the moment at which each subject at a certain point in his mental development makes his entry into it.[43]
>
> — *Écritis: A Selection*, p. 163

The interpretation of a sequence for placing the primary models (letters and the like) thereby obtaining a displaced term in the structures is one of the basic propositions that is advanced by Lacan. Letter in that regard is an initial circumstance in which the effect of coherence or incoherence could be seen and obtained and the creation of a letter for a discourse would be almost valuaised provided the model that is acting at the behest of unconscious is brought to recognition yet by far the task has proved to be very difficult. On that account the magnitude of letter as the smallest interactive form of sensation isn't a very inquisitive fact. For the similar reason, Lacan believes it to be a part of "material support". Consciously or unconsciously the term of action and act of inaction involved make a complete break with the primordial object rooted in the reception of the language routed in the unconscious and accordingly the nature of effect generated would be randomly pursued in the inconstancy or unconstancy of the entire experiential situation. The morphological terms that are elaborated by generating a word from a letter, a sentence from the words and a paragraph from the sentences would similarly be embodied in indefinite moments of conception as an illusion of primordial authority if a letter is material, word, of necessity, would be material and the production of multiple illusions would none the less be a conceptual and stylistic disruption conjuncting the whole range of prepositions. This

43. Jacques Lacan, *Écritis: A Selection*, tr. Alan Sheridan, 1989, Routledge Classics, London $E_{C4p4}EE$, p.163.

methodology of finding an interpretation of language as an act of action and effect of unconscious upon conscious, so as to resolve an unconscious into unconscious, is basically a development of an idea in which the following equative terms are generated:

$$\Sigma = A - A = A + A = A \,/\, A = A^{\ldots\ldots n}$$

$$= \text{Random} \quad \frac{\text{Unconscious}}{\text{Conscious}}$$

$$a = A \,/\, B = A \text{ or } B$$

$$= A^{n} B^{n}$$

We can understand that in Lacanian understanding, the creation of a fact or a model of language, and consequently the resolution of fact and model into value concept, will continue to be randomly conceived inasmuch as the unconscious authority from which these situations are derived won't facilitate the effect of certainty upon the situation, hence primordial and conscious form would conceive only and on inconsequential imperceptions in relation to the entire structural event. The formation of a word through composite letter, becomes an exercise of relegating more and more illusory effects to the necessity of conjunction of a letter with the word and for that matter there cannot be any systematic emergence of a concrete or coherent universal. Lacan supports the claim by admitting that the division of an image by a concept is the basic constitution of the irrationality contained in prospective meaning hence:

> To pinpoint the emergence of linguistic science we may say that, it is contained in the constitution movement of an algorithm that is its foundation. This algorithm is the following:

$$\frac{S}{s}$$

> which is read as signifier over signified, "over" corresponding to the bar separating the two stages.
>
> One cannot go further along this line of thought that to demonstrate that no signification can be sustained other than by reference to another signification: in its extreme form this amounts to the proposition that there is no language (langue) in existence for which there is any question of its inability to cover the whole field of the signified, it being an effect of its existence as a language (langue) that it necessarily answers all needs.[44]
>
> — *Écritis: A Selection*, pp. 164-65

The incoherence and abruption caused by division is related to the search for an original model of comprehension of language as the division is intended. It is expected that there cannot be any fixed formula to define the nature of generated value. The random perception caused on account of the aberration involved in both signifier and signified could exactly invert the whole proposition by one complete rotation and at that the variant for the signified. The necessity of conceiving a formal definition of deviance intended in Lacan's intention can have an imperfect manipulation for the entire figural as well as formal motivations and the admission of inversion can destroy the possibility of finding out a meaning for the situation. It now seems worth our while to see the situation in a rather new perspective and at that the idea of language must be interpreted through a legitimate and conscious model created in speech and writing. Speech is an effect of audition inasmuch as the utterances produced and

---

44. Jacques Lacan, *Écritis: A Selection*, tr. Alan Sheridan, 1989, Routledge Classics, London E_{C4p4}EE, pp.164-65.

created derive themselves from the imaginary source material and source material in turn is prohibited to display the essential nature of the objects by virtue of being constantly open to evolution and mutation. For example, water is associated in its primordial form with regeneration, yet the source that creates this concept is never necessitated to be known or understood and in that way the division of water by regeneration would obliquely dismantle the synthesis potential of all the attributes and variants included in it. It would mean that language cannot afford to receive and present the content in a reversible manner rather it will have to open up a segment for the general production of unsaturated meaning. In fact, the nature of speech as an effect of sound must be confined within the progress of the same sound in erratic medium in so far as the magnitude of volume of a sound and the other sound are distinct. Lacan suggests a situation for which the aberration in the medium and the content of the original sound could be sufficiently displaced yet the emergence of meaning cannot as such be authenticated.

In Lacan, the categorical interpretation of experience as a category occupies a worthy place inasmuch as Lacan deals with located and dislocated versions of an experience, accordingly, the experience is a sensory attitude built through the irregularity of sensation or feeling and at that it is constantly in a state of evolution.[45] At the beginning the child who imbibes

45. The qualitative nature of experience is indefinite inasmuch as it begins with a division and it ends also with a division, on that account division reduces the association of the contents:

> Lacan's most famous dictum is "the unconscious is structured like a language"... Lacan .... embraced Saussure's semiotic model of a fluid system of signs, in which meaning is assigned subjectively to empty signifiers by an unconscious process of signification. The Lacanian unconscious resides in this gap between symbol and significance, constituting the associative link. The key point is that meanings are not fixed; mental representations may acquire new connotations for the individual or be used to signify something →

this attitude compels the construction and deconstruction of the attitude by interpreting the necessary forms through an internal interruption only. As it happens in the case of language, the primitive model functions quite abruptly and there are frequent changes in the manner and authority of communication of the term and its meaning. It so happens that the evolving attitude is perceptibly destroyed by the conjunction of an authoritarian object formation within the child itself and for this reason the resolved and resultant forms of attitude are always at variance with the projected situation. Lacan observes about the entire structural necessity in the following manner:

> But in either case the efficacy of the unconscious does not cease in the waking state. The psychoanalytic experience does nothing other than establish that the unconscious leaves none of our actions outside its field. The presence of the unconscious in the psychological order, in other words in relation to functions of the individual, should, however, be more precisely defined: it is not co-extensive with that order for we know that if unconscious motivation is manifest in conscious psychical effects, as well as in unconscious

→ else entirely. As the unconscious system of signification develops during childhood, the ideas of *self, other, society* and *gender* are constructed in accordance with, or opposition to, the basic psychosexual notions of the phallus, the mother and the "names-of-the-father". This has an important consequence for . . . conscious representations, including their most fundamental ideas, can vary between individuals, change with context, and evolve over time. Interpretation is not a matter of consulting a look-up table of fixed symbolic meanings. Instead one must understand the individual's history and context in order to grasp the true significance of their ideation. Symbols can become confused, or disconnected from their conventional meanings, and the underlying thoughts and desires may be expressed in cryptic ways.

— An Introduction by Sean Homer Routledge, 2004, Metapsychology Online Reviews: Review by Sam Brown, Ph.D. 20, June 2006 (vol. 10, Issue 25), Review - Jacques Lacan — Philosophy,view_doc.php?type=book&id=3154&cn=394.]

> ones, conversely, it is only elementary to recall to mind that a large number of psychical effects that are quite legitimately designated as unconscious, in the sense of excluding the characteristic of consciousness are none the less without any relation whatever be the unconscious in the Freudian sense.[46]
> — *Écritis*: A Selection, p. 180

An example, in this regard, has to be conceived as progressing from an elementary attitudinal inaction to a preliminary demotivated action and the appropriate length of attitude acquired by a perception could be rightly transformed into an imperception inasmuch as the threefold states of developmental form — id, ego, and super-ego — do not commit any relationship or interrelationship in the face of the lack of a fixed model. The point that is to be understood is not how an attitude becomes different from the proposed variance of the mediums. In either of the situations, the worth of an example must be noticed to have created a better form of presentation through actual, right and condensed inception of the formation.

Lacan's position in upholding the continuous regression of an attitudinal motive by the displacement of a model of evolution could be explained in an artistic situation through a compulsory commitment that it could assign to any character or any event:

ततः श्रुत्वा महाराजः कैकय्या दारुणं वचः ।
चिंतामभिसमापेदे मुहुर्तं प्रतताप च ।।1।।
"किं नु मेऽयं दिवास्वप्नश्चित्तमोहोपि वा मम ।
अनुभूतोपसर्गो वा मनसो वाप्युपद्रवः"।।2।।[47]

tataḥ śrutvā mahārajaḥ Kaikayyā dārunaṁ vachaḥ।
cintāmabhisamāpede muhurtaṁ pratatāpa ca ।।1।।

46. Jacques Lacan, *Écritis: A Selection*, p. 180.

47. Rahul Sankrityayan, *Sanskrit Kāvyadhārā*, p. 158.

kiṁ nu meyeṁ divāsvapniścattamohopi vā mam
anubhūtopasargo vā manso vāpyudravaḥ ॥2॥

— *Sanskrit Kāvyadhārā*, p. 158

The monarch, as Kaikeyī pressed
With cruel words her dire request,
Stood for a time absorbed in thought
While anguish in his bosom wrought.
Does some wild dream my heart assail!
Or do my troubled senses fail!
Does some dire portent scare my view?
Or frenzy's stroke my soul subdue?[48]

In these two artistic events based on scriptural and religious functions assigned to the divine forms, it may be possible to comprehend the situation by interpreting the conscious and unconscious versions as an unconscious effect of the perception. Daśaratha (the king) builds up a set of correlated attitudes, yet could not modify the attitude, into perception inasmuch as interactive id, ego and super-ego thwart the progress of perception. Hence, he falls upon 'चिंतामभिसमापेदे मुहुर्तं प्रतताप च (*cintāmabhisamāpede muhurtaṁ pratatāpa ca*)'. The object function assigned to the attitude conception is only felt as a part of the regressed thinking and for this reason Daśaratha considers a possibility of division of the signified (मुहुर्तं *muhurtaṁ*) with the signifier (कैकय्या *Kaikayyā*) and hence comes to a conclusion that "अनुभूतोपसर्गो वा मनसो वाप्युपद्रवः (*anubhūtopasargo vā manaso vāpyudravaḥ*)" the consequent metaphors in मुहुर्तं (*muhurtaṁ*) and 'दिवास्वप्न (*divāsvapna*)' are precisely conjugated through an extraordinary release of deviant perception. To say that the necessity of attitude creates a fragmentary version of experience creates resolved antithetical necessities in the wholesome sensation and the contention of Lacan seems to be meriting the whole proposition.

It is now worth the while to suggest that the usual

48. .... internet

definitions of language and experience have been consciously incoherent while the effect of resolution is estimated inasmuch as the language becomes object deficient and the experience is attitude deficient. This appears to be one of the major contributions made by Lacan in sustaining the post-structuralist tradition[49] of an inquiry into the primordial categories.

Manner of Examining Language and Experience in the Post-structuralist Tradition

The manner of examining language and experience in the post-structuralist tradition primarily confirms the loss of a definite function of both the language and the experience, and, for that matter, the situational urgency that attempts the whole categorical presentation is basically mounted on the extreme dysfunction that comes to occupy its place in the scheme of the things. Foucault, for the similar reasons, is a post-structuralist thinker who interprets both the categories in relation to the historical origins and the development of time as a primary notion. Time is both a functional and a dysfunctional event associated with the origin and growth of several attending events and situations. For example, the history, as one of the basic formations of time, could only be called history if the events in which history is conceived are misappropriated with a greater margin. There are certain ways to understand how the wholesome system of knowledge is conceived and composed through a legitimate and perfect understanding of language and experience. By language, Foucault means a dispersal of the unities that are supposed to

49. In post-structuralism the resolution of the categories (language and experience) is obviously a methodical perspective built around the perspective of reduction hence the conduct of change is of necessity to disperse the poetic contents towards infinity.

— Roland Barthes, — *Mythologies*, tr. Annette Lavers, Hill and Wang, New York, 1984, MYTH TODAY, The Athenaeum Library, Athenaeum Reading Room http://evans-experientialism.freewebspace.com/barthes04.htm

unify and integrate and correlate the structure of thought, therefore, the matter of language is always a continuity rather than fixed and static; while it is continuous, it derives the thought matters from infinity and precisely becomes an effect of regression. For example, in order to obtain **A** one must return to **A**, and, because of that, the growth or continuity, although, intending to be continuous, will fall back upon the reduction of wholesome event till the time it is converted into a supra-reduced entity and the equation will hold the merit inasmuch as the factor **A** having a composite function at **A** will have a permanent dysfunction by making a random association with the regressed variable only to be found at random at **A**. This method of viewing the matter doesn't guarantee a precise formulation of a concept, rather it disorients the movement towards authority. For example, consider the following observation:

> Continuous history is the indispensable correlative of the founding function of the subject: the guarantee that everything that has eluded him may be restored to him; the certainty that time will disperse nothing without restoring it in a reconstituted unity; the promise that one day the subject — in the form of historical consciousness — will once again be able to appropriate, to bring back under his sway, all those things that are kept at a distance by difference, and find in them what might be called his abode.[50]
>
> — *The Archaeology of Knowledge*, p. 12

It means that the action of thought and intention of thought both could be divided into a natural form of language that obtains a division into subject and predicate, yet however, the collective function of the subject and predicate would

50. Michel Foucault, *The Archaeology of Knowledge*, tr. from French by A.M. Sheridan Smith, Tavistock Publications, London, EC_4P_4EE, 1972, p. 12.

intentionally discredit the synthesis that is supposed to be brought about inasmuch as each would assume an independent position. This situation can be viewed in terms of the players playing a football match and one single movement intended to be carried on by the footballers has enlisted participation from so many players. In other words, the movement of the ball is dispersed inasmuch as the authority of participation attracts the manner of approval through different hands and different manners. On the field and all along the field the diverse, disparate and digressive turns, even within the movement, could be understood. Foucault, relaying on this, could authenticate the whole situation by saying that the subject, and for that matter even predicate, are both, the by-products of a continuous time moment and the term continuity at length revives the primordial forms in infinity and endlessness. For this reason, subject cannot be made to inhere upon a single continuous movement, rather, almost like the state of the ball on the football ground it will accord a variation within the movement. To this extent there cannot be any fixed and permanent subjection of the situation, hence the discontinuity in forming the subject and the predicate is always the significant option available. This is perhaps one of the things to be understood. The nature of subject is built around the formal function of the statements or the facts or the situations or the events or event formations presented collectively or individually to the consideration of time. The fact is only an authority of perception. On the other hand, the foundation of perception doesn't have any concrete existence. It is issued only at the behest of indeterminate sequence of the situation. There is only a motive to be presented and performed inasmuch as the observation made for the sake of perception could not guarantee any formal construction of the ideas. Before it could become a part of the idea, it moves and keeps moving without any presupposition for creating the content or expressing the notion, statement or fact. For this, reason could have only an optional view of the matter and it is most certainly an event that decomposes the preliminary strength built around. This appears to be a rather distinct process of abandoning the roots of conceptualisation while the event of thought conception is launched; the purpose of perception is to suggest a basis for observation, hence the resolution of perception must be in the carefully felt sensation. Yet, however, the loss of fixation around content disengages the associated meanings involved and there can't be any full-fledged activity as such. It only disregards the conception. Foucault could only present a view that language that generates facts, statements ideas or anything of the sort, is obviously marked by the progress of implied division within itself. For example, if **A** is an act of perception and **B** is an event of resolution, then the interrelationship between **A** and **B** would be pursued through an account established in this regard by the adhesive principle having cumulative forms; for this, it will have the following version of presentation:

$$\underline{A}$$

$$\underline{A^{a}}$$

$$\underline{A^{b}}$$

$$\underline{A^{c}}$$

$$\underline{A^{-n}}$$

$$= B = B^{-n}$$

In this equative measure the purpose of obtaining a significant relation is effectively built around the intra-associated cumulative division leading to regression and reduction till the time a variant in **B** is obtained and the last stretch of resolution compulsorily adds to the effect of a deviance in the sequence of composite perception. This would mean that Foucault has a typical conception of language, and accordingly, a full-scale definition could be approached by saying that the insignificance of conceptual idea presenting an indirect interaction with the time motives and time expressions are also the expressions of language at any particular movement of time. This attribute is very radical and compulsive in nature.

In Foucault's understanding of the term, the necessity of finding value and concept together with a principal determinant doesn't proceed through a path of geometrical arrangement of the coordinates. The position of the observer, length of concept and strength of value, both are distributed heterogeneously all along the spatial environment, and for this, a correspondence could never be brought about. The observer will observe, the concepts will be made and values will continue to be generated, yet the essential arrangement of the sequence would only be an aberration; therefore, the presentation of meaning cannot be predicated with any authenticity. It is possible now to find a valid illustration for the situation by intercepting the terms obtained in the following utterances:

या मयासीन्न संबुद्धा कदाचिदपि मंदया ।
पिता दानवराजो मे भर्ता मे राक्षसेश्वरः ।। 39।।
पुत्रो मे शक्रनिर्जेता इत्यहं गल्र्वता भृशम् ।[51]

yā mayāsinna saṁbuddhā kadācidapi mandaya ।
pitā dānavarājo main bhartā main rākṣaseśvaraḥ
putro main śakranirjetā etyaḥ garlṛvtā bhṛṣaṁ ।
— *Sanskrit Kāvyadhārā*, p. 194

51. Rahul Sankrityayan, *Sanskrit Kāvyadhārā*, p. 194.

That which I never even thought.
My father king of Demons, My husband god of Demons.
My son the victor over Indra, Thinking this I used to be proud.

In these formations, the sensory embodiment, although very powerfully generated, marks the creation of determinate objects at the several junctions. For this purpose, we can understand three important object sensations "दानवराजो *dānavarājo*", "राक्षसेश्वर: *rākṣaseśvaraḥ*", "शक्रनिर्जेता *śakranirjetā*" and in each the functions of value and concept together with form and content do not entail or achieve merit inasmuch as दानवराजो *dānavarājo* being Rāvaṇa has been rendered formless, "राक्षसेश्वर: *rākṣaseśvaraḥ*" being Rāvaṇa once again is now denotatively an abstraction only and the stretch of infinity in both is exceptionally received in "शक्रनिर्जेता *śakranirjetā*" (being Meghanāda) and has entered into an indistinct interrelationship with abstraction inasmuch as he is now very formless. The point is established as to how the origination of an idea at the site of sensation can withhold the exact replication of the terms absolutely.

In that way the considerable amount of diversion and deviance is made to be situated when an experience tends to be created. For the same reason, there is by and large, an impossibility in presupposing either a value or a concept for the sensory acquisitions. In the same context, Foucault's idea on the experience as a category is only a presentation of random and abstract functioning of the figures as different as the medium, content, observer and observation. In each we could only understand how the motive of truth isn't the function of an idea inasmuch as idea doesn't have a function. The fact or statement made through will have no meaning precisely in consequence as such. Foucault's understanding of a coherent and composite situation determining the term of an event within the fact or statement or discourse altogether confers a score of motivated perceptions on language suitable for the linguistic forms, and accordingly, by language he would mean a process of determination of letter, syllable, word, sentence or for that matter the whole paragraph. From this it would follow that the process of determination is, perhaps, an unethical situation for the reason that no letter, no syllable no word and no sentence could be determined through its own existence, rather in order to find its value, we will have to look at its connection and inter-connection either with the preceding form or with the succeeding event. Hence, there cannot be any method of knowing the primary existence of a linguistic form, consequently, self-determination would be an illusive term. Foucault observes:

> The associated field that turns a sentence or a series of signs into a statement, and which provides them with a particular context, a specific representative content, forms a complex web. It is made up first of all by the series of other formulation within, which the statement appears and forms one element. . . . The associated field is also made up of all the formulations to which the statement refers, (implicitly or not), either by repeating them, modifying them, or adapting them. . . . Generally speaking, one can say that a sequence of linguistic elements is a statement only if it is immersed in an enunciative field, in which it then appears as a unique element.[52]
>
> — *The Archaeology of Knowledge*, pp. 98-99

The focus falls upon two things. In the first place, there cannot be any arbitrary fixation of the form of language inasmuch as the strength and capacity to generate value would be lost through radical projection, and secondly, the length of modification of a syllable into word or a word into sentence could only be a possibility if it is covered by a separate mechanism of relationship and interrelationship, primarily.

52. Michel Foucault, *The Archaeology of Knowledge*, pp. 98-99.

Foucault suggests that the inclusive functioning of any necessary form of language could only be successful when it has a strong cause and effect relationship, yet the figures which conclude an event in a language may necessarily not be in possession of this ideal of practice. Word cannot be a cause, at the most it can serve as an effect. On the other hand, the experiential medium that would suggest the beginning of the process of a function in language has its own inter-notational problems inasmuch as the primitive object of experience enters into a regular displacement.

In so far as language is concerned, the event of evolution is manifested obviously through the process of presupposition. Every minor term presupposes the major term and for that matter letters, syllables presuppose words and sentences. Yet, however, presupposition is not a fact but a probability of the fact. Look at the following:

> Whereas grammatical construction needs only elements and rules in order to operate; whereas one might just conceive of a language (*langue*) — an artificial one, of course — whose only purpose is the construction of a single sentence; whereas the alphabet, the rules of construction and transformation of a formal system being given, one can perfectly well define the first preposition of this language (*langue*). There is no statement that does not presuppose others; there is no statement that is not surrounded by a field of coexistences, effects of series and succession, a distribution of functions and roles.[53]
>
> — *The Archaeology of Knowledge*, p. 99

Foucault's concern for the language has both necessity and purpose in reviving and dispersing conscious semiological facts and uncertain semantic suppositions, hence he suggests that the principle of evolution is technically impossible with regard

53. Michel Foucault, *The Archaeology of Knowledge*, p. 99.

to the language as generative event since it will call for coexistence and presupposition. While we can admit coexistence, presupposition as a functional term in synthesis and synchronisation of certain principles would altogether be beyond conception. For the similar reasons the idea of generating a context for meaning and even a content for value cannot be rightly presupposed. All the letters and nearly all the units of language exist on the principle of a conjunction through association and an injunction through correspondence. For example, the meaning of "horse" is specific; primarily because it is presupposed by a definite form that is obtained by a distinction between "horse" and a "cat". The meaning of "horse" does not owe anything to its immediate perception as a "horse". Looking at this situation there cannot be any abstraction involved in the formative sequence appearing on behalf of the language. On the whole, we can understand the following exclusive and distinct characteristics of the language according to Foucault:

I. Language is a compulsive system with no independent facility to generate the terms for value and concept.

II. There is a constant displacement of the unity that keeps the various elements of language together hence the system as such is not open for modifications and changes.

III. The units of language are unrealistic for this reason presentation of a statement or fact or discourse of language halts at the inception only.

IV. Figural and formal sequence of the units of language is at variance with one another hence nothing definite could be presupposed.

V. Only at the extraordinary socio-cultural or politico-historical changes, does language assume a unified meaning.

While we look at Foucault's conception of language, the essential circumstance of post-structuralism, according to him, can be understood in that post-structuralism focuses on elevation and designation of language and experience to the status of discourse, and for that matter, it could always suggest an inherence of the statement and fact in both the language and experience. None the less, these two categories are not evolved as being conditioned by independence and autonomy. Thus the structure of language and experience cannot fix themselves through a common object of perception and in consequence there cannot be any presupposition of value and concept for each of these.

The constitutive principles inherent upon the structure and function of *rasa* and post-structuralism could well be advanced through both condition and situation that operate the principles of (a) Synthesis, (b) Exposition, (c) Cognition and (d) Presentation of the various categories. In *rasa*, for example, the continuity of change, modification, transformation and transmutation of one category into the other and other into yet another, is a basic form of evolution for the creation of an ideal artistic situation. It would mean that *bhāva* evolves into *sthāyī bhāva* and *sthāyī bhāva* in turn is modified into *vibhāva* and *vibhāva* in turn becomes *anubhāva*, hence *sañcārī bhāva* and on that account the process of idealisation of *rasa* as a single, wholesome, assertive form is complete. In *rasa*, thus one understands how transformation intends the generation of concrete, rational, solid, truthful absolute and perfect form inasmuch as the participating categories create almost an independent universal for each.

While in post-structuralism the nature of categories, primarily language and experience are modified with a view to enlisting a method for regression, accordingly, the language and experience, both enter into modification and disperse right at the point at which the resolution is to be effective in meaning there by object and event both are supra-rationalised and excess of reason intends an aberration of meaning although the motive of transformation is imminent.

3

Applicatory Principles I

In *rasa* and post-structuralist theoretical tradition, the range of artistic comprehension varies from universal to local, situational to occasional and ideal to abstract, and for that matter, while producing recognisable evidence in the adopted terms one has to have prejudices and favour for a theory that turns to record the eminence of transformation, cognition, correlation, conjunction and comprehension as the basic effects of presentation. In the following pages we will have to find out under what circumstances the credit of prejudice has to be distinctly assured for *rasa* and not at all for post-structuralism.

A valid literary theory is always one that has practical applications. A literary theory is about literature and unless it can be applied, it has very little practical relevance. It must be flexible enough to take the wear of time to be malleable to interpretations and newer needs. The *rasa* theory fulfils most of these conditions. In fact, it is considered the soul of literature. The strength of this theory lies in the fact that it deals with what is common to all mankind at all times — emotions; various kinds of emotions and how they are depicted, inferred and transmitted through a work of art, which is also the main problem that confronts a critic, i.e. to find out how, in a work, emotion is depicted, suggested and how it is finally communicated to the reader or the audience or *sahṛdaya*. Considerate of the entire literary process, from its very conception in the mind of the artist or poet for that matter to its final perception in the heart of the perceiver or reader, it has tremendous linguistic potential too (*dhvani*).

In assessing the suitability of the observations which we have made, it is worthwhile to take up for discussion, one by one, all the nine *rasas*, and in the first place, we will take up the primary concrete universal emotion, the *śṛṅgāra rasa*.

Śṛṅgāra Rasa

Ānandavardhana in *Dhvanyāloka* observes:

> शृङ्गार एवं मधुरः परः प्रह्लादनों रसः।
> तन्मयं काव्यमाश्रित्य माधुर्यं प्रतितिष्ठति॥7॥[1]
>
> — p. 48

The *śṛṅgāra* (erotic) indeed is the sweetest and the most delectable of all sentiments or emotions for that matter and the poetry which is full of *śṛṅgāra* is abounded securely or, to say so, is full of the quality of sweetness. According to Bharatamuni whatever in the ordinary world is bright, pure (*medhya*) shining or beautiful is associated with love.

Rati (love) is the *sthāyī bhāva* of *śṛṅgāra*. Dhanañjaya in *Daśarūpaka* defines *rati* as:

> रम्यदेशकलाकालवेषभोगादिसेवनैः॥
> प्रमोदात्मा रतिः सैव यूनोरन्योन्यरक्तयोः।
> प्रहृष्यमाणश्शृङ्गरो मधुरश्शृङ्गविचेष्टितेः॥48॥ [2]
>
> — p. 334

Thus *rati* (love) is delight manifested in fondness for lovely places, arts, occasions, garments, pleasures and the like and the feeling on the part of two young persons mutually

---

1. *Dhvanyāloka* of Ānandavardhana, 1974, ed. K. Krishnamoorthy, Motilal Banarsidass, Delhi, p. 48.
2. *Daśarūpaka* of Dhanañjaya with *Avaloka* of Dhanika, ed. R.S. Tripathi, Vishwavidyalaya Prakashan,Varanasi, p. 334.

> enamoured, so that, it is gladsome and is manifested by tender gestures, constitutes the *śṛṅgāra*.[3] — p. 130

Here, one thing which is very important from the point of view of *śṛṅgāra* is that *rati*, the *sthāyī bhāva* of *śṛṅgāra* is to be considered so; only when it is mutual, is bright, is pure, is shining, is virtuous and good as opposed to evil or lust for that matter which cannot be pure, virtuous and beautiful and hence cannot be true love — true love is always identified with purity. One-sided love or impure love or evil love or forcible love will give rise to disgust (*bībhatsa*) and if one's love (in one-sided love) is pure it will lead to sacrifice; which will be further manifested through sorrow (*karuṇa*). *Śṛṅgāra* is always supposed to lead to love-in-union (for love-in-separation finally leads to reunion), all other forms of love will naturally lead to *karuṇa* or *bībhatsa* — all rather than *śṛṇgāra*.

Śṛṅgāra rasa in the *Nāṭyaśāstra* has been broadly divided into two categories: *saṁbhoga śṛṅgāra* or love-in-union and *vipralambha śṛṅgāra* or love-in-separation. But according to Mammaṭa though the former is to be the considered one the latter is of five types. He says:

> तत्र शृङ्गारस्य द्वौ भेदौ। संभोगो विप्रलम्भश्च।
> तत्राद्य: परस्परावलोकनालिङ्गनाद्यरपानपरिचुम्बनाधानन्तत्वादपरिच्छेद्य एक एव गण्यते।
> अपरस्तु–अभिलाषविरहेर्ष्याप्रवासशापहेतुक इति पंचविध:।[4]
>
> — *Kāvyaprakāśa*, pp. 63-64

> Love in union (*saṁbhoga*) is to be counted as one only, any classification of it being impossible by reason of the endless variety of its manifestations in the form of mutual glances, kissing, embraces and so forth but love in

---

3. *Daśarūpaka* of Dhanañjaya, by George C.O. Haas, 1962, Motilal Banarsidass, Varanasi, p. 130.
4. Mahāmahopādhyāya Sir Ganganatha Jha, *Kāvyaprakāśa* of Mammaṭa with English translation (revised), 1996, Bharatiya Vidya Prakashan, Varanasi, pp. 63-64.

> separation (*vipralambha*) is of five kinds, the feeling being due to (a) longing, (b) separation, (c) jealousy, (d) residence abroad, and (e) curse.

The various *vibhāvas* (excitants or determinants), *anubhāvas* (ensuants or consequents) and *sañcārī bhāvas* (variants or transitory emotions) of *śṛṅgāra* have already been discussed in the first chapter.

Saṁbhoga Śṛṅgāra (Love-in-union)

Let us discuss *saṁbhoga śṛṅgāra* or love-in-union first. Defining the state of love-in-union Dhanañjaya in *Daśarūpaka* writes:

> अनुकूलौ निशेवेते यत्रान्योन्यं विलासिनौ।
> दर्शनस्पर्शनादीनि स संभोगो मुदान्वितः।।69।।[5]
>
> — *Daśarūpaka*, p. 355

> Love-in-union (*saṁbhoga*) is that blissful state in which the two playful lovers are in complete agreement, enjoy seeing or touching each other and the like.[6]
>
> — The *Daśarūpaka*, p. 140

To take examples of love-in-union from the Western literature, we find a very apt manifestation of it in the following lines from Milton's *Paradise Lost*, where Adam and Eve are making love (after eating the forbidden fruit):

> *But come, so well refreshed, now let us play,*
> *As meet is, after such delicious fare;*
> *For never did thy beauty since the day*
> *I saw thee first and wedded thee, adorned*
> *With all perfections, so inflame my sense*
> *with ardour to enjoy thee, fairer now*
> *Than ever, bounty of this virtuous tree.*
> *So said he, and forbore not glance or toy*
> *of amorous intent, well understood*
> *of Eve, whose eye darted contagious fire*
> *Her hand he seized, and to a shady bank,*

5. *Daśarūpaka* of Dhanañjaya with *Avaloka* of Dhanika, p. 355.
6. *Daśarūpaka* of Dhanañjaya, by George C.O. Haas, p.140.

Thick over head with verdant roof embowered
He lead her nothing loth; flowers were the couch,
Pansies, and violets and asphodel,
And hyacinth, earth's fresnest softest lap.
There they their fill of love and love's disport
Took largely, of their — till dewy sleep
Oppressed them, wearied with the amorous play.[7]

— Book IX, lines 1027-45

Here the first overture comes from the man and then various *vibhāvas*, *anubhāvas* and *sañcārī bhāvas* contribute to the advent of *śṛṅgāra* and the whole scheme can very well be presented through the following graphical design, which we have discussed in the first chapter:

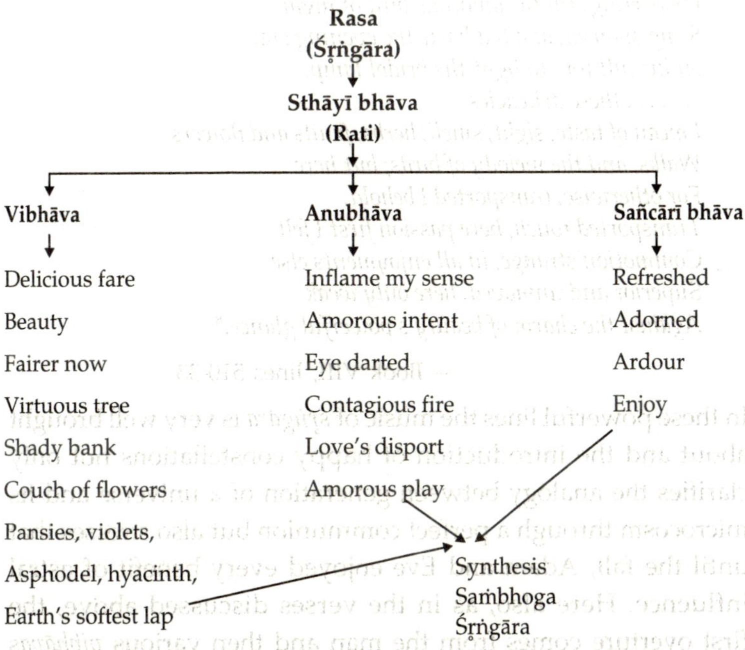

***fig.* 2.1: Saṁbhoga śṛṅgāra in *Paradise Lost*, Book IX, lines 1027-45.**

7. *The Poems of John Milton*, ed. John Carey and Alastair Fowler, Longman Group Limited, New York, 1968, pp. 915-16.

To further elaborate on it, let us take another example, again from Milton's *Paradise Lost*, where the whole universe seems to be drenched in the shower of love, rather seems to be dancing in the rhythm of *śṛṅgāra* and not only dancing but taking part in it and leading to *śṛṅgāra*:

To the nuptial bower
I led her blushing like the morn: all heaven,
And happy constellations on that hour
Shed their selectest influence; the earth
Gave sign of gratulation, and each hill;
Joyous the birds; fresh gales and gentle airs
Whispered it to the woods, and from their wings
Flung rose, flung odours from the spicy shrub,
Disporting, till the amorous bird of night
Sung spousal, and bid haste the evening star
on his hill top, to light the bridal lamp.
. . . . these delicacies
I mean of taste, sight, smell, herbs, fruits and flowers,
Walks, and the melody of birds; but here
For otherwise, transported I behold,
Transported touch, here passion first I felt,
Commotion strange, in all enjoyments else
Superior and unmoved, here only weak
Against the charm of beauty's powerful glance.[8]

— Book VIII, lines 510-33

In these powerful lines the music of *śṛṅgāra* is very well brought about and the introduction of happy constellations not only clarifies the analogy between generation of a universe and its microcosm through a perfect communion but also stresses that until the fall, Adam and Eve enjoyed every benefit of astral influence. Here also, as in the verses discussed above, the first overture comes from the man and then various *vibhāva*s like "happy constellations", "joyous birds", "fresh gales", "gentle air", "odours from spicy herbs", "spousal of amorous

8. *The Poems of John Milton*, ed. John Carey and Alastair Fowler, Longman Group Limited, New York, 1968, pp. 841-43.

birds", "flowers" and "fruits"; *anubhāva*s like "blushing", "transported", "touch" and "beauty's powerful glance"; and *sañcārī bhāva*s like "vehement desire", "gratulation", "passion" and "enjoyment" contribute to the advent of *śṛṅgāra*. We can very well understand the music of *śṛṅgāra* evolving through the divine communion of Adam and Eve through the following graphical design:

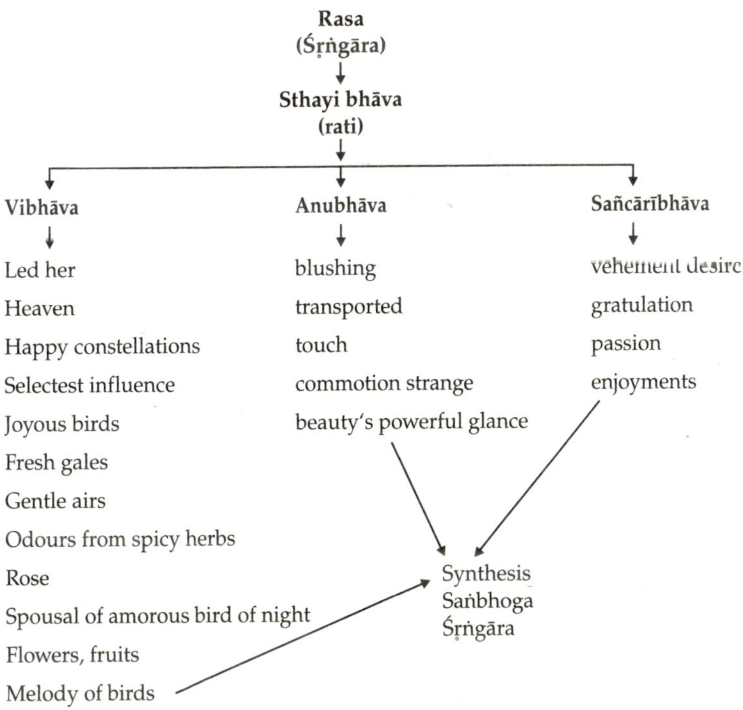

***fig.* 2.2: *Saṁbhoga śṛṅgāra* in *Paradise Lost*, Book VIII, Lines 510-33**

When it comes to applying *rasa* theory to the modern Western literature, a striking feature we come across is the problematic nature of love or eroticism depicted in it. Whatever we look at — fiction, drama or poetry, what we see is violence, unnatural love (incest, homosexuality, etc.) and unnatural separation. Not that, simple straightforward examples approving the theme of *rasa* theory cannot be found, but to prove the universality of *rasa* theory it is necessary that we touch upon this aspect. In the context of *śṛṅgāra* of course, to such problematic literature, it is worth our while to first take an example of love-in-union from the modern Western literature approving the *rasa* theory in its context; if not fully at least partially:

> In the brown dining-room, its perfumed air
> Full of the smell of wax and fruit, at ease
> I gathered a plate of who knows what Belgian
> Dish, and marvelled in my enormous chair.
>
> Eating I listened to the clock — silent, happy.
> The kitchen door opened with a gust,
> — And the serving girl came in, who knows why,
> Shawl half-off, hair dressed cunningly.
>
> And, touching her little finger tremblingly
> To her cheek, a pink and white velvet-peach,
> And making a childish pout with her lips,
>
> She tidied the plates to put me at my ease:
> — Then, just like that — to get a kiss, for certain —
> Whispered: "Feel: It's caught a cold, my cheek . . ."[9]
>
> — Rimbaud, *Selected Poems: The Sly Girl*

Here in the above poem all the *vibhāvas*, *anubhāvas* and *sañcārī bhāvas* are present to establish it as an example of love-in-union. But the two things which bother us are: first the poet is passive; no involvement, besides his relishing the food and a happy state of mind, has been conveyed and the situation for *saṁbhoga śṛṅgāra* demands it to be mutual; the second thing that bothers us is that the girl, the cause of *śṛṅgāra* seems to be inviting the poet, but there is nothing to rule out the possibility that the relationship being explored is purly incestuous and

9. Rimbaud, *Selected Poems*, "*The Sly Girl*" A.S. Kline © 2002, 2008 http://www.poetryintranslation.com/PITBR/French/Rimbaud1.htm

without any emotional involvement. An essential condition for generation of *śṛṅgāra rasa* is purity of the relationship. *Śṛṅgāra rasa* demands love to be pure and virtuous and not just impure and incestuous.

Even though the relationship being explored here holds the possibility of being purely incestuous but when we apply the scheme of *śṛṅgāra* to it, we find *saṁbhoga śṛṅgāra* in it, to put it graphically:

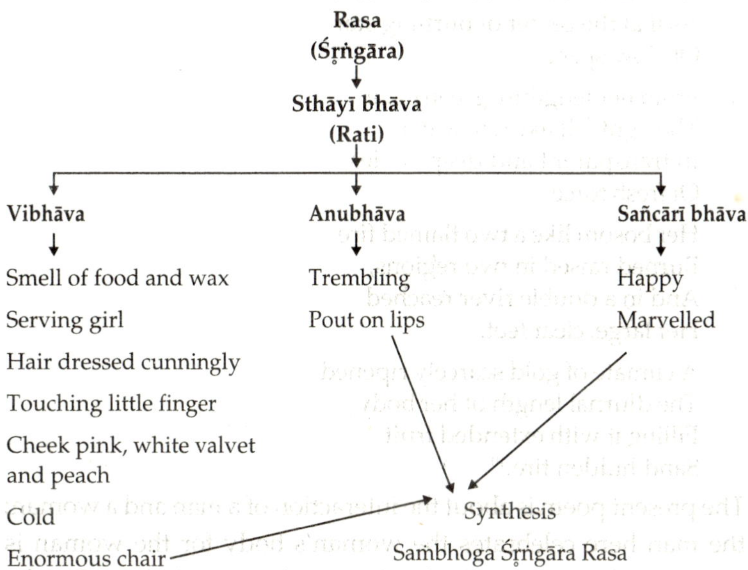

fig. **2.3:** ***Saṁbhoga śṛṅgāra* in Rimbaud's *The Sly Girl***

Saṁbhoga śṛṅgāra demands pure, virtuous and complete agreement on the part of playful lovers. It can be understood that unnatural love, incestuous relationships, etc. cannot lead to *śṛṅgāra* since the unnatural aspect when highlighted gives rise to disgust and not to *śṛṅgāra*, at least, in the Indian context. Besides, true love has always or universally been considered to be pure and virtuous. But love in the modern literature is intriguing. There is a lot of unnaturalness in it, viz. intervention of intellect, depictions of abnormal relations, violent and unusual cosummations and incomplete relationships, etc.

To further illustrate the point, let us take into consideration a poem with an unnecessary intervention of intellect — Pablo Neruda's *Adonic Angela*:

> Today I stretched out next to a pure young woman
> As if at the shore of a white ocean,
> As if at the center of burning star
> Of slow space.
>
> From her lengthily green gaze
> The light fell like dry water,
> In transparant and deep circles
> Of fresh force.
>
> Her bosom like a two flamed fire
> Burned raised in two regions,
> And in a double river reached
> Her large, clear feet.
>
> A climate of gold scarcely ripened
> The diurnal length of her body
> Filling it with extended fruit
> Sand hidden fire.[10]

The present poem is about the interaction of a man and a woman; the man here celebrates the woman's body for the woman is passive, at least, is not depicted as participating in love. But the perception is hampered by the use of intellectual language. The description is unusual, a kind of private and arbitrary language (unconventional) is used in expressions like "lengthily green gaze", "burning star", "dry water", "double river", "gold scarcely ripened", "diurnal lengths", "extended fruits" and "hidden fire". It is only when the language is grasped on the intellectual level pertaining to the difference in convention, that

10. Pablo Neruda's *Adonic Angela*, 1904-1973, http://www.pierdelune.com/neruda9.htm

the emotional enjoyment is possible. Once having done so, the possibilities of consummation become clearly discernible besides the unusual description. But remarkably we find our graphic scheme still to be befitting the poem and the poem in turn leading to the advent of *saṁbhoga śṛṅgāra,* i.e. love-in-union:

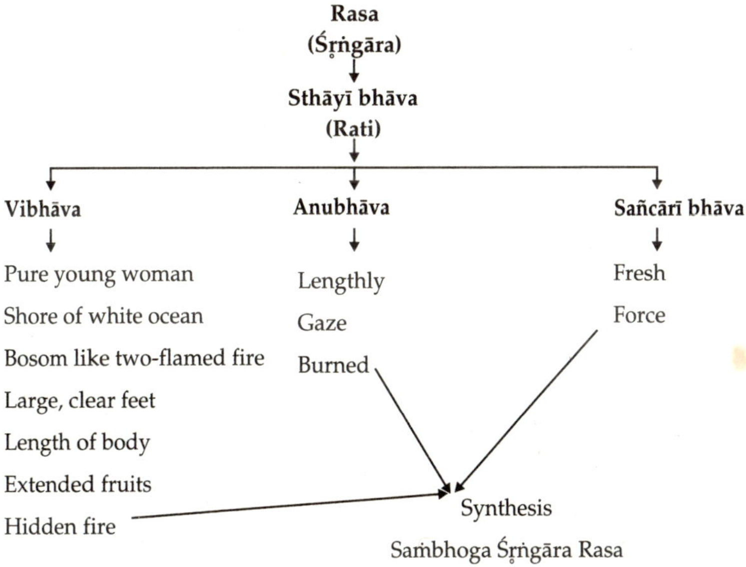

fig. **2.4:** ***Saṁbhoga śṛṅgāra*** **in Pablo Neruda's** ***Adonic Angela***

Now let us take another important feature of the modern literature, i.e. quest of abnormal and unusual relationships. To a great extent the delight in exploring the abnormal or unusual or unnatural relationships is of a sensational kind — pleasure at relishing the forbidden. But once the inhibitions are quietened and the excitement for the forbidden vanishes (and it is accepted in the convention), the aesthetic qualities can be clearly noticed. As the *rasa* theory deals with the creation, manifestation, evolution and realisation of *rasa* therefore, the prime consideration in the above-discussed situations should be that whether the manifestation of love (*rati*) has been successfully handled or not.

Vipralambha Śṛṅgāra (Love-in-Separation)

In love-in-union the very possibility of any negative factor is removed from the air, as we saw from the *vibhāva*s listed: spring, garlands, festivity, etc. but in *vipralambha śṛṅgāra* or love-in-separation, the same *vibhāva*s no longer look appealing in the absence of the lover. They rather add to the pain; and the manifestations of this are very much closer to *karuṇa* (the difference being that in *karuṇa* there is no hope of reunion while love-in-separation keeps revolving between hope and despair and mostly leads to re-union). In love-in-union there is always the fear of separation and in love-in-separation the hope of union. In love-in-union fear intensifies love while in love-in-separation fear of losing and longing, both get intensified in the absence of the loved object. The manifestations of love-in-separation are listlessness, worry, longing, etc. sharply in contrast with those of love-in-union, viz. coyness, shyness, a faint smile and so on. To illustrate the point let us take into consideration the following verses from Rimbaud's *The Song of the Highest Tower*:

Let it come, let it come
The day when hearts love as one.

I've been patient so long
I've forgotten even
The terror and suffering
Flown up to heaven,
A sick thirst again
Darkens my veins.

Let it come, let it come
The day when hearts love as one.

So the meadow
Freed by neglect,
Flowered, overgrown
With weeds and incense,
To the buzz nearby
Of foul flies.

Let it come, let it come
The day when hearts love as one.[11]

— Rimbaud, From *Une Saison en Enfer*

Here the lover is longing for, is desperate for re-union with his beloved. The *anubhāvas* which had been stimulating in the presence of beloved are visibly no more appealing now; rather they add to the pain, the agony of separation and therefore, the meadow "freed by neglect" is overgrown with "weeds and incense" and "the buzz" is that of "foul flies" and not the song of some humming bird or nightingale. The terror is that of losing the beloved and suffering caused due to separation. The poet is so much in pain that he has lost the sense of time and has even forgotten how long it has been to his suffering. The only thing he now longs for is his union with the beloved. To put the whole scheme graphically:

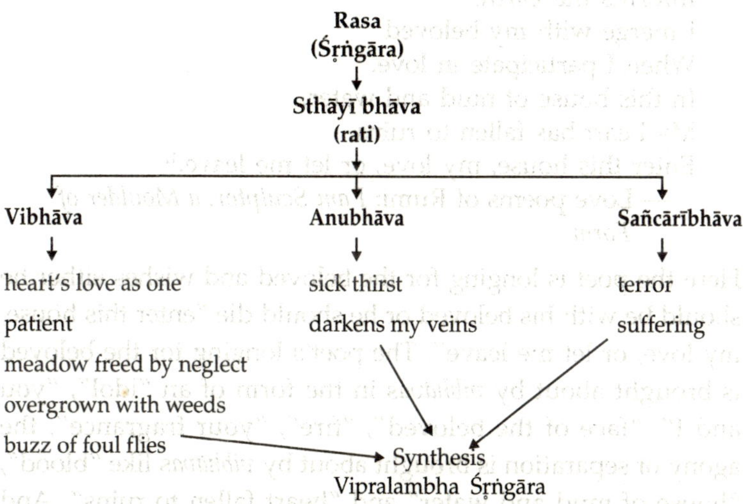

fig. 2.5: Vipralambha śṛṅgāra* in Rimbaud's *The Song of the Highest Tower.

11. Rimbaud: *Selected Poems.*

Love-in-separation can arise out of longing, separation, jealousy, residence abroad and curse. One or two, or even all together can be instrumental in the arousal of the feeling of *vipralambha* in a situation or an object. To further illustrate the point let us take the following poem:

I am sculptor, a moulder of form.
In every moment I shape an idol.
But then, in front of you, I melt them down
I can rouse a hundred forms
And fill them with spirit,
But when I look into your face,
I want to throw them in the fire.
My soul spills into yours and is blended.
Because my soul has absorbed your fragrance,
I cherish it.
Every drop of blood I spill
Informs the earth.
I merge with my beloved
When I participate in love.
In this house of mud and water,
My heart has fallen to ruins.
Enter this house, my love, or let me leave.[12]

— Love poems of Rumi: *I am Sculptor, a Moulder of Form*

Here the poet is longing for the beloved and wishes either he should be with his beloved or he should die "enter this house, my love, or let me leave". The poet's longing for the beloved is brought about by *vibhāva*s in the form of an "idol", "you and I", "face of the beloved", "fire", "your fragrance", the agony of separation is brought about by *vibhāva*s like "blood", "house of mud and water" and "heart fallen to ruins". And these *vibhāva*s with *anubhāva*s in "spill", "merge" and *sañcārī*

12. *Rumi's Divan of Shems of Tabriz: Selected Odes (Element Classics of World Spirituality)* by Jalal Al-Din Rumi (Author), Maulana Jalaluddin Rumi (Author), James Cowan (Author, Translator) Love Poems of Rumi, http://www.khamush.com/love_poems.html.

bhāvas in "absorbed", "cherish" lead to the generation of *vipralambha*.

Significant condition in *vipralambha* is that both hope and despair co-exist in it. When there is no hope of re-union *śṛṅgāra* will no longer remain *śṛṅgāra* but will naturally lead to *karuṇa*. Besides, the sorrow generated by love is very distinctly different from other kinds of sorrows. The essence of *śṛṅgāra*, as stated earlier, is fulfilment-mutal, and therefore, even in *vipralambha śṛṅgāra*, after a delay that causes suffering, there is union. To further illustrate the point it is worth our while to consider the following lines by Rumi from the *rasa* perspective at this juncture:

> Because I cannot sleep
> I make music at night.
> I am troubled by the one
> Whose face has the colour of spring flowers.
> I have neither sleep nor patience,
> Neither a good reputation nor disgrace.
> A thousand robes of wisdom are gone —
> All my good manners have moved a thousand miles away.
> The heart and the mind are left angry with each other.
> The stars and the moon are envious of each other.
> Because of this alienation the physical universe
> Is getting tighter and tighter.
> The moon says, "How long will I remain
> Suspended without a sun?"
> Without love's jewel inside me,
> Let the bazaar of my existence be destroyed stone by stone
> O love, you who have been called by a thousand names,
> You who know now to pour the wine
> Into the chalice of the body, . . .
> Give me a glass from your bottle, . . .
> Remove the cork once more

. . . then the addict will be breed of craving
And will be resurrected,
And stand in awe fill judgement day.[13]

— Love poems of Rumi: *Because I Cannot Sleep*

The poem opens on a strong note "because I cannot sleep I make music at night" the *vibhāvas* in "music" and "I" are those of *śṛṅgāra* but *anubhāva*s in "cannot sleep" and "am troubled" specify at the very beginning that the situation or state is that of *vipralambha* and the beloved, the "one whose face has the colour of spring flowers" is the *vibhāva* of *vipralambha* in the situation. The first section of the poem is about the agony of separation; all the *anubhāva*s and *sañcārī bhāva*s of *vipralambha śṛṅgāra* like sleeplessness, impatience, loss of all wisdom and good manners, envy and alienation are present here. But out of this agony, this despair the poet could look forward in hope to the possible union with the beloved and therefore the second half of the poem speaks of hope of reunion and the manifestations of the state are to be found in *vibhāvas*, *anubhāva*s and *sañcārī bhāva*s like "love", "wine", "chalice of the body", "prostrate", "addict", "breed of craving", "resurrected" and "awe".

Dhanañjaya identifies ten stages of privation in *vipralambha śṛṅgāra*:

दशावस्थः स तत्रदावभिलाषोऽथ चिन्तनम् ।। 51।।
स्मृतिर्गुणकथोद्वेगप्रलापोन्मादसंज्वराः ।
जडता मरणं चेति दुरवस्थं यथोत्तरम् ।। 52।।[14]

— *Daśarūpaka*, p. 342

It has ten stages. At first [there occurs] in it longing (*abhilāṣā*),

13. *Rumi's Divan of Shems of Tabriz: Selected Odes* (*Element Classics of World Spirituality*) by Jalal Al-Din Rumi (Author), Maulana Jalaluddin Rumi (Author), James Cowan (Author, Translator) Love Poems of Rumi, http://www.khamush.com/love_poems.html.

14. *Daśarūpaka* of Dhanañjaya with *Avaloka* of Dhanika, p. 342.

> then anxiety (*cintana*), recollection (*smṛti*), enumeration of (the loved one's) merits (*guṇakathā*), distress (*udvega*), raving (*pralāpa*), insanity (*unmāda*), fever (*sañjvara*), stupor (*jaḍatā*), and death (*maraṇa*); those are the unfortunate stages in due order.[15]
>
> — *Daśarūpaka*, p. 132

The fact that there are ten stages (of privation) is generally agreed upon by many learned scholars; endless examples of it are to be seen in the works of the canonical poets of both the Eastern and Western tradition. For example, we can take into consideration the following lines from Shakespeare's *Hamlet*, in which Polonius is describing the effect of Hamlet's separation from Ophelia on Hamlet:

> And he, repulsed — a short tale to make —
> Fell into a sadness, then into a fast,
> Thence to a watch, thence into a weakness,
> Thence to a lightness, and by this declension
> Into the madness wherein now he raves
> And all we mourn for.[16]
>
> — *The Plays and Poems of William Shakespeare*, p. 274

To take another example from a lesser known poet, let us take the following poem by Aditya Neal. The poem begins with the description of the stages of anxiety and longing:

> She couldn't stand the silence,
> She couldn't stand the tears,
> She couldn't stand her life,
> After only thirteen years. He was her entire world,

Then there is recollection:

---

15. *Daśarūpaka* of Dhanañjaya, by George C.O. Haas, p. 132.

16. *The Plays and Poems of William Shakespeare*, by William Shakespeare, James Boswell, Edmond Malone, Alexander Pope, Samuel Johnson, William Warburton, Edward Capell, Theobald (Lewis), George Steevens, Richard Farmer, Thomas Hanmer, Nicholas Rowe, Isaac Reed, Arthur Brooke, George Chalmers, Pub. R.C. and J. Rivington, 1821, p. 274.

She gave him all she possessed,
He did the same in return,
They were thought to be obsessed. . . .
From two they became one
They made each other whole,

Then we find enumeration of merits:

They filled each others voids,
They filled each others souls.
Everything was perfect,
Everything was great,

Then the events turn the other way and there comes distress in love:

Until one day,
They were told they'd have to wait.

Her parents were moving her,
To a distant place,
They'd be torn apart,
Couldn't see each others face.

They swore they'd make it work,
Vowed to stay together
. . . . But he slipped away,
While she was thinking of him,
He had found another,

The obvious result of this infidelity is raving:

She was devastated,
Her heart was torn straight out,
She'd been such a fool,
. . . . every day she'd cry,
She tried to fight off all the pain,
. . . . it just shot through every rain.

The raving further slips into *unmāda* (insanity):

. . . . She only grew worse.
. . . . This was love's curse.
It finally overtook her,
. . . . She grabbed a picture of him,
and snuck out the front door

The *unmāda* is then lingered into fever and then stupor:

She walked into the woods,
Found a secluded place,
Kept thinking of the past.
And how she'd been replaced

Then finally comes the tenth stage i.e. death, and strictly in adherence to the views of Bharatamuni, the death is not depicted but we are informed:

Hours later she was found,
In a pool of her blood,
And beside her they found,
His picture in the mud
....
It was obvious how she died
It was from a broken heart.[17]

— Aditya Neal: *She Couldn't Stand the Silence*

Now two things trouble us; first, since this love finally leads to endless suffering and death, is it evil, and secondly, in the poem, what inevitably follows is tragic and therefore the question that naturally follows is whether the final emotion manifested in the poem is that of *śṛṅgāra* or *karuṇa rasa*?

The solution can be found in looking at the treatment. How is love treated? There is death, true, but does it suggest evil or does it generate disgust? The answer will be relevant. Here death becomes secondary, the agony of separation, *vipralambha* becomes the primary thing; or even if finally *karuṇa* is considered to be the outcome, *vipralambha śṛṅgāra* does have its moments of intensity in it. Keeping in mind the ten stages attributed to *vipralambha* by Dhanañjaya we can say that in the poem it is the *vipralambha* that is essentially highlighted.

Besides, in a long work, it is always possible that two or

17. *Tamilrorrents: Poems Love & Friendship*, Love, She Couldn't stand the silence, http://www.tamiltorrents.net/forums/archive/index.php/t-8656.html

even more *rasa*s reach their peaks. While finally a chief *rasa* can be the outcome, other *rasa*s too can have their moments of intensity in it.

Hāsya Rasa

The second important universal, absolute and complete form of realisable situation or experience listed by Bharatamuni is *hāsya*. It is generated, created or produced when action, costume and speech or language for that matter bring forth some unusual, strange or incongruent relation. *Hāsya* is something different from what we know as joy, generated when some lost friends meet or something pleasing or wonderful is achieved. This joy, can be found in *rasa*s like *śṛṅgāra*, *vīra* or *adbhuta*.

Bharatamuni while describing *hāsya rasa* says:

> विकृत परवेशालङ्कारधाष्टर्य लौल्यकुहकासत्प्रलापव्यङ्ग
> दर्शानदोषोदाहरणादिभिर्विभावैरुत्पद्यते[18]
>
> — *Nāṭyaśāstra* of Bharatamuni

Thus *hāsya rasa* arises from *vibhāva*s such as wearing clothes and ornaments that belong to someone else or do not fit (*vikṛta*), shamelessness (*dhṛṣṭya*), greed, tickling sensitive parts of the body, telling fantastic tales, seeing some (comic) deformity (*vyaṅga*) and describing faults (*doṣodāharṇa*). The further discussion of *hāsya rasa* enumerated in detail in *Bhāratīya Nāṭyaśāstra*, *Sāhityadarpaṇa* of Viśavanātha Kavirāja, *Vāgbhaṭālaṁkāra* of Vāgbhaṭa, *Daśarūpaka* of Dhanañjaya and the like is really very remarkable inasmuch as it covers every possible situation or condition in *hāsya* and is as varied as *smita* (gentle smile), *hasita* (smile), *vihasita* (laughter), *upahasita*

18. *Gaṅgānāthajhā-Granthamālā* (vol. 14), *Nāṭyaśāstra* of Bharatamuni (Part Two) with *Abhinavabhāratī* by Abhinavaguptācārya & *Manoramā* (Hindi Commentary) by Pārasanatha Dvivedī, 1996, ed. Pārasanatha Dvivedī, Sampurnanand Sanskrit University, Varanasi.

(laughter with ridicule), *apahasita* (uproarious laughter) and *atihasita* (convulsive laughter).

While elaborating on these Dhanañjaya in *Daśarūpaka* observes:

> स्मितमिह विकासिनयनम्, किञ्चिल्लक्ष्यद्विजं तु हसितं स्यात्
> मधुरस्वरं विहसितम्, सशिरःकम्पमिदमुपहसितम् ।।76।।
> अपहसितं सास्राक्षम्, विक्षिप्ताङ्गं भवत्यतिहसितम्।
> द्वे द्वे हसिते चैषां ज्येष्ठे मध्येऽधमे क्रमशः ।।77।। [19]
>
> — *Daśarūpaka*, p. 363

> Thus a gentle smile (*smita*) is opening the eyes wide; a smile (*hasita*) is showing the teeth to some extent; laughing (*vihasita*) is making a soft sound; laughter (*upahasita*) is the same, accompanied by shaking of the head; uproarious laughter (*apahasita*) is *laughter* accompanied by tears; and convulsive laughter (*atihasita*) is laughter with shaking of the body. Two of these varieties of laughter are characteristic of the higher creed (noble born), two of the middle (ordinary) and two of the lower (characters), in the order named. This division of laughter in terms of dignity of the individuals can be roughly equated to what in the West is known as "high" and "low" or farcical comedies. Sometimes the laughter is witty and gentle and gives rise to humour (a smile). At other times it is boisterous, more physical (funny action) and gives rise to violent laughter (in the text as well as in the reader). [20] — *Daśarūpaka*, pp. 143-44

One significant condition for generation of laughter is that it involves trivialising the subject. If evil is taken too seriously, outcome will obviously be *bhayānaka* or *bībhatsa*. Hence, in a satire, there is a trivialisation of all things. When the satire is on the entire mankind or class, it also involves the reader as

---

19. *Daśarūpaka* of Dhanañjaya with *Avaloka* of Dhanika, p. 363.
20. *Daśarūpaka* of Dhanañjaya by George C.O. Haas, p. 143-44.

well as the narrative voice, and hence here we find the possibility of laughter. For instance let's take the following lines from *The Rape of the Lock* by Alaxendar Pope, where Ariel's conjectures regarding the disaster that threatens Belinda (the herden), are stated in some of the most amusing lines in the poem:

> Whether the nymph shall break Diana's law,
> Or some frail china jar receive a flaw;
> Or stain her honour, or her new brocade;
> Forget her prayers, or miss a masquerade;
> Or lose her heart, or necklace, at a ball;
> Or whether Heaven has doom'd that shock must fall.[21]
>
> — *The Rape of the Lock,* lines 253-58

Laughter in the above given situation has become a possibility only because the moral bankruptcy of the ladies is trivialised and made to seem less serious by the ridiculous contrasts of the above given paired calamities.

Where there is possibility of order, possibility of disorder too is to be found there, only and this disorder — when of a relatively harmless kind — gives rise to laughter. Thus, the essential condition for generation of *hāsya* through the element of disorder or deformity is that it should essentially be of a harmless kind and must not lead to any cruelty. To take an apt example of it let us take into consideration the following lines again from Alexander Pope's satirical masterpiece *The Rape of the Lock*:

> And now, unveiled, the toilet stands displayed.
> Each silver vase in mystic order laid.
> First, robed in white, the Nymph intent adores
> With head uncovered, the cosmetic Powers.
> A heavenly image in the Glass appears,
> To that she bends, to that her, eyes she rears;
> Th' inferior Priestess, at her Altar's side,

21. Alexander Pope and Geoffrey Tillotson, *The Rape of the Lock*, 3rd edn. revised, Routledge, 2004, p. 17.

Trembling, begins the sacred Rites of Pride.
Unnumbered Treasures open at once, and here
The various offerings of world appear;
From each she nicely culls with curious Toil,
And decks the Goddess with the glittering spoil.
This Casket India's glowing Gems unlocks,
And all Arabia breathes from yonder Box.
The Tortise here and Elephant unite
Transformed to combs, the speckled and the white.[22]

— *The Rape of the Lock*, pp. 52-53

Pope in these verses delights in the "artificial beauty" that he describes. At the toilet table Belinda, the heroine, is lavishing on her own beauty, the adoration which should be reserved for a higher object, is hence quite incongruous. And this *vikṛta* (disorder) in the description of Belinda's dressing up in as pompous a manner as "Achilles arming" is instrumental in the generation of laughter. When we put the above given situation or example in our scheme of graphical design the outcome is:

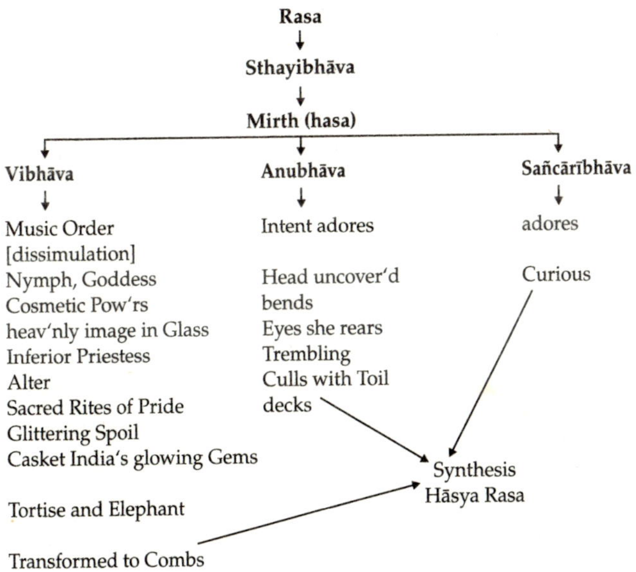

fig.* 2.5: *Hāsya rasa* in Pope's *The Rape of The Lock

22. Alexander Pope and Geoffrey Tillotson, *The Rape of the Lock*, p. 36.

Vikṛta, when innocuous and harmless, often has the potential of generating an uproarious laughter. For instance, let us take into consideration the following poem by Shel Silverstin:

"I cannot go to School today,"
Said little Peggy Ann Mckey;
"I have the measles and the mumps,
A gash, a rash, and purple bumps.
My mouth is wet, my throat is dry,
I'm going blind in my right eye.
My tonsils are as big as rocks,
I've counted sixteen chicken pox
And there's one more — that's Seventeen,
And don't you think my face looks green?
....
My temperature is one-o-eight.
My brain is shrunk, I cannot hear,
There is a hole inside my ear.
I have a hangnail, and my heart is . . .
What's that? What's that you say?
You say today is — Saturday?
G'bye, I'm going out to play!"[23]

— Shel Silverston: *Sick*

Poor little Peggy innocently citing all the possible reasons or diseases or explanations she could think of just to skip the school (*vikṛta*) makes one hold one's stomach and laugh but the funniest incongruity in the situation comes when she is told it's Saturday, the holiday and forgetting all the severe sign's of illness she was citing just a moment before, she says goodbye and runs out to play.

"Shamelessness" has been listed as another element having the potential for generation of laughter. An important point to note here is that shamelessness can lead to laughter only and only when it does not threaten the accepted conventions and norms of the society, when it is creating some minor

23. *Shel Silverstein: Poems and Drawings;* originally appeared in *Where the Sidewalk Ends* by Shel Silverstein. http://www.poets.org/viewmedia.php/prmMID/16480.

disorder, a major disorder (for instance a man going about naked in the streets) will lead to utter disgust. The reader or the perceiver should not feel threatened by the shamelessness that he perceives. Let us, for instance, take the following lines from *Beggar to Beggar Cried* by William Butler Yeats:

> "Time to put of the world and go somewhere
> And find my health again in the sea air",
> Beggar to beggar cried, being frenzy-struck,
> "And make my soul before my pate is bare-
> And get a comfortable wife and house
> To rid me of the devil in my shoes",
> Beggar to beggar cried, being frenzy — struck,
> "And the worse devil that is between my thighs."
> And though I'd marry with a comely lass,
> She need not be too comely — let it pass
> "Nor should she be too rich, because the rich
> are driven by wealth as beggars by the itch;
> Beggar the beggar cried, being frenzy-struck.
> And cannot have a humorous happy speech.[24]
>
> — W.B. Yeats, *Beggar to Beggar Cried*

Here, in the above given situation, *vikr̥ta, dhr̥ṣṭya* and *vyaṅga* all three combine and prove instrumental in the generation of *hāsya*. A beggar looking forward to getting an attractive wife, a comfortable house and gaining health, present a situation which is incongruous (*vikr̥ta*); his public acceptance of his physical and mental urge "And the worse devil that is between my thighs" is a shameless act (*dhr̥ṣṭya*) and the whole situation is a satire (*vyaṅga*) well brought out in the lines "rich are driven by wealth as beggars by the itch". The incongruent juxtaposition of wealth and itch too leads to a rapturous laughter in the situation. One thing evident from the discussion in the foregoing is that an element of cruelty lurks behind the element of laughter. The old woman's laughter on Han Shan's

24. *Beggar to Beggar Cried* by William Butler Yeats, http://www.poemhunter.com/poem/beggar-to-beggar-cried/

poverty is cruel and equally cruel is the laughter on the state of the beggar in the present instance. But laughter has become a vivid possibility in these instances, only because the objects of imitation (the poor poet and the beggar) themselves participate in the laughter, overlooking the cruel development they manage to look at the funnier side of things.

"Greed" is another element which is largely associated with shamelessness. When greed leads to some minor mishap and no major disaster, it is funny. As we find in the poem *When I, Good Friends, Was Called to Bar* by W.S. Gilbert:

> In Westminster Hall I danced a dance,
> .... For I thought I should never hit on a chance
> Of addressing a British jury
> But I soon got tired of third-class journeys,
>
> And dinners of bread and water;
> So I fell in love with a rich attorney's
> Elderly, ugly daughter.
> The rich attorney, he wiped his eyes,
> And replied to my fond professions;
> "You shall reap the reward of your enterprise",
> The briefs came trooping gaily,
> And everyday my voice was heard
>
> At the Sessions or Ancient Bailey.
> All thieves who could my fees afford
> Relied on my orations,
> And many a burglar I've restored
> To his friends and his relations.
>
> At length I became as rich as the Gurneys
> An incubus then I thought her,
> So I threw over that rich attorney's
> Elderly, ugly daughter.
> The rich attorney my character high
> Tried vainly to disparage
> And now, if you please, I'm ready to try
> This Breach of Promise of Marriage ![25]

25. W.S. Gilbert, *When I, Good Friends, was Called to Bar,* Full Text of W.S. Gilbert, http://www.archive.org/stream/wsgilbert000491mbp/wsgilbert000491mbp_djvu.txt

Here, the lawyer who has himself made a "breach of promise of marriage" makes out a case of *Breach of Promise of Marriage* and this incongruity in the situation leads to laughter. Further, he is greedy and shameless — he ditches the rich lawyer, who has sponsored him, the first chance he gets in his efforts to rise, i.e. to make good livelihood in life. But all lawyers being considered greedy, it seems funny that one lawyer manages to cheat the other (for only a lawyer can cheat a lawyer). Greed can also lead to funny behaviour — stuffing oneself with food or gold, or trying to steal too many things and stumbling and falling, etc. Moreover his shameless acceptance of his act of treachery, disloyalty and betrayal too leads to generation of laughter (as it is nothing new, many people try such things to get early success in life, but only a few accept the guilt).

"Tickling sensitive parts of the body" leads to a laughter that is generated by direct contact. In the perceiver, this can lead to sympathetic laughter. This can be understood in view of the fact that in an environment of laughter, one finds oneself laughing even without any known cause or reason.

"Telling fantastic tales" can, beyond any doubt, lead to comic. "Deformity" when temporary, harmless or simulated can be comic. If a lip on teeth does not fit, this deformity will give rise to either a sense of sorrow or the grotesque, but if the lips are twisted and made to look grotesque, this as it is, both temporary and harmless, will lead to laughter.

"*Doṣodāharaṇa* (describing faults) has been listed as another *vibhāva* of *hāsya*. But the essential condition or a pre-requisite for it to lead to laughter is that it should be clothed in such a manner that a certain incongruity, a certain distortion (which is not too harsh) is noticeable. To put it in other words, while describing faults, the focus should be on relatively less serious defects which a perceiver, if possible, shares and so can find somewhat funny. The treatment should be such that the relatively serious problems seem much less serious as is noticeable in the following lines from *The Rape of the Lock*:

> The hungry Judges soon the sentence sign,
> And wretches hang that jury-men may dine
> The merchant from the exchange returns in peace
> And the long labours of the Toilet cease.[26]
>
> — Canto III, lines 20-25

These brilliant lines which couple by incongruity the worlds of the bourgeoisie and the proletariat with that of the leisure class could have almost seemed ominous had there not been this controlled juxtaposition (of worlds). Thus it is the treatment that is important or it is the vein in which the faults are seen or made to be seen in a work that determines the true nature of satire. Even so, a satire can become grotesque, and seem so serious that the comic element no longer emerges prominent and then what we will have instead is the "Comedy of Grotesque" as is to be seen in the works of T.S. Eliot.

The various accompanying states or *vyabhicārī bhāva*s of *hāsya rasa*, as already discussed in chapter II, are dissimulation, laziness, drowsiness, *(tandrā)* sleep, dreaming, awakening, envy, etc.

"Dissimulation", always holds the potential of mirth as we saw in the cheating of one lawyer by the another.

"Laziness", "dreaming", "drowsiness" (when caused by drinking), "sleep" and "awakening" (sudden awakening of a lazy of foolish man can lead to incongruent action and hence generate laughter) have comic potentials beyond doubt. In Pope's satirical masterpiece *The Rape of the Lock* we can find all the *vyabhicārī bhāva*s discussed here leading to *hāsya*. To illustrate the point we can take examples of them one by one:

> Now lap-dogs give themselves the rousing shake,
> And, sleepless lovers, just at twelve, awake:

26. Alexander Pope and Geoffrey Tillotson, *The Rape of the Lock*, p. 47.

Thrice rung the bell, the slipper knocked the ground.
And the pressed watch returned a silver sound.
Belinda still her downy pillow pressed,
Her guardian sylph prolonged the balmy rest.[27]

—*The Rape of the Lock,* lines 15-20

Here in these verses amusing presentation of the laziness and sleeping habits of the aristocratic ladies and gentlemen of the time lead to generation of laughter. Further in this poem dreaming and dissimulation lead to comic in:

Fairest of mortals, thou distinguished care
— if ever one vision touched thy infant thought,
of all the nurse and all the priest have thought;
of airy *elves* . . . . or virgins visited by angel-powers,
. . . Hear and believe! thy own importance know,
. . . Some secret truths, from learned pride concealed,
To maids alone and children are revealed.[28]

— *The Rape of the Lock,* lines, 27-38

And dreaming and awakening lead to mirth in:

This to disclose is all thy guardian can:
Beware of all, but most beware of man!
He said, when Shock, who thought she slept too long,
Leaped up, and waked his mistress with his tongue.
'Twas then, Belinda, if report say true,
Thy eyes first opened on a billet — doux;
Wounds, charms, and ardours were no sooner read,
But all the vision vanished from thy head[29]

— *The Rape of the Lock,* lines, 114-20

These satirical lines with humour and wit expose to ridicule the laziness, idleness, frivolities, follies and shallowness of the aristocratic ladies and gentlemen of the time.

In all the *vyabhicārī bhāvas* of *hāsya rasa* "envy" seems to be a bit problematic, as the natural outcome of envy are — hatred, treachery and disaster — which are inimical to *hāsya*. Laughter

27. Alexander Pope and Geoffrey Tillotson, *The Rape of the Lock*, p. 28.
28. Ibid., p. 29.
29. Ibid., p. 35.

can be generated out of envy only and only when the cruel aspect is subverted. For instance in Pope's *The Rape of the Lock* Clarissa's jealousy of Belinda's beauty and fame prompt her to offer a pair of scissors to the Baron in order to assist him in his wicked design (cutting of Belinda's lock of hair). But the outcome of this wicked act is painted in such a pompous manner that it generates laughter instead of sorrow or pain. For instance, take a look at the presentation of Belinda's anger and grief on this wicked act:

> Then flashed the living lightning from her eyes,
> And screams of horror rend the affrighted skies.
> Not louder shrieks to pitying heaven are cast,
> When husbands, or when lap-dogs breathe their last[30]
>
> — *The Rape of the Lock*, lines 445-48

> Or the Baron's rejoice on the same:
> Let wreaths of triumph now my temples twine,
> (the victor cried) the glorious prize is mine!
> While fish in streams, or birds delight in air,
> . . . As long as Atalantis shall be read,
> Or the small pillow grace a lady's bed
> . . . So long my honour, name, and praise shall live![31]
>
> — *The Rape of the Lock*, lines, 451-60

One thing which comes out evidently, from the discussion in the foregoing, is that for generation of laughter it is important that pity is never given a scope to emerge. This is done by putting the reader in opposition (and not in sympathy with) to the object that causes laughter. It is this distancing from the object of laughter that leads to the possible generation of mirth. In fact, even when a person laughs at himself; he manages to distance himself from himself, i.e. see himself from outside. The reader or the *sahṛdaya* must also be able to do so.

As we have stated again and again, in the *rasa* theory; it is

30. Alexander Pope and Geoffrey Tillotson, *The Rape of the Lock*, p. 55.
31. Ibid., p. 56.

the treatment, the way of looking at things (even a corpse) that will decide the *rasa*.

Karuṇa Rasa

The third important generative condition or concentrated form of realisable emotion or experience, capable of participating in the creation of an ideal artistic situation, as listed by Bharatamuni in the *Nāṭyaśāstra* is *karuṇa*. Dhanañjaya in *Daśarūpaka* while describing *karuṇa rasa* says:

इष्टनाशादनिणक्षै शोकात्मा करुणोऽनुतम् ।
निश्वासोच्वसरुदितस्तम्भप्रलपितादयः ।।81।।
स्वापापस्मारदैन्याधिमरणालस्यसम्भ्रमाः ।
विषादजडतोन्मादचिन्ताद्या व्यभिचारिणः ।।82।।[32]

— *Daśarūpaka*, p. 366

> The pathetic sentiment (*karuṇa*) with [the permanent State] sorrow (*śoka*) as its essence, [results] from the loss of something cherished and from attaining something undesired. In consequence of [there occur] heaving of sighs, drawing of sighs, weeping, paralysis, lamentation and the like [as consequents]; the transitory states [occurring in connection with it] are sleep, epilepsy, depression, sickness, death, indolence, agitation, despair, stupor, insanity, anxiety and so forth[33] — *Daśarūpaka*, p. 146

According to the *Nāṭyaśāstra*, *karuṇa*, the compassionate or the pathetic *rasa*, comes from the primary *rasa* of *raudra* or the furious:

> The result (*karma*) of the furious should be known as the aesthetic experience of compassion.[34]
>
> — *Aesthetic Rapture*, p. 48

---

32. *Daśarūpaka* of Dhanañjaya with *Avaloka* of Dhanika, p. 366.
33. *Daśarūpaka* of Dhanañjaya, by George C.O. Haas, p. 146.
34. J.L. Masson and M.V. Patwardhan, *Aesthetic Rapture*, 2 vols., Poona: Deccan College, 1970., vol 1, p. 48.

The word *karma* here apart from meaning result also signifies (a string of) other connotations like "deed", "consequence", etc. Thus, *raudra* becomes the cause and *karuṇa* the effect, and *anubhāvas* of *raudra* in turn become, or to put it more aptly, lead to or prove instrumental in the generation of *karuṇa rasa*. A man's mistakes can at any moment lead to a disaster and disaster in turn leads to tragedy. Further, the realisation of the waste of good in tragedy leads to sorrow and hence to the *karuṇa*. For instance, in Coleridge's *The Rime of the Ancient Mariner*, mariner's killing of the albatross brings about a deep crisis in his life and leads to terrible, dreadful, parlous, serious and turbulent suffering and sorrow:

> The many men, so beautiful!
> And they all dead did lie:
> And a thousand thousand slimy things
> Lived on; and so did I
>
> . . . .
>
> I looked to heaven, and tried to pray;
> But or ever a prayer had gusht,
> A wicked whisper came and made
> My heart as dry as dust.
>
> . . . .
>
> An orphan's curse would drag to hell
> A spirit from on high,
> But oh; more horrible than that
> Is a curse in a dead man's eye!
> Seven days, seven nights, I saw that curse,
> And yet I could not die.[35]
>
> — *The Rime of the Ancient Mariner*, pp. 25-26

To look at another instance let us take one from Dante's *The Divine Comedy*, where Dante describes the state he finds in the hell. In the first circle of the hell Dante finds those men suffering, who have lived their life with lack of baptism. The

---

35. Samuel Taylor Coleridge, *The Rime of the Ancient Mariner*, Electronic Text Center, University of Virginia Library, http://etext.virginia.edu/toc/modeng/public/Col2Mar.html, p. 25-26.

only thing he can hear in the first circle of the hell are their sighs:

> . . . . no plaint was heard
> Except of sighs, that made the eternal air
> Tremble, not caused by tortures, but from grief
> Felt by those multitudes, many and vast,
> Of women, and infants[36]
>
> — *The Divine Comedy,* Canto IV, lines 24-28

The sight is so abominable and tormenting that the poet himself gets filled with grief:

> Sore grief assailed
> My heart at hearing this, for well I knew
> Suspended in that Limbo many a soul
> Of mighty worth.[37]
>
> — *The Divine Comedy,* Canto IV, lines 39-42

"Many a soul of mighty worth" signifies the cause of *karuṇa* in these lines. The realisation of the waste of good (here in this instance suffering of mighty people) leads to the generation of *karuṇa rasa*. The same fact (realisation of the waste of good) keeps filling the poet with grief, sorrow and suffering again and again, throughout his journey through the hell:

> My sense reviving that erewhile had dropped
> With pity for the kindered shades, whence grief
> O'er came me wholly, straight around I see
> New torments, new tormented souls, which way
> Soe'er I move, or turn, or bend my sight.[38]
>
> — *The Divine Comedy,* Canto VI, lines 1-5

There almost seems no way out from this endless grief, sorrow and suffering for the inhabitants of the hell, as there isn't any for Coleridge's mariner:

36. Alighieri Dante, *The Divine Comedy*, tr. Henry Francis Cary with 109 illustrations by John Flaxman, 1910, Geoffrey Cumberlege, Oxford University Press, Amen House, London E.C.4, p. 11.
37. Ibid., p. 12.
38. Ibid., p. 19.

Since then, at an uncertain hour,
That agony returns;
And till my ghastly tale is old,
This heart within me burns.[39]

— *The Rime of the Ancient Mariner*, p. 46

This brings to the light an important fact about *karuṇa rasa* that there is virtually no hope in it.

The question well deserving our consideration at this juncture is that whether it is to be universally established that there is complete loss of hope in *karuṇa*? For when a man loses his position or wealth, he might get it back. When a man is imprisoned, he might come out of the jail. Yet is the suffering felt by them completely nullified when the original positions are restored? In *vipralambha śr̥ṅgāra* the separation is temporary and most importantly the separated lovers too know it and hence in separation, in agony of separation too, they get certain pleasure and so do the sympathetic reader or the *sahr̥daya*.

In a tragedy too the possibility of some achievement, fulfilment, some glory or some retribution can be seen. When, in the end, good is destroyed, some evil is also destroyed along with it which leads to the cathartic effect. Thus what will determine that whether a tragedy is in the *karuṇa rasa* or not? It can be answered thus: that whether the *sthāyī bhāva* of a tragedy is *śoka* (sorrow) or not will be decided by; what dominates at the end — the sense of waste or something positive. In this context it is worth our while to take into consideration Milton's *magnum opous* the *Paradise Lost*. Right at the beginning of the great epical poem, Milton declares his subject to be:

Of man's first disobedience, and the fruit
of that forbidden Tree, whose mortal taste
brought death into the world, and all our woe,
with loss of Eden.[40]

— *Paradise Lost*, Book I, lines 1-4

39. Samuel Taylor Coleridge, *The Rime of the Ancient Mariner*, p.46.
40. *The Poems of John Milton*, p. 458.

Thus, in the very beginning we know that the cause of the poem or the *vibhāvas* of the poem are to be those of *karuṇa* with loss of something cherished (loss of Eden) and attainment of something undesired (death and woe). But when he further states,

> . . . till one greater Man
> Restore us, and regain the blissful seat[41]
> — *Paradise Lost,* Book I, lines 4-5

We know that the final end of the poem is to be something positive instead of generating the sense of waste and hence is not *karuṇa*. In Book XII when Adam and Eve go hand in hand towards the future, we can very well understand that loss of the "paradise" is seen as the humanity's gain. Although they walk out of the "paradise" with complete or full knowledge of the impending disasters and fresh memories of the old sorrow and suffering but there isn't any sense of waste in it; rather there is an image of gain through loss:

> The world was all before them, where to choose
> Their place of rest, and Providence their guide:
> They, hand in hand, with wandering steps and slow,
> through Eden took their solitary way [42]
> — *Paradise Lost,* Book XII, lines 647-50

This establishes the point that the poem is not to be in *karuṇa rasa,* i.e. the *sthāyī bhāva* of the great epical poem is not *śoka*. But *karuṇa rasa* does find its moments of the highest intensities in it. For example, when after the full celebration of their amorous play (lust), Adam and Eve start realising the evil that the "fruit of knowledge" of "the forbidden tree" has cast on them:

> False in our promised rising; since our eyes
> Opened we find indeed, and find we know
> Both good and evil, good lost and evil got,

41. *The Poems of John Milton,* p. 458

42. Ibid., p. 1060.

Bad fruit of knowledge, if this be to know,
Which leaves us naked thus, of honour void,
Of innocence, of faith, of purity,
Our wonted ornaments now soiled and stained,
And in our faces evident the signs
Of foul concupiscence; whence evil store;
Even shame, the last of evils; of the first
Be sure then.[43]

— *Paradise Lost,* Book IX, lines 1070-80

With penality in the form of curse pronounced on them, with their honour, innocence, purity (righteousness) and faith (confidence) lost forever they are filled with sorrow, grief, utter despair and gloom. Unable to retain or hold the agony anymore within him; Adam bursts out:

O miserable of happy! Is this the end
Of this new glorious world, and me so late
The glory of that glory, who now become
Accurst of blessed, hide me from the face
Of God, whom to behold was then my highest
Of happiness: yet well, if there would end
The misery, I deserved it, and would bear
My own deservings; but this will not serve;
All that I eat or drink, or shall beget,
Is propagated curse. O voice once heard
Delightfully, I increase and multiply,
Now death to hear! For what can I increase
Or multiply, but curses on my head?
Who of all ages to succeed but feeling
The evil on him brought by me, will curse
My head. . . . .
. . . . . . .O fleeting joys
of Paradise, dear bought with lasting
. . . .
All I received, unable to perform
Thy terms too hard, by which I was to hold
The good I sought not. To the loss of that

43. *The Poems of John Milton*, pp. 918-19.

Sufficient penalty, why hast thou added
The sense of endless woes?[44]
— *Paradise Lost*, Book X, lines 720-54

Here, in these verses we find what can be called a perfect example of *karuṇa rasa*. With the fatal mistake committed, disaster already occurred, fatal judgement or penality or curse pronounced, all peace and happiness robbed and the absolute loss of hope; not only in the present but for all the time, all the ages or generations to come "for what can I increase or multiply, but curses" we get a situation ideal for the generation of *karuṇa*. Applying the above verses to our scheme of graphics we find:

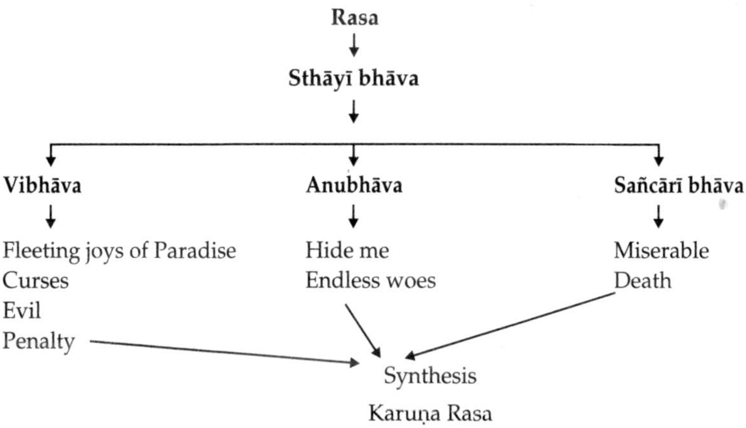

fig. **2.6: *Karuṇa* in *Paradise Lost*, Book X, lines 720-54**

Karuṇa rasa arises when man has lost all hope or when he is left with no courage or no will to fight. The relishment of *karuṇa* on the part of the reader comes through sympathy and identity. If on the one hand a cruel tyrant suffers, his suffering will seem justified and hence shall generate no sympathy, but on the other hand, the destruction and devastation by war or

44. *The Poems of John Milton*, pp. 964-65.

suffering caused by poverty, would certainly generate sympathy and hence lead to *karuṇa rasa*.

As discussed earlier also, the nature of *rasa* depends upon the nature as well as the treatment of the object. A nightmare can lead to *karuṇa* as well as to *bhayānaka rasa*. In a situation like war, possibilities of *karuṇa, bībhatsa, vīra, raudra* and *bhayānaka* all are to be found. *Karuṇa* surfaces where the work indicates no hope or spirit or ability or will to fight left. In British war poet, Wilfred Owen's (who himself died in the First World War) poem *Strange Meeting* he describes his meeting with an enemy soldier in the hell, where the enemy soldier tells him:

> The pity of war, the pity war distilled.
> Now men will go content with what we spoiled,
> Or, discontent, boil bloody, and be spilled.
>
> . . . .
>
> Even with truths that lie too deep for taint.
> I would have poured my spirit without stint
> But not through wounds; not on the cess of war.
> Foreheads of men have bled where no wounds were.[45]
>
> — Wilfred Owen, *Strange Meeting*

The obvious reaction to the poem is that of mixed aversion for the great waste caused by the War. The *vibhāva*s in the form of war, blood, wounds and death have the possibilities of both *bībhatsa* and *bhayānaka*. But the focus is upon the great waste caused by the war and when the poet says "Now men will go content with what we spoiled/Or, discontent, boil bloody, and be spilled", "Foreheads of men have bled where no wounds were" the obvious outcome is *karuṇa* instead of *bībhatsa* or *bhayānaka* which comes out even more markedly in the last lines:

> I am the enemy you killed, my friend.
> I knew you in this dark: for so you frowned

45. Wilfred Owen (1893-1918): *Futility*, http://users.fulladsl.be/spb1667/cultural/owen/futility.html.

Yesterday through me as you jabbed and killed.
I parried; but my hands were loath and cold.
Let us sleep now . . .[46]

— Wilfred Owen, *Strange Meeting*

Thus, the consequences of the ruthless monster, war — pity and sorrow — are focused or brought into light.

Poverty and agony generated by it (as discussed earlier) has great potential for generating pity and sorrow or *karuṇa*. To further illustrate the point, we can take Rainer Maria Rilke's *The Beggar's Song* for analysis:

I always go from gate to gate,
Soaked to the bone and all burned up;
All of a sudden I'll lay my right ear
In my right hand.
Then my own voice sounds to me
as if I had never known it.

Then I don't know for sure, who it is that's screaming,
Me or just somebody else.
I'm screaming about next to nothing, really.
Poets scream about more.

Finally, I close my face
With both eyes shut;
Which looks as if it's in my hands
With its whole weight, and resting.
That's so that they don't think
I don't have a proper place,
To lay down my head.[47]

In the above verses the manifestations of the suffering caused by poverty are miserable — "soaked to the bone and all burned up" and the maniac state of the begger as evident from — "my own voice sounds to me/as if/had never known

46. Wilfred Owen (1893Ḥ1918): *Strange Meeting*, deviantART: geaannunziata journal, http://geaannunziata.deviantart.com/journal/22625525/.

47. Rainer Maria Rilke, *The Beggar's Song*, *Poetry Connection*, http://www.poetryconnection.net/poets Rainer_Maria_Rilke/3230.

it", "I'm screaming about next to nothing" and in "looks as if it is in my hand" and so on — create an ideal condition for the generation of *karuṇa*.

Abhinavagupta while commenting on *Dhvanyāloka* in *Locana* says that sorrow which is the *sthāyī bhāva* of *karuṇa* has been capable of being aesthetically appreciated through sympathy and identity. Here it must be understood that the sorrow experienced in a work of art is different from that experienced in the real life. The first is a pleasurable experience while the second is painful. Sorrow, depicted in a work of art is relished principally and primarily because of the aesthetic distancing of the sympathetic reader or the *sahṛdaya* which enables him to relish even the negative emotions or states which when aesthetically transmuted no longer seem to be negative any more.

Raudra Rasa

The fourth universal, absolute, concrete form of realisable experience as listed by Bharatamuni in the *Nāṭyaśāstra* is *raudra*. Bharatamuni says:

> Now (the *rasa*) called *raudra* has anger for its permanent emotion. Demons, monsters and violent men are its characters. It is caused by battles. It arises from such *vibhāvas* as anger, provocative actions (*ādharsana*), insult (*adhikṣepa*), lies, assaults (*upaghāta*), harsh words, oppression (*adhidroha*) or according to Abhinava "murderous intent" and "envy".[48]
>
> — *Aesthetic Rapture*, vol. I, p. 53

This anger, the *sthāyī bhāva* of the *raudra rasa*, when justly felt due to injustice and oppression might lead to the end of evil but when generated by "violent men", "demons", and "monsters" can lead to generation of evil. For instance, we

48. J.L. Masson and M.V. Patwardhan, *Aesthetic Rapture*, vol 1, p. 53.

can take into consideration Milton's *Paradise Lost* where Satan's (the devil) anger gives rise to a dance of evil throughout the poem.

Satan as described by Milton in *Paradise Lost* was first of the created beings who, for endeavouring to be equal with the highest, for making a war in the heaven against the creator seeking to overthrow him and seize his throne, was hurled down to the hell. He was baffled and the anger, the fury, the *raudra* in him led him to think of a new war and revenge:

> What though the field be lost?
> All is not lost: the unconquerable will,
> And study of revenge, immortal hate,
> And courage never to submit or yield.[49]
>
> — *Paradise Lost*, Book I, lines 105-08

Here Satan displays firm determination and courage — heroic qualities — but his intentions are certainly evil. He is prompted by undying hatred for God and a desire for revenge. He is baffled but not confounded; he has a matchless strength of mind and body. His anger has made him even stronger and therefore rising from the lake of fire he declares that the rebels must make the most of the dreadful place where they find themselves:

> The mind is its own place, and in itself
> Can make a Heaven of Hell, a Hell of Heaven.
> ....
> To reign is worth ambition, though in Hell:
> Better to reign in Hell, than serve in Heaven[50]
>
> — *Paradise Lost*, Book I, lines 254-64

Angry Satan plans to mobilise his disordered army to establish a dark evil kingdom of his own and what naturally follows, is a dance of evil through *raudra*. He gives a powerful and loud call to his followers:

---

49. *The Poems of John Milton*, p. 468.

50. Ibid., p. 476.

He called so loud that all the hollow deep
of Hell resounded[51]

— *Paradise Lost*, Book I, lines 314-15

Issuing the call to take up the fight once more, and assert their strength and courage:

Awake, arise, or be for ever fallen![52]

— *Paradise Lost*, Book I, lines 330

They all rise to his call and with mighty labours speedily build the huge palace of Pandemonium, Hell's capital. They then hold a conference to plan some vast revenge and decide to find the compensation for the loss of infinite happiness (heaven) in the form of inflicting infinite misery on others (especially man):

. . . There is a place
(If ancient and prophetic fame in Heaven
Err not), another world, the happy seat
Of some new race called man, about this time
To be created like to us, though less
In power and excellence, but favoured more
Of him who rules above . . . . . .
Thither let us bend all our thoughts, to learn
What creatures there inhabit, ...
. . . Here perhaps
Some advantageous act may be achieved
By sudden onset: either with Hell-fire
To waste his whole creation, or possess
All as our own, and drive, as we were driven,
The puny inhabitants; or, if nor drive,
Seduce them to our party, that their God
May prove their foe, and with repenting hand
Abolish his own works.[53]

— *Paradise Lost*, Book II, lines 346-70

---

51. *The Poems of John Milton*, p. 481.
52. Ibid., p. 482.
53. Ibid., pp. 523-25.

Satan in the due course of the epic succeeds in his evil design. And we find him declaring his mischief, the deplorable act gloriously to his followers:

> The new created world, which fame in heaven
> Long had foretold, a fabric wonderful
> Of absolute perfection, there in man
> Placed in a paradise, by our exile
> Made happy: him by fraud I have seduced
> From his creator, and the more to message
> Your wonder, with an apple; he thereat
> Offended, worth your laughter, hath given up
> Both his beloved man and all this world,
> To sin and Death a prey, and so to us,
> Without our hazard, labour, or alarm,
> To range in, and to duell, and over man
> To rule, as over all he should have ruled.[54]
>
> — *Paradise Lost*, Book X, lines 481-93

As Satan deceived Adam and Eve in the shape of a serpent, so he and his followers all turned into serpents (as a punishment) and *raudra* in turn leads to *bhayānaka*:

> So having said, a while he stood,
> expecting . . . . high applause. . . .
> To fill his ear, when contrary he hears
> On all sides, from innumerable tongues
> A dismal universal hiss[55]
>
> — *Paradise Lost*, Book X, lines 504-08

The act of deceit generates a series of fleeting emotions in Adam and Eve, but the realisation of the evil, its deplorable outcome, the disaster that has befallen on them generates *raudra* in Adam and baffled and confounded in a fury he bursts out on Eve:

> Out of my sight, thou serpent, that name best
> Befits thee with him leagued, they self as false

54. *The Poems of John Milton*, pp. 950-51.

55. Ibid., p. 951.

And hateful; nothing wants, but that thy shape,
Like his, and colour serpentine may show
Thy inward fraud, to warn all creatures from thee.[56]
— *Paradise Lost*, Book X, lines 867-71

His anger does not stop at it, he goes on to the extent of even questioning the God, the supreme: for having created a fallible feminine creature as Eve:

O why did God,
Creator wise, that peopled highest heaven
With spirits masculine, create at last
This novely on earth, this fair defect
Of nature, and not fill the world at once
With men as angles without feminine
Or find some other way to generate
Mankind?[57]
— *Paradise Lost*, Book X, lines 888-95

This *raudra* gradually subsides into *karuṇa*, as both Adam and Eve lament, weep, regret, bewail till exhausted from it, reach into a momentry state of *śānta* as will be described in our forthcoming discussion on *śānta rasa*.

An important point which comes out as evident from the foregoing discussion is that *raudra* in Satan manifests itself comparatively less in words and more in violent deeds, whereas, that in Adam manifests itself more or less only in words rather than in deeds.

As stated earlier, *raudra* can usually be associated with injustice and oppression. In modern literature, this kind of injustice, oppression and cruelty is very much felt, especially in literatures like that of Rimbaud, Verline and Allen Ginsberg. But anger, as evident from the above instances, if in excess of its cause (fury suggests this), can inflict pain and cause sorrow and *bhaya* (As is evident from Satan's words (speeches) and

56. *The Poems of John Milton*, p. 971.
57. Ibid., p. 972.

deeds in Milton's *Paradise Lost* discussed in the foregoing). On the other hand, if choked, it might lead to incomprehension, disjunction and hold the possibility of *bībhatsa.*

The various *sañcārī bhāva*s of the *raudra rasa* are (*Nāṭyaśāstra,* VI.6.3):

> Correct perception (*asaṁmoha*), dynamic energy (*utsāha*), panic, resentment, rashness, violence, pride, sweat, trembling, horripilation, stuttering (*gadgada*) and so forth.[58]
>
> — *Aesthetic Rapture,* vol. I, p. 53

"Correct perception" along with being the *sañcārī bhāva* of the *raudra* is also the cause of *vīra rasa*. Here, it can mean that when injustice, oppression, etc. are perceived there might be the need for fury. Hence, it is indicated here that "correct perception" leads not only to heroic action but also to anger. Raudra is also related to *vīra rasa* in other ways. In heroic actions, the element of fury is perceivable, if not always, at least sometimes. It is, for this reason, that Abhinavagupta has related *utsāha* or dynamic energy, which is the primary state or the *sthāyī bhāva* of *vīra,* to anger or *krodha* (*Aesthetic Rapture,* vol. II, p. 89). This can be justified by the fact that even a meek man, furious at some injustice, can act courageously. Both the *rasa*s involve action, "dynamic energy" and "correct perception".

One might ask, if *vīra* and *raudra rasa*s are so similar, what is it that differentiates them? A close look shows that the primary states (*sthāyī bhāvas*) of the two are different, i.e. dynamic energy and anger respectively. Anger the *sthāyī bhāva* of *raudra rasa* is a state which is more or less blind. In other words, "correct perception" might get blocked by anger. Hence, there is the possibility of some wrong action. Besides, anger need not necessarily be correctly channelised. Fury might lead to a lot of words, but no action as is the case with

58. J.L. Masson and M.V. Patwardhan, *Aesthetic Rapture*, vol. 1, p. 53.

the *raudra rasa*. But in case of *vīra rasa*, the dynamic energy will either be reserved or correctly channelised and therefore, will always lead to a positive state or emotion.

Raudra is very closely associated with *bhayānaka* as well. We have seen that the manifestations of the furious are the following: "beating", "splitting", "crushing", "ripping open", etc. All these have suggestions of blood and mutilation. Such actions give rise to fear, and also to disgust. Thus, *raudra* is also related to *bībhatsa*.

While discussing the *vīra rasa* and its relation with other *rasas* Bharatamuni in the *Nāṭyaśāstra* says that:

> The awesome aesthetic experience comes from the heroic. . . The result of the furious should be known to be an aesthetic experience of compassion.[59]
>
> — *Aesthetic Rapture*, vol. I, p. 48

What the first part of the passage suggests is that wherever heroism is manifest, *raudra* will accompany as an accessory. Besides, the heroic emotion is the source of the awesome. This need not always be true. A man burdened by sorrow cannot become furious; he might whimper. This is so, for the moment one gives vent to sorrow, he has lost his positive frame of mind, his strength to fight back. Similarly, a man who is afraid cannot at the same time become furious. Thus, even with a bad man or with a monster, the important thing is a courageous frame of mind. Even though the actions of a bad man or a monster are not heroic, the frame of mind is one that is ready to take up any challenge.

Raudra is always associated with violence and destruction. But it is not necessarily productive. The moment it is channelised in a positive direction, it becomes *vīra*. Hence, in *raudra*, the central emphasis is upon the turmoil, the fury, and

59. J.L. Masson and M.V. Patwardhan, *Aesthetic Rapture*, vol. 1, p. 48.

its consequences. It is thus that *raudra* will invariably lead to *karuṇa rasa*. So, it is not surprising that the effects or *anubhāvas* of *raudra* are also similar to the *anubhāvas* of *karuṇa*, i.e. tears, fear, trembling, etc. *Raudra* is a very vital element in the modern Western literature. But it has a tendency to dissolve or get transformed into something else. It cannot sustain itself for a long time, after its moments of intensities it gives way to either sorrow or action and this action is essentially devastating. And when the fury, the anger, of *raudra* is impotent, it usually leads to a sense of incomprehension — the *absurd*.

Vīra Rasa

Gleams that untravell'd world whose margin fades
For ever and for ever when I move.
How dull it is to pause, to make an end,
To rust unburnish'd, not to shine in use!
.... Where all too little, and of one to me
Little remains; but every hour is saved
From that eternal silence, something more
.... And this gray spirit yearning in desire
To follow knowledge like a sinking star,
Beyond the utmost bound of human thought.[60]

— Tennyson's *Ulysses*, lines, 20-33.

On reading the above given lines the sympathetic reader or the *sahṛdaya* experiences a kind of dynamic energy which completely engrosses him. To put it in other words, every part of his body becomes active to put whatever he thinks, in practice. This is called *maitrībhāvanā* and this comes into existence when there is *utsāha* and *ācārya*. Here in the above-given verses this *utsāha* and *ācārya* is instigated by what we know as *vīra rasa*. The experience of the *ānanda* in the *vīra rasa* is different from that in the other *rasas*. As is evident from the above example in the *vīra rasa*, *citta* gets *vistāra* (spreads in the whole body of *sahṛdaya*).

60. *The Victorian Web*, http://www.victorianweb.org/authors/tennyson/ulyssestext.html

Bharatamuni said that *vīra rasa* is of the form of *utsāha* (*utsāhātmaka*). According to him, men of noble character (*uttama prakṛti*) would naturally have *utsāha*. *Utsāha* is the *sthāyī bhāva* of the *vīra rasa* and:

> Asaṁmoha (not to get perturbed), *adhyavasāya* (determination), *naya* (foresight), *vinaya* (modesty), *bala* (strength), *parākrama* (prowess), *śakti* (strength of mind), *pratāpa* (valour) and *prābhava* (grandeur) are its *vibhāvas*.[61]
>
> — *Nāṭyaśāstra* 6.39

One's inclination towards the bad (or worldly) things is known as *Saṁmoha* and *Asaṁmoha* is its absence. *Naya* can be explained as the good knowledge of the statecraft and *vinaya* is the control over senses. To further illustrate on these, it is worth our while to take again into consideration a few lines of Alfred Tennyson's *Ulysses*, a great poem expressive of an indomitable will, summoning up every reserve of resolute courage and seeking new worlds to conquer.

Ulysses, the hero of the Trojan War, returned to his island state of Ithaca after twenty years. He has been ruling his state for some time, but the life of peace, devoid of adventure, does not suit him (*asaṁmoha*). In the poem, he is supposed to be standing at the coast of the sea, surrounded by his sailors whom he exhorts to follow him in the quest of more knowledge and experience:

> . . . My Mariners,
> Souls that have toil'd, and wrought, and thought with me,
> That ever with a frolic welcome took
> The thunder and the sunshine, and opposed
> Free hearts, free foreheads, — you and I are old;
> Old age hath yet his honour and his toil.
> Death closes all, ...
>
> — Tennyson's *Ulysses*, lines, 46-52

61. *Nāṭyaśāstra* 6.39.

Tis not too late to seek a newer world.
. . . . tho'much is taken, much abides and tho'
We are not now that strength which in old days
Moved earth and heaven, that which we are, we are.
One equal temper of heroic hearts,
Made weak by time and fate, but strong in will
To strive, to seek, to find, and not to yield.[62]
— Tennyson's *Ulysses*, lines, 58-71

Here *asaṁmoha* (not to get perturbed) in "with a frolic welcome took/The thunder and the sunshine", *vinaya* (control over the sense) in "oppossed free hearts, free foreheads", *naya* (foresight) in "old age hath yet his honour and his toil", *prābhava* (grandeur) in "tis not too late to seek a newer world" and *parākrama* (prowess) and *pratāpa* (valour) in "To strive, to seek, to find, and not to yield, (*śakti*) strength in "that strength which in old days, moved earth and heaven" and "heroic hearts" lead to an overflow of dynamic energy in the reader which is naturally a manifestation, in the reader, an experience of *vīra rasa*.

According to Bharatamuni the *anubhāva*s of the *vīra rasa* are:

> *sthiratā* (firmness), *dhairya* (boldness), *śaurya* (show of might), *tyāga* (charity) and *viśāradatā* (skill).[63]
> — *Nāṭyaśāstra* 6.39

To again consider the examples from the *Ulysses* as discussed above we can say that Ulysses's speech and actions manifest everything his firmness, boldness, might, skill and charity, all the *anubhāva*s of the *vīra rasa*. About the *vyabhicārī bhāva*s of the *vīra rasa*, Bharatamuni in the *Nāṭyaśāstra* says that:

> *Dhṛti* (courage), *mati* (thinking), *garva* (pride), *āvega* (mental agitation), *ugratā* (fierceness), *amarṣa* (anger), *smṛti*

62. *The Victorian Web*.

63. *Nāṭyaśāstra* 6.39.

(recollection) and *romāñca* (horripilation) are its *vyabhicārī bhāvas*.[64]
— *Nāṭyaśāstra* 6.39

Ulysses's courage and firm determination to take up new challenges despite old age, his thinking in — "old age hath yet his honour and his toil/death closes all", his mental agitation in "rust unburnish'd, not to shine in use", his recollection of the successful ventures of the past -- "in old days moved earth and heaven" and the resultant (horripilation) manifest the *vīra* in the situation to the full.

In *vīra rasa* the person what is to be vanquished is the *ālambana vibhāva* and its actions are the *uddīpana vibhāva* which rouse the *utsāha* and raise it to the state of *rasa*. Dhanañjaya in *Daśarūpaka* says that the person who is the *ālambana vibhāva* of *vīra rasa* should be of the *dhīrodātta* type. According to him a man of *dhīrodātta* type is *mahāsattva* (high minded) which means, he is not easily overcome by anger and distress, etc. He is *gambhīra* (deep) and is of forgiving nature. He is not boastful but at the same time in his assertions and actions (*dṛḍha vrata*). Though conscious of his greatness he does not show his *ahaṁkāra* (egoism):

महासत्त्वोऽतिगम्भीरो क्षमावानविकत्थनः।
स्थिरो निगूढाहङ्कारो धीरोदात्तो दृढव्रतः ।।[65]

— Cited in *Some Unexplored Aspects of The Rasa Theory*, p.82

An important point, to be kept in mind, while discussing *vīra rasa* is that *vīratā* (being *vīra*) is not confined to the battle and adventure only. It has a wider scope. The word *udātta* in *dhīrodātta* indicates this only. *Vīratā* in fact is associated, related or connected with all the great qualities like *dayā* (kindness), *dāna* (charity), Dākṣiṇya (politeness) and *śaurya* (show of valour), etc.

64. *Nāṭyaśāstra* 6.39.

65. B.M. Chaturvedi, *Some Unexplored Aspects of the Rasa Theory*, tr. P. Sri Ramachandrudu, Vidyanidhi Prakashan, Delhi, 1996, p. 82.

A man cannot be called a *vīra* merely by defeating the enemy in the battle; for being called *vīra* he should have such great qualities as discussed above. It is only when these *guṇa*s appear; that there would be *vistāra* of *citta* and *utsāha* would prevail everywhere. It is because of this reason that the words of Jīmūtavāhana in *Nāgānanda* make the *utsāha* pervade in the spectre but not *karuṇa*:

> शिरामुखैः स्यन्दत एवं रक्तमद्यापि देहे मम मांसमस्ति ।
> तृप्तिं न पश्यामि तवापि तावत् किं भक्षणात्त्वं विरतो गरुत्मन् ॥
>
> O! Garutman! There is still blood flowing through the ends of my veins; still there is flesh in my body. I do not think you are satisfied; why did you stop eating.[66]
>
> — Cited in *Some Unexplored Aspects of The Rasa Theory*, p. 83

What is witnessed here is the real sign of *vīratā* and as is evident from it, the real sign of *vīratā* when expressed leads to the overflow (uncontrolled) of *sāttvika utsāha* (positive energy) in the reader or the spectator.

Based on the qualities associated with *vīratā*, in the Indian tradition we have many varieties of *vīra* — *dānavīra*, *dharmavīra*, *dayāvīra* and *yuddhavīra*, etc. (and numerous examples of each can be cited from both Indian and Western tradition). It is because of this reason that in Sanskrit literature not only the victorious persons like Rāma, Kr̥ṣṇa, Arjuna and Candragupta, etc. but also persons like Buddha, Mahāvīra, Jīmūtavāhana, Dadhīci, Karṇa, Yudhiṣṭhira and Paraśurāma are all considered as great *vīra*s.

The scope of the *vīra rasa* is not confined only to *dayā*, *dharma*, *dāna* and *yuddha*, but on close examination we can see how it overshadows and envelops all the *rasa*s like *śr̥ṅgāra*, etc. also. In the *Abhinavabhāratī* it has been indicated that the *vīra rasa* only has got the capacity to produce all the *rasa*s. A *mahāpuruṣa* shows *utsāha*, i.e. a high-minded and noble person

---

66. B.M. Chaturvedi, *Some Unexplored Aspects of the Rasa Theory*, tr. P. Sri Ramachandrudu, Vidyanidhi Prakashan, Delhi, 1996, p. 83.

shows the dynamic energy, strength, might, courage and valour to achieve something great in this world and this can lead to the possible generation of all the *rasa*s. As stated by Abhinavagupta *vīra rasa* is the one which has the other *rasa*s as the objects aspired for:

यस्तु रसो रसान्तरं फलत्वेनाभिसन्धाय
प्रवर्तते तस्योदाहरणं वीरः।[67]

— Cited in *Some Unexplored Aspects of The Rasa Theory*, p. 84.

What can be understood from this is that the *utsāha*, the *sthāyī bhāva* of *vīra* is found only in a person of nobility. It reaches its climax in the personality of a *mahāpuruṣa*. Only a *mahāpuruṣa* (person of nobility) shows *utsāha* (dynamic energy) to achieve a very important object (result) connected with this world, the result of his act can lead to all the *rasa*s depending on the difference of the *ālambana* (the opponent). To illustrate the point it is worth our while to take into consideration the following verses from Tulasīdāsa's *Rāmacaritamānasa*, where he has very skilfully shown how *vīra* can lead to or produce all other *rasa*s. Rāma climbed the stage and is about to break the *śivadhanuṣa*:

उदित उदयगिरिमंच पर रघुवर बाल पतंग ।
विकसे संत सरोज बन, हरषे लोचन भृंग ॥

चाप समीप राम जब आये। नरनारिन्ह सब सुकृत मनाये ॥
सबकर संसय अरू अजानू। मंदमहीपन्ह कर अभिमानू ॥

भृगुपति केरि गरब गरूआई । सुखरन्ह केरि कदराई ॥
सियकर सोचु जनक पछतावा । रानिन्ह कर दारून दुखपावा ॥

संभुचाप बड़ बेहितु पाई । चढ़े जाइ सब संग बनाई ॥
रामबाहुबल सिंधु अपारू । चहत पार नहिं कोउ कड़हारू ॥[68]

— Cited in *Some Unexplored Aspects of The Rasa Theory*, p. 85.

---

67. B.M. Chaturvedi, *Some Unexplored Aspects of the Rasa Theory*, tr. P. Sri Ramachandrudu, Vidyanidhi Prakashan, Delhi, 1996, p. 84.

68. Ibid., p. 85.

> When Rāma drew near to the bow, men and women present there invoked on his behalf the help of gods as well as on account of their own past good deeds. The doubts and ignorance of all those who had assembled there, the arrogance of the foolish kings, the proud pretensions of Paraśurāma (the chief of Bhṛgu's race), the apprehensions of gods and the great sages, the distress of Sītā, King Janaka's remorse and the fire of the queens' terrible agony —all these boarded together the great bark of *śivadhanuṣa*, with whose help they sought to cross the boundless ocean of Srī Rāma's strength of arm; but there was no helmsman to steer the ship.

Here we can see that how although, Rāma, the *mahāpuruṣa*, the *āśraya* of *utsāha* is one but reactions of different persons to the situation when the *śivadhanuṣa* is broken are different. Different *sthāyī bhāva*s appear among different people as a reaction to the *utsāha* of Rāma, *vismaya* in the ordinary people, *rati* in Sītā, fear and aversion (about themselves) in other princes, *krodha* in Paraśurāma, *karuṇa* in Janaka and his wives, and *hāsa* in Viśvāmitra. This magnificent illustration, beyond doubt, proves the point that *vīra rasa* is at the centre of all the *rasa*s and that all the *rasa*s are or can be produced by it, directly or indirectly. This may be said to be a reason why all the heroes in literature (fiction of all kinds, epics and all) are *dhīrodātta*s, i.e. *vīra*s only, no matter whether the predominant *rasa* in them (or in the work) is *śṛṅgāra* or any other.

A significant question put forth many times is that if the *vīra rasa* is the source of all the *rasa*s then why *adbhuta* only is said to be born out of it; Abhinavagupta has answered it in the *Abhinavabhāratī*: *vīrasya samyak nikaṭāni yatphalāmi so'dbhutam — śṛṅgāro api vīrasya anantaram phalam.*[69] The first general reaction to *vīra* is wonder, and therefore *adbhuta* is said to be

---

69. B.M. Chaturvedi, *Some Unexplored Aspects of the Rasa Theory*, tr. P. Sri Ramachandrudu, Vidyanidhi Prakashan, Delhi, 1996, p. 85.

the direct product of *vīra*. *Rati*, *hāsa* and other *bhāva*s appear as reactions of *vīra*, only after wonder and so they are connected with *vīra* indirectly.

An important point to be kept in mind while discussing *vīra rasa* is that in *vīra rasa* the dynamic energy must be channelised in the right direction through "correct perception" as we discussed in detail in our discussion on *raudra rasa*.

The scope of the *vīra rasa* is very wide. Numberless examples of *vīra rasa* can be cited from all old medieval and modern writings (Achilles of *The Iliad*, Beowulf of *The Beowulf*, Odysseus of Homer's *Odyssey*, Bilbo Baggins of Tolkien's, *The Hobbit*), but here it must be kept in mind that *utsāha*, the *sthāyī bhāva* of *vīra* is an emotion which can be found even among the common people. This we see in Ernest Hemmingway's *The Old Man and the Sea*:

Santiago, the hero of Heminway's *The Old Man and the Sea* is an old fisherman, a common man. But he is a veteran fighter prepared for anything and everything. And what is remarkably important about him is that he never gives up hope:

> He was an old man who fished alone in a skiff in the Gulf Stream and he had gone eighty-four days now without taking a fish. In the first forty days a boy had been with him. But after forty days without a fish the boy's parents had told him that the old man was definitely and finally *salao*, which is the worst form of unlucky. . . . It made the boy sad to see the old man come in each day with his skiff empty. . .[70]
>
> — *The Old Man and the Sea*, p. 2

The situation is inevitably that of *karuṇa* but what holds our attention is the "never say die" or "never say no" spirit of the old man, his stubborn perseverance. When the narrative begins he is going out for the eighty-fifth time without a fish. His

70. Hemingway, Ernest, *The Old Man and the Sea*, www.asiaing.com

single-minded and dogged determination becomes even clearer as the narrative proceeds.

The old man is battle-scarred and there are marks of sea-battles (with fishes) upon him:

> . . . his hands had deep-creased scars from handling heavy fish on the cords. But none of these scars were fresh. They were as old as erosions in a fishless desert.
>
> Everything about him was old except his eyes and they were the same colour as the sea and were cheerful and undefeated. — *The Old Man and the Sea*, p. 2

Thus we can see that the "old Man" is a warrior with nerves of steel. Even after eighty-four days out of luck, his eyes are still undefeated. The old man has full control over him and never gets angry; not even when he is ridiculed: "many of the fishermen made fun of the old man and he was not angry" *(The Old Man and the Sea*, p. 7.) He had learnt his lesson from life that the ultimate essence of heroism is "humility" and "forgiveness":

> He was too simple to wonder when he had attained humility. But he knew he had attained it and he knew it was not disgraceful and it carried no loss of true pride.
>
> — *The Old Man and the Sea*, p. 4

We importantly see here that pride and humility are resolved into one man. Thus, he is a man Dhanañjaya calls of the *dhīrodātta* type and response to him therefore is of *adbhuta* type as manifested in the reaction of the boy who considers Santiago the best fisherman in the world:

> There are many good fishermen and some great ones. But there is only you.
>
> Thank you. You make me happy. I hope no fish will come along so great that he will prove us wrong.
>
> — *The Old Man and the Sea*, p. 9.

But on the eighty-fifth day, when the old man goes deep into the sea, actually a big marlin, very big in fact, comes along his way and challenges him. What follows is a battle of courage, patience and intelligence. The old man is "shrewd" and skilful. But he soon realises that the fish is also a "shrewd" old fish, the way it dives in and threatens to capsize Santiago's skiff makes us realise that it is equally experienced in this game. The battle turns slowly into a test of patience and endurance, a war of attrition. Even after an entire day and a night neither is ready to give up:

> "Fish", he said softly, aloud, "I'll stay with you until I am dead." — *The Old Man and the Sea*, p. 19.

And the process makes us wonder at the courage and endurance of the two warriors (old fish and old man) when Santiago appreciates the fighting calibre of the fish:

> "Fish", he said, "I love you and respect you very much. But I will kill you dead before this day ends."
>
> — *The Old Man and the Sea*, p. 19

As the day progresses, finally the fish comes out and he kills him, but on his way back the dead fish is attacked by sharks. He fights with them with his harpoon, and when it is gone, with a knife and then with the tiller. But in the night they eat most of his great fish and he almost seems to be giving up in despair but immediately he recovers and says:

> "But man is not made for defeat,". . . . "A man can be destroyed but not defeated. I am sorry that I killed the fish though. . . ." — *The Old Man and the Sea*, p. 38

As readers we feel sorry for both the fish and the "old man" but more than that we feel wonder and admiration at the indomitable spirit, courage strength and endurance of the "old man".

Vīra, in itself can lead to a state of "happiness" when it achieves something great, as happens when the "old man" finally kills the fish in *The Old Man and the Sea*. In that moment of achievement there is a moment of wonder and complete satisfaction of *śānta* and *adbhuta rasa*.

Bībhatsa and Bhayānaka Rasa

About *bībhatsa rasa* Dhanañjaya writes:

> बीभत्सः कृमिपूतिगन्धिवमथुप्रायैर्जुगुप्सैकभू-
> रुद्वेगी रुधिरान्त्रकीकसवसामांसादिभिः क्षोभणः।
> वैराग्याज्जघनस्तनादिषु घृणाशुद्धोऽनुभावैर्वृतो
> नासावक्त्रविकूणनादिभिरिहावेगार्तिशन्नदयः ॥73॥[71]
>
> — *Daśarūpaka*, p. 358

> The odious sentiment (*bībhatsa*) has [the permanent state] disgust (*jugupsā*) as its sole basis, it causes distress (*udvega*) chiefly by means of worms, stinking matter, and nausea; it causes horror by means of blood, entrails, bones, marrow, flesh, and the like; it causes unmixed aversion in the case of the hips, breasts, and so forth [of women] because of renunciation it is accompanied by contraction of the nose, mouth, and so on as consequents, in it [there occur] agitations, sickness, apprehension, and the like [as transitory states.[72]
>
> — *Daśarūpaka*, pp. 141-42

Disgust on the physical or metaphysical plane is born when familiar things become unknown, the real becomes the unreal, the natural the unnatural, for instance, when a living body decomposes, it is not the object in itself that generates repulsion, it is the transformation from the known to the unknown, from the recognisable to the unrecognisable. To illustrate the point it is worth our while to consider a few lines from Coleridge's, *The Rime of the Ancient Mariner*. In *The Rime of the Ancient Mariner* killing of the Albatross, leads to a

71. *Daśarūpaka* of Dhanañjaya with *Avaloka* of Dhanika, p. 358.
72. *Daśarūpaka* of Dhanañjaya, by George C.O. Haas, p. 146.

series of disasters, the boat comes to a standstill at a monstrous or seemingly haunted place in the sea, after many heart-drying events all the men of Mariner's troops drop dead one by one except the Mariner who is left helplessly alive but alone:

> I looked upon the rotting sea,
> And drew my eyes away;
> I looked upon the rotting deck,
> And there the dead men lay.
> . . . .
> I closed my lids, and kept them close,
> And the balls like pulses best;
> For the sky and the sea, and the sea and the sky
> Lay like a load on my weary eye.
> And the dead were at my feet.
> The cold sweat melted from their limbs,
> Nor rot nor reek did they:
> The look with which they looked on me
> Had never passed away.[73]
>
> — *The Rime of the Ancient Mariner*, lines 241-257

Here the repulsion, or the disgust is caused due to transformation of known into unknown, recognisable into unrecognisable, of sea into rotting sea, deck into rotting deck, men into dead men, sweat into cold sweat and the like. It is natural for the dead bodies to rot; but these dead bodies of the Mariner's deck, neither rot nor reek, hence it is unnatural and therefore the situation causes repulsion.

Disgust need not necessarily arise only from a physical displacement. In fact, in all cases, the disillusionment is the result of realisation of the gap between the ideal and the real, between the natural and the unnatural, between what it ought to be and what things really are. In T.S. Eliot's *The Hollow Men*, it is the disillusionment at the modern man's metaphysical position on mechanical state that leads to disgust and hence the expression:

---

73. Samuel Taylor Coleridge, *The Rime of the Ancient Mariner*, p. 47.

We are the hollow men
We are the stuffed men
Leaning together
Head piece filled with straw, Alas![74]

— T.S. Eliot: *The Hollow Men*

The displacement of men into hollow men, of men into stuffed men is the displacement of the inner stuff of man. A little later this displacement becomes even clearer when Eliot says:

Shape without form, shadow without colour,
Paralysed force, gesture without motion;
Those who have crossed
With direct eyes, to death's other kingdom
Remember us — if at all — not as lost
Violent souls, but only
As the hollow men
The stuffed men.[75]

— T.S. Eliot: *The Hollow Men*

In the above verses it is the lack of courage in "shape without form", "shadow without colour", "paralysed force" and "gesture without motion" that brings forth the inert disillusionment of the modern man — at his own cowardice and impotency for that matter.

This element of distortion comes out even more evidently in Samuel Beckett's pantomime *Waiting for Godot*. This play has everything in it to be called a "dark comedy" but the implications of the state of the tramps depicted in it are much more terrifying than would immediately seem. The physical condition of the two tramps who are waiting, who have no other way out but to wait, for an unknown mysterious entity — Godot — evokes both pity and disgust. Nothing material happens in the play and the essence of this nothingness is to be found in following words of Estragon: "Nothing happens,

74. T.S. Eliot, *The Hollow Men*, American Poems, http://www.americanpoems.com/poets/tseliot/1076.

75. Ibid.

nobody comes, nobody goes, it's awful" *(Waiting for Godot*, Act 1). The dark comedy evident in the play at times becomes so disgusting that it hurts:

Vladimir: Oh, Gogo, that's too bad. But where are your old boots?

Estragon: (confused) My boots? I... I... I have no idea.

Vladimir: (also puzzled) Wait just a second, you never remember anything! How can you say "It was horrible, as usual?"

Estragon: (now terribly confused) I did say that, didn't I?

Vladimir: It's a paradox!

Estragon: A paradox!

Vladimir: A most ingenious paradox!

Estragon: Wait, what's the paradox?

Vladimir: (wrinkles his brow) I don't know, I forgot.

Estragon: Forgot what?[76]

— *Waiting for Godot*, Act 3

What leads to disgust in the above given situation is the unnecessary confusion or to put it in other words the unnatural or unobvious confusion depicted in the comprehension of the objects and the situation; depicted in an equally disgusting manner.

Whatever is "ugly", "unpleasant", and "unclear" or "undesired"; can cause repulsion and hence lead to disgust. "Ugly" is disgusting because normalcy is distorted in it and it equally applies to "unpleasant", "unclear" and "undesired". A break of order or hormany, a disruption in the order of things can lead to both disgust and fear. For normalcy when distorted will naturally lead to a feeling of alienation, which

76. Samuel Beckett, *Waiting for Godot*, Act 3, *Waiting for. . . Mustadio* by Mark Matarazzo, http://raptox.us/fanfic/wfg3/wfg3.html.

if incomprehensible will lead to fear — fear of the unknown. Thus the final outcome in such a case would be terrifying and hence the *rasa* generated from it will be or can be *bhayānaka* as well.

About *bhayānaka rasa*, it is said in *Daśarūpaka* that:

> विकृतस्वरसत्त्वादेर्भयभावो भयानकः ।
> सर्वांवेपथुस्वेदशोषवैवर्ण्यलक्षणः ।।
> दैन्यसम्भ्रमसंमोहत्रासादिस्तत्सहोदरः ।। 80।।[77]
>
> — *Daśarūpaka*, p. 364

> The terrible sentiment (*bhayānaka*) with fear (*bhaya*) as its [permanent] state (*bhaya*), [results] from change in voice, loss of courage, and the like [as determinants]; it is characterised by trembling of all the limbs, sweating, being parched, and fainting [as consequents]; its associated [transitory states] are depression, agitation, distraction, fright and the like.[78] — *Daśarūpaka*, p. 145

Fear can be transmuted to the audience in two different ways. First, if one is sufficiently distanced, one will perceive the manifestation of fear in the work; he will recognise and perceive it in two different ways. First, if one is sufficiently distanced, one will perceive the manifestation of fear in the work, and he will recognise and perceive fear through the emotions and states of fear (*anubhāva*s like trembling of all the limbs, sweating, etc.) manifested within the work. But if he, instead of distancing himself, is able to share the fear of the victim, he will feel an empathetic response of fear himself as is visible in the case of horror fiction.To further elaborate the point we can take into consideration a few lines from Dante's *The Divine Comedy*.

In *The Divine Comedy* the very opening lines of canto III of "Inferno", which warn us about the torments and dangers

77. *Daśarūpaka* of Dhanañjaya with *Avaloka* of Dhanika, p. 364.

78. *Daśarūpaka* of Dhanañjaya, by George C.O. Haas, p. 145.

impending in the hell, have the potential of generating the *bhayānaka rasa*. Dante is just about to enter into hell when he reads the following lines depicted at the entrance gate:

> Through me you pass into the city of woe:
> Through me you pass into eternal pain:
> . . . . All hope abandon ye who enter here[79]
>
> — *The Divine Comedy*, lines, 1-10

Fearful and hesitant or reluctant to enter at first, Dante is persuaded by his master (Virgil) and finally dares to enter into hell only to find the air there to be filled with sighs, moans, lamentations and so on and so forth:

> Here sighs, with lamentations and loud moans,
> Resounded through the air pierced by no star,
> That e'en I wept at entering. Various tongues,
> Horrible languages, outcries of woe.
> Accents of anger, voices deep and hoarse,
> With hands together smote that swelled the sounds,
> Made up a tumult, that for ever whirls
> Round through that air with solid darkness stained,
> Like to the sand that in the whirlwind flies[80]
>
> — *The Divine Comedy*, Canto III, lines, 20-29

The sight of hell with its torments, cries, moans and woes is both fearsome and disgusting and the natural response of the poet to it is that of fear, agony and incomprehension well manifested in the following lines:

> I then, with error yet encompassed, cried:
> "O master! What is this I hear? What race
> Are these, who seem so overcome with woe?
> . . . .
> . . . What doth aggrieve them thus,
> That they lament so loud?[81]
>
> — *The Divine Comedy*, Canto III, line, 30-43

79. Alighieri Dante, *The Divine Comedy*, p. 8.

80. Ibid., p. 8.

81. Ibid., pp. 8-9.

But this is not all, even more horrible, woeable and fearsome sight is to be seen by the poet throughout his journey through hell and the following lines suggest that the plight to forthcome can chill the blood of any sound man:

> And lo ! toward us in a bark
> Comes on an old man, hoary white with eld,
> Crying, 'woe to you, wicked spirits! Hope not
> Ever to see the sky again I come
> To take you to the other shore, across,
> Into eternal darkness, there to dwell
> In fierce heat and in ice[82]
>
> — *The Divine Comedy,* Canto III, lines, 77-80

The physical manifestations of the announcement and other sights are obviously those of the *bhayānaka rasa*:

> This said, the gloomy region trembling shook
> So terribly, that yet with clammy dews
> Fear chills my brow. The sad earth gave atlast,
> That, lightning, shot forth a vermillion flame,
> Which all my senses conquered quite, and I
> Down dropped, as one with sudden slumber seized.[83]
>
> — *The Divine Comedy,* Canto IV, lines 122-26

The response of fear is a response of repulsion. It is so also with disgust. One tends to move away from what is fearsome or disgusting. At the root of both these responses is a certain sense of alienation, of lack of recognition. Since this cannot be rejected or substituted (by renunciation as in Indian tradition), it has to be endured or at least experienced.

Disgust, fear and repulsion, etc. are so closely intermixed that it is hard to distinguish among them. This is nothing unusual as various accompanying states or *vyabhicārī bhāvas* of the two *rasas* are similar. In *bhayānaka* they are (*Nāṭyaśāstra*, VI, 68):

---

82. Alighieri Dante, *The Divine Comedy*, p. 9.
83. Ibid., p. 11.

> Paralysis, sweating, stuttering, horrification, trembling, a break in the voice, change of colours, anxiety, confusion, depression, panic, rashness, lifelessness, fright, apoplexy, death and so forth.[84] — *Aesthetic Rapture*, vol. I, p. 54

The *vyabhicārī bhāvas* of *bībhatsa* are the following (*Nāṭyaśāstra*, VI.72):

> Apoplexy, agitation (*udvega*), panic, confusion, sickness, death and the like. — *Aesthetic Rapture*, vol. I, p. 55

Since many of the accompanying states are identical, often disgust and fear are intermixed. As is evident from Coleridge's, *The Rime of the Ancient Mariner* and other examples.

Adbhuta Rasa

Dharmadatta in his work says:

> The essence in *rasa* is the *camatkāra* experienced at every step. In that *camatkāra* which is the essence, it is the *adbhuta* experienced everywhere.[85] — *Sāhityadarpaṇa*, III p. 1

Viśvanātha in *Sāhityadarpaṇa* explains *camatkāra* to be consisting in the expansion of the *citta*; it is otherwise called the *vismaya* (wonder). *Camatkāra* or delight is a very important element in the reader's response to a work of art. Art is considered to be the expression of perfection towards the true, the good and the beautiful and therefore has always been regarded as something mysteriously wonderful. Our admiration of a work of art inevitably also involves an admiration of the skill of the artist. In a work of art, what is transmitted through every other *rasa* is a kind of delight at the wonderful reorganisation of the material and the skill of

---

84. J.L. Masson and M.V. Patwardhan, *Aesthetic Rapture*, vol. 1, p. 54.
85. *Sāhityadarpaṇa* of Viśvanātha Kavirāja with *Vimlā* (Hindi commentary) by Śrī Śalgramshastri, 1956, Motilal Banarasidas, Nepali Khapra, P.O. Box. No: 75,Varanasi, (U.P.) India, p. 1.

the artist in doing so. This may be the reason why Bhānudatta went on to the stage of considering *camatkāra* to be present in every *rasa* as its ancillary.

About *adbhuta rasa* Dhanañjaya in *Daśarūpaka*, writes:

अतिलोकैः पदैः स्याद्विस्मयात्मा रसोऽद्भुतः।।78।।
कर्मास्य साधुवादाश्रुवेपथुस्वेदगद्गदाः ।
हर्षावेगधृतिप्राया भवन्ति व्यभिचारिणः ।।79।।[86]

— *Daśarūpaka*, p. 363

The marvellous sentiment (*adbhuta*), whose essence is [the permanent state] astonishment (*vismaya*), [is caused] by supernatural things [as determinants]; it has as its result (*karma*) or consequents exclamations of surprise, weeping, trembling, sweating, and stammering; the transitory states (occurring in connection with it) are generally joy, agitation and contentment.[87] — *Daśarūpaka*, p. 145

To illustrate the point let us take into consideration the Canto XXXIII of Dante's *The Divine Comedy* where Dante is describing his wonder, astonishment and awe at the glimpse of the great mystery: the trinity and the union of Man with God:

Thenceforward what I saw,
Was not for words to speak, nor memory's self
To stand against such outrage on her skill.
As one, who from a dream awakened straight,
All he hath seen forgets; yet still retains.
Impression of the feeling in his dream;
E'en such am i: for all the vision dies,
As 'twere, away; and yet the sense of sweet,
That sprang from it, still trickles in my heart.[88]

— *The Divine Comedy*, Canto, XXXIII, lines 52-60

Visibally the *adbhuta* is generated at the divine vision or the

---

86. *Daśarūpaka* of Dhanañjaya with *Avaloka* of Dhanika, p. 363.
87. *Daśarūpaka* of Dhanañjaya, by George C.O. Haas, p.105.
88. Alighieri Dante, *The Divine Comedy*, p. 355.

revelation of truth and the obvious manifestations of it are those of *adbhuta* — "dream awakened", "vision dies", "all he hath seen forgets", "retains impression of the feeling in his dream" — Such is the relish of the *adbhuta* that even when "all the vision dies" "the sense of sweet that sprang from it, still trickles" in the heart of the poet and through his words this blissful relish is also transferred to the *sahṛdaya*, the sympathetic reader.

Such is the effect, the *camatkāra* of this *adbhuta* vision of the living ray, the universal form, that the poet thinks he would have been lost if he turned away from it: He cannot but keep on watching awestruck the universe unfolding it in front of him:

> Such keenness from the living ray I met,
> That, if mine eyes had turned away, me thinks,
> I had been lost; but, so emboldened, on
> I passed, as I remember, till my view
> Hovered the brink of dread infinitude.
> O grace, unenvying of thy boon! That gavest
> Boldness to fix so earnestly my ken
> On the everlasting splendour, that I looked,
> While sight was unconsumed; and in that depth,
> The universe unfolds; all properties
> Of substance and of accident, beheld,
> Compounded, yet one individual light
> The whole[89]
>
> — *The Divine Comedy*, Canto, XXXIII, lines, 71-85

The relish of the wonderful vision is such that the poet's sense of time, place and speech, all is lost and yet he cannot but speak of it:

> I do not but speak of it, my soul dilates
> Beyond her proper self; and, till I speak,
> One moment seems a longer lethargy,
> Than five — and — twenty ages had appeared

89. Alighieri Dante, *The Divine Comedy*, pp. 355-56.

To the emprize, that first made Neptune wonder
At Argo's shadow darkening on his flood[90]
— *The Divine Comedy*, Canto, XXXIII, lines, 87-92

The effect of this *camatkārika* vision justifies itself to be called to be that of the *adbhuta*:

With fixed need, suspense and motionless,
Wondering gazed; and admiration still
Was kindled as I gazed.
— *The Divine Comedy*, Canto, XXXIII, lines, 93-95

The more the poet describes the divine vision of the eternal light of that abyss of radiance, clear and lofty "of the three orbs of triple hue, clipt in one bound" the less apt it seems and the poet regrets the speech for being so feeble and hence inferior:

. . . O speech!
How feeble and how faint art thou, to give conception birth.
— *The Divine Comedy*, Canto, XXXIII, lines, 112-114

The poet says that all he described here is "less than little to what he saw of that eternal light" and therefore he could but admit at last that:

Here vigour failed the towering fantasy:
But yet the will rolled onward, like a wheel
In even motion, by the love impelled,
That moves the sun in heaven and all the stars [91]
— *The Divine Comedy*, Canto, XXXIII, lines 132-35

In *Nāṭyaśāstra*, it is said that *adbhuta rasa* comes from *vīra rasa*. What this involves is an admiration — either inside the text, or on the part of the *sahṛdaya* and the "joy" born out of this. For instance let us consider Richard Bach's, *Jonathan Livingston Seagull*.

---

90. Alighieri Dante, *The Divine Comedy*, p. 356.

91. Ibid., p. 357.

Jonathan Livingston Seagull is a remarkable and courageous seeker who can do anything, who can go through any amount of difficulty to learn what he wants.

What is striking here is that in an attempt to be extraordinary, to fly beyond his normal capacity, he would stop at nothing not even when he becomes an outcast:

> Why, Jon why?" his mother asked
> "Why is it so hard to be like the rest of
> the flock, Jon?, why can't you leave
> Low flying to the pelicans, the albatross?
> Why don't you eat? Son, you're bone and feathers!"

But Jonathen replies:

> "I don't mind being bone and feathers,
> Mom. I just want to know what I can
> Do in the air and what I can't, that's
> All. I just want to know."[92]
>
> — *Jonathan Livingston Seagull,* pp. 13-14.

He risks his life, but soon knows all about speed, high-flying and low-flying. He is thrown out of the flock but still keeps meditating about flying to heights never touched before. This dedication leads him to reach a higher level of understanding. The transcendence of an ordinary being into a Seagull gives rise to both wonder and admiration and flying peacefully alone and alone Jonathan one day leaves the world:

> They came in the evening, then, and found Jonathan gliding, peaceful and alone, through his beloved sky. Without a word, Jonathan put them to his test, a test that no gull had ever passed. He twisted his wings, slowed to a single mile per hour above stall. The two radiant birds slowed with him. At last he turned that speed straight up into a long vertical slow — roll. They rolled with him, smiling.

He recovered to level flight and was quiet for a while before he spoke: "Very well," he said, "who are you?"

92. Richard Bach, *Jonathan Livingston Seagull.*

> "We're from your flock, Jonathan. We are your brothers." The words were strong and calm. "We've come to take you higher, to take you home."
>
> — *Jonathan Livingston Seagull*, pp. 52-53

It is thus that Jonathan reaches heaven. But he is disappointed since he finds that even there things have a limit:

> In the days that followed, Jonathan saw that there was as much to learn about flight in this place as there had been in the life behind him. But with a difference. Here were gulls who thought as he thought. For each of them, the most important thing in living was to reach out and touch perfection. . . .
>
> — *Jonathan Livingston Seagull*, p. 60

And with the help of the Elder Jonathan learns:

> "Chiang, this world isn't heaven at all, is it?"
>
> The Elder smiled in the moonlight. "You are learning again, Jonathan Seagull." He said.
>
> . . . . Is there no place as heaven?
>
> "No, Jonathan, there is no such place. Heaven is not a place, and it is not a time. Heaven is being perfect." He was silent for a moment. "You are a very fast flier, aren't you?"
>
> "I . . . I enjoy speed," Jonathan said, taken aback but proud that the Elder had noticed.
>
> "You will begin to touch heaven, Jonathan, in the moment that you touch perfect speed. And that isn't flying a thousand miles an hour, or a million, or flying at the speed of light. Because any number is a limit, and perfection doesn't have limits. Perfect speed, my son, is being there."
>
> — *Jonathan Livingston Seagull*, pp. 64-65

Thus, Jonathan learns of transcendence, where one is not limited since he does not believe that a limit exists, and reaches perfection. But he does not stop there. He comes back to his old flock and guides the ones who have the inclination towards perfection. This is not unusual. Any kind of seeking can lead to *adbhuta* and then a *śānta rasa*, for all seeking are directed towards perfection. Once it is achieved, transcendence is achieved as well. But all seeking involve "steadfastness", "patience", and "courage" and, hence, are heroic. This perseverance as well as the transcendence to an intenser world (which is unusual and hence wonderful) generates *adbhuta rasa*.

Śānta Rasa

As compared with the relish of other *rasa*s the relish of the *śānta*, the ninth *rasa* is deeper with long-lasting effects. *śānta* is that stage of *rasa* which is devoid of any *vṛtti* (earthly touch) found in other *rasa*s. It is transcendental and therefore is connected with *mokṣa*, the greatest *puruṣārtha*. Bharatamuni in *Nāṭyaśāstra* says that the *bhāva*s as the *rati*, etc. are the transformations (*vikāra*s) whereas the *śānta* is the original nature (*mūla prakṛti*):

> भावा विकारा रत्याद्याः शान्त स्तु प्रकृतिर्मतः [93]
>
> — *Nāṭyaśāstra*, ch. 6.

The transformations have come out of this original nature and finally merge into it.

> स्वं स्वं निमित्तमासाद्य शान्ताद्भावः प्रवर्तते ।
> पुनर्निमित्तापाये तु शान्त एव प्रलीयते ॥
>
> — *Nāṭyaśāstra*, ch. 6.

He further says that just as the effects (*kāryas*), created out of some material cause (*prakṛti*) merge and disappear on that cause itself so also the *bhāva*s which have come into existence from the *śānta rasa*, the *mūla prakṛti*, due to the presence of some instrumental causes (*nimitta*), disappear on the *śānta rasa* itself at the disappearance of those instrumental causes.

93. http://libru/RBACH/seagullengl.txt

Abhinavagupta also opines that the experience of every *rasa* ends in *śānta* when the senses get aversion for the worldly objects. The *sthāyī bhāva* of *śānta rasa* is *śama*. *Śama* means the cessation of all the *cittavṛttis* (modifications of the mind) instrumented by the five restless senses. The cause for the instigation of *śānta* is *nirveda* (detachment) produced by the *tattvajñāna* (spiritual or true knowledge). Thus, correct or true knowledge is the *vibhāva* of the *śānta rasa*. The absence of the *bhāvas* like *kāma* and *krodha* is considered as the *anubhāva* of the *śānta rasa* by Abhinavagupta. According to him just as the *rati* for the elders and the gods cannot turn into *śṛṅgāra* but only the *rati* for the beloved develops into that form (*śṛṅgāra*) so also only the *nirveda* produced by the *tattvajñāna* can develop into *śānta rasa* but not the one produced by poverty, etc.

Śānta rasa implies a state of calm or of equilibrium; a state of tranquillity or of repose. But this tranquillity, equilibrium, calm or repose cannot be achieved effortlessly, it comes only after a lot of struggle and therefore in the presentation of the *śānta rasa* all other *rasas* are contributory factors. The point noteworthy here is that it is possible to move to *śānta rasa* from all other emotional states or *sthāyī bhāvas* like *rati, hāsa, śoka, krodha, utsāha, bhaya, jugupsā* and *vismaya*. And from whatever *sthāyī bhāva* one moves to *śānta*; two possible ways are to be seen. One, when there is a fulfilment and hence the end of desire. Secondly, when from and due to excessive indulgence or denial, there is disgust and thus a rejection which leads one away from the state of excitement and away from desire, to *nivveda* (detachment) and hence to *śānta*.

Thus an important point to keep in mind while discussing *śānta rasa* is that "right knowledge" is the prerequisite of *śama*. Only right knowledge, realisation of truth according to Abhinavagupta can lead one to the purity of mind and detachment or *vairāgya*. To illustrate the point it is worth our while to once again take into consideration Dante's *The Divine*

Comedy. Dante in *The Divine Comedy* by his journey through hell, purgatory and then paradise comes to realise that; once worldly occupation and wrong indulgences cost one penality after death in the form of eternal suffering and penance in the hell and one's good deeds finally lead one to divine or eternal bliss of the paradise. This realisation purges him of all his previous faults and through true पश्चाताप — *paścātapa* (repentence) he is elevated to that level of eternal bliss of the *śānta rasa* where all desires come to an end:

> I, meanwhile, who drew
> Near to the limit, where all wishes end,
> The ardour of my wish (for so behoved)
> Ended within me.[94]
>
> — *Divine Comedy,* Canto XXXIII, lines, 44-46

It is worth our while to here illustrate through apt examples how *śānta* can be reached at from all other *rasa*s. Let's first take the case of *śṛṅgāra rasa*. In the case of *śṛṅgāra rasa* there is the possibility of moving to *śānta,* not only through disgust but also through a positive transcendence in union. In *Bṛhadāraṇyaka Upaniṣad* (N, 3.21) we have an instance where the realisation of *Brahman* is compared to a state of union with one's wife:

> Just as when a man is embraced by his wife, he knows nothing outside or anything inside; similarly when the individual self is embraced by the universal self, he knows nothing outside nor anything inside; for he has attained an end which involves the fulfilment of all other ends, being verily the attainment of *ātman* which leaves no other end to be fulfilled[95]

As we have already discussed earlier the discrepancy between the ideal and the real, the realisation of how things

94. Alighieri Dante, *The Divine Comedy*, p. 355.
95. *A Constructive Surve of Upaniṣadic Philosophy*, p. 255.

are different from what they seem to be — "oddity" — can generate laughter as in case of the poem by Han-Shan:

Once at Cold Mountain, troubles cease —
No more tangled, hung up mind.
I idly scribble poems on the rock cliff,
Taking whatever comes, like a drifting boat.
Some critic tried to put me down —
"Your poems lack the Basic Truth of Tao."
And I recall the old timers
Who were poor and didn't care.
I have to laugh at him[96]

— *Cold Mountain,* p. 19-20

The poet's insight into the true nature of sorrow helps him to move beyond it and therefore he finds it possible to laugh on the oddity of the situation but this realisation without question holds the possibility of a disillusionment that can lead one to *nirveda* (detachment) and thus to *śānta*. Thus we find that in laughter in the above situation there is possibility of the *śānta*.

Śoka or sorrow can lead to *śānta* when the desire to escape from the world of sorrows one reaches into a state of disillusionment and detachment. In Milton's *Paradise Lost* on realisation of their fatal flaunt (eating the forbidden fruit of knowledge) sink into deep and still deeper sorrow. The manifestation of this sorrow leads to the possibility of *śānta* first in the plight of Eve then through her in Adam:

She ended weeping, and her lowly plight,
Immovable till peace obtained from fault
acknowledged and deplored, in Adam wrought
commiseration; soon his heart relented
Towards her, his life so late and sole delight,
Now at his feet submissive in distress,
Creature so fair his reconcilement seeking,
His counsel whom she had displeased, his aid;

96. R.D. Ranade, *A Constructive Survey of Upanisadic Philosophy*, Bombay: Bhartiya Vidya Bhavan, 1968.

As one disarmed, his anger all he lost,
And thus with peaceful words unpraised her soon.[97]

— *Paradise Lost*, Book X, lines, 937-46

According to Abhinavagupta from *krodha* (anger) one can move towards *śānta* if one:

> . . . . perceives the happenings of the world as harmful to his spiritual well-being (and angry with them desires to conquer them). . . .[98]
>
> — *Śānta Rasa*, p. 129

The main argument here is that anger which arises from the refutation of desires or the bereavement of desired objects, may lead one to detachment when the anger, rage or madness is overcome giving way to the realisation of truth. As we see in Milton's *Paradise Lost*, when Adam's anger is washed away by Eve's grief, the obvious, disillusionment from a fairer realisation of truth leads them to *śānta*:

But rise, let us no more contend, nor blame
Each other, blamed enough elsewhere, but strive
In offices of love, how we may lighten
Each other's burden in our share of woe;
Since this day's death denounced, if aught I see,
Will prove no sudden, but a slow-paced evil,
A long day's dying to augment our pain.[99]

— *Paradise Lost*, Book X, lines, 958-64

About the relation of *utsāha* (of *vīra rasa*) with *śānta*, Abhinavagupta says that *utsāha* can lead to *śānta* if one:

> . . . . resorts to extraordinary energy dominated by the

97. Han-Shan, *Cold Mountain*, tr. Gary Synder, http://www.hermetica.info/hanshan.htm
98. *The Poems of John Milton*, pp. 973-74.
99. Masson and M.V. Patwardhan, *Santa Rasa and Abhinavagupta's Philosophy of Aesthetics*, Bhandarkar Oriental Series no. 9, Bhandarkar Oriental Research Institute, Poona, 1969, p. 129.

> absence of delusions (in order to overcome worldly temptations).[100] — *Śānta Rasa*, p. 129

The *vibhāva* of both *vīra* and *śānta* are similar as *vīra* is instigated by correct perception and *śānta* by "realisation of truth". Both have "steadfastness", "determination", "patience", etc. among their *vyabhicārī bhāvas*. But the basic difference between the two is that while in *vīra* there is the affirmation of ego (due to pride), in *śānta* ego gets diluted in the realisation of the supreme in realisation of the bigger self. But to attain this,

> Self-realisation, a lot of difficulties, temptations, etc. have to be overcome — which requires courage, a basic ingredient of *vīra rasa*. In Hemmingway's *The Old Man and the Sea* Santiago, the Old Man, filled with composure, perseverance, goods tactics, valour and power from his life of courage learns humility:
>
> He was too simple to wonder when he had attained humility. But he knew he had attained it and he knew it was not disgraceful and it carried no loss of true pride.[101]
>
> — *The Old Man and the Sea*, pp. 9-10

Thus, we see the *vīra* leading him finally to *śānta* and when in the end after being cheated by the world of what he won and almost broken by it, Santiago is found planning of his next fishing expedition with better weapons and new "tricks", the spectators and readers too along with him experience the universal relish named *śānta rasa*.

Bhaya or fear, too, can lead to *śānta* in various ways. First of all the realisation that the objects of senses lead to pain and suffering and fear of those senses in turn can lead one to disillusionment and hence to *vairāgya* (or detachment or renunciation). For instance Gautama Buddha in Aśvaghoṣa's

---

100. *The Poems of John Milton*, p. 974.
101. Masson and Patwardhan, *Santa Rasa and Abhinavagupta's Philosophy of Aesthetics*, p. 129.

Buddhacarita, after seeing the four great signs realises the profound truth, "one must die" (*The Bible of the World*, p. 192) and later waking up in the middle of sleep perceives the "magnificent apartment, as splendid as the palace of *sakka* filled with beautiful courtesans to be like a cemetery filled with dead bodies impaled and left to rot[102]. . . ." (*The Bible of the World*, p. 194).

Secondly, when one is terrified, it might lead to a desire to overcome this terror (*vīra*) and thus through this heroic effort in overcoming fear one can attain *śānta* as we see in Milton's *Paradise Lost* where Adam and Eve, when expelled from the paradise after the curses being pronounced, with full knowledge of the impending disasters are the sufferings and torments to come in their new life (on earth) instead of being totally shattered from it, soon recover from it and walk out of the paradise with a calm and composed mind.

> With dreadful faces thronged and fiery arms:
> Some natural tears they dropped, but wiped them soon;
> The world was all before them, where to choose
> Their place of rest, and providence their guide
> They hand in hand with wandering steps and slow,
> Through Eden took their solitary way[103]
>
> — *Paradise Lost*, Book XII, lines, 644-49

Visibly in the above given lines we find the fear, the terrible leading to heroic and heroic in turn leading to *śānta*.

In the illustration from Aśvaghoṣa's *Buddhacarita* we saw how *śṛṅgāra* due to change in outlook gets reversed into *bībhatsa* and *bībhatsa* in turn leads to *śānta*.

According to Abhinavagupta, *vismaya* or wonder can also lead to *śānta*:

---

102. Ernest, Hemingway, *The Old Man and the Sea*, www.asiaing.com.

103. Aśvaghoṣa, *The Buddhacarita*, *The Bible of the World*, ed. Robert O Ballow, et al., New York: Avon Books, 1970.

> . . . . If he feels astonished at his unprecedented realisation of his own self.[104]
>
> — *Śānta Rasa*, p. 129

Wonder at the unique nature of the realisation of *mokṣa*, the greatest *puruṣārtha*, can lead one to *śānta* as we find in Dante's *The Divine Comedy* where when Dante is finally admitted to a glimpse of the great mystery; the Trinity, and the Union of man with god. The *adbhuta* (wonderful) leads him to that deeper and long-lasting relish of peace which we know as *śānta*:

> Thenceforward, what I saw,
> Was not for words to speak, nor memory's self
> To stand against such outrage on her skill.
> As one, who from a dream awakened, straight,
> All he hath seen forgets; yet still regains
> Impression of the feeling in his dream;
> E'en such am I: for all the vision dies,
> As'twere away; and yet the sense of sweet,
> *That sprang from it, still trickles in my heart.*[105]
>
> — *Divine Comedy*, Canto XXXIII, lines, 52-60

Śānta, the state of the highest happiness, is one that cannot really be shown. As stated in *Nāṭyaśāstra*:

> It should be acted out by means of the *anubhāvas*, such as *yama* and *niyama*, meditation on the self, concentration of the mind on the self (*dhāraṇā*), devotion (*upāsanā*), compassion towards all creatures and the wearing of religious paraphernelia (*liṅgarahaṇa*)[106]
>
> — *Śānta Rasa*, p. 92

Yama "abstentions" refer to the five abstentions mentioned in Patañjali's *Yoga-Sūtra* — *ahiṁsā* (non-violence), *satya* (truth), *asteya* (absence of the desire to steal), *bramhacarya* (celibacy)

---

104. *The Poems of John Milton*, p. 1060.
105. Masson and Patwardhan, *Santa Rasa and Abhinavagupta's Philosophy of Aesthetics*.
106. Alighieri Dante, *The Divine Comedy*, p. 355.

and a *parigraha* (non-possession). These *yamas* when achieved result in detachment of oneself from all the worldly desires which naturally leads to state of eternal bliss — *śānta*.

Similarily, *niyamas* or "observations", *śaucac* (cleanliness), *santoṣa* (sense of fulfilment), *tapas* (meditation), *svādhyāya* (study of the Vedas or the pursuit of knowledge) and *īśvara praṇidhāna* (contemplation of the Almighty), meditation on the self, "devotion", "compassion towards all creatures", etc. are manifested only when the divine bliss (*śānta*) is achieved.

About the *vyabhicārī bhāvas* of the *śānta rasa* Abhinavagupta says that:

> Its *vyabhicārī bhāvas* are disgust with the world (*nirveda*) remembrance, firmness of mind, purity in all the four stages of life (*āśrama*), rigidity (of the body) (*stamba*), horripilation, etc.[107]
>
> — *Śānta Rasa*, p. 92

"Disgust with the world" leads one to the abatement or the rejection of desire. Purity of mind persisting through "firmness of mind" leads one to *śānta*. The division of the stages of life into *āśramas* according to the Indian tradition, namely *brahmacarya, gārhasthya, vānaprastha* and *saṁnyāsa* also imply renunciation of desires that leads finally towards *mokṣa*, the realisation of the Ultimate Truth.

It is evident from the foregoing discussion that all the eight *sthāyī bhāvas* — *rati, hāsa, śoka, krodha, bhaya, utsāha, jugupsā* and *vismaya* have the potential of leading to *śānta*. According to Abhinavagupta, any sustained work of literature must inevitably lead to *śānta*. He, in this context, cites the example of the *Mahābhārata* where the epic war (where almost everyone is destroyed) leads to a disillusionment with the world — power, lust, desires — and thus to *śānta rasa* (*Śānta Rasa*, p. 106.)

107. Masson and Patwardhan, *Santa Rasa and Abhinavagupta's Philosophy of Aesthetics*, p. 129.

In the Indian tradition it is believed that all arts lead to *mokṣa*. In *Bhagavad Gītā* it is said that one can attain *mokṣa* (self-realisation) through *karma* (one's work or profession), *bhakti* (devotion) as well as through *jñāna* (knowledge). The obvious implications of this are that, any art — dance, music, literature, painting (one's *karma*) can lead to *mokṣa*. In fact, any path followed earnestly can lead to *mokṣa*.

In the Chinese Taoist tradition a painter pursues self-realisation through the principles of Tao; similarly, Japanese and Chinese poets and painters seek transcendence through the principles of Zen. T'ai Chi, the Chinese martial art, concentrates on tranquillity in movement; in it movement occurs while there is stillness inward — the kind of feeling attributed to *śānta rasa*. In an explanation of the martial aspect of T'ai Chi we come across the following lines:

> As a martial art, T'ai Chi is externally a soft exercise, but internally hard,. . . .When we have mastered sticking, adhering, connecting and following, we will naturally progress from conscious movement to interpreting energy and finally spiritual illumination and the realm of absolute transcendence.[108]
>
> — Douglas Wile, *Lost T'ai-chi Classics from the Late Ch'ing Dynasty*

Thus, we see that the martial art (generally practised for health benefits and fitness besides fighting) finally leads to spiritual illumination and the realm of absolute transcendence.

It establishes the fact that all arts finally lead to *śānta*; to *mokṣa*. Our examination of the Western canonical epics and works of literature in the foregoing text too proves the point

---

108. ^ a b c Wile, Douglas (1995), *Lost T'ai-chi Classics from the Late Ch'ing Dynasty (Chinese Philosophy and Culture)*. State University of New York Press. http://en.wikipedia.org/wiki/Tai_chi_chuan_philosophy#cite_note-Wrile1995-1.

that all kinds of seekings finally lead to detachment with the worldly desires and thus to *śānta rasa*. And therefore a sympathetic reader or a *sahṛdaya*, through the path of literature too can attain *mokṣa* with the help of appropriate works like Dante's *Divine Comedy*, Milton's *Paradise Lost* and the like.

4

Applicatory Principles II

THE comprehension of structure and the strength of the contents of structure are precisely the formal methods through which we can undertake an examination of situated, realised, exposed and communicated possibilities enriched as parts of theoretical formulation. The necessary evidence of such a possibility is governed primarily on account of assertion and compulsive manner of interpretation and in a theory the likelihood of application is generated via content and medium implantation of the principles of conceptualisation. In *rasa,* as is evident from the discussion in the foregoing, the actual conduct of the categories and the subsequent reception of the magnitude of medium and content formation by any artistic principle are merited through nearly every range of perception, accordingly, the transformation is completed and upheld as a basic methodology of propagating the strength of artistry. On the other hand, in post-structuralist theories, there is an emphasis on deviating and diverting, both the medium and the content, so as to disengage language and experience as the forms of disintegration and never of conjunction or association. At the instance of inception, the composition of language and experience is assuredly not derived from the primitive forms, rather the suggestive possibilities are rounded off just at the instance of segregated value formations, thus there isn't any substance of value that could enlist an effect of merit on the language or on experience and accordingly there is a gradual fall in the possibility of enrichment.

In post-structuralism the conditions favouring the formation of an artistic principle become manifest through inter-constitutional disassociation in language and experience and it is for this reason that Derrida, Foucault, Lacan and later Barthes adopt a view to the effect that appearance of a category isn't really the reality of realisation and therefore the effect of understanding in respect of the situation will have to be assorted through diversions of the content-oriented possibilities and obviously not by focusing an intention on reviving the convergence of the contents in a certain direction of revival. It is because of this that the form of content and the motive of the content both are separated generally at the points of associative formations.

This is really one of the terms of extraordinary significance in our valuation of post-structuralism[1] as a condition and event and the following verses by Bhartṛhari's *Śṛṅgāraśataka* will prove the point to certain excellence:

> वियदुपचितमेघं भूमयः कन्दलिन्यो
> नवकुटजकदम्बामोदिनो गन्धावाहाः ।
> शिखिकुलकलकेकारावरम्या वनान्ताः
> सुखिनमसुखिनं वा सर्वमुत्कण्ठयन्ति ॥1॥[2]
>
> — Bhartṛhari's *Śṛṅgāraśataka*, p. 125.

Sky filled with clouds and joyous earth aggravate the desire of pleasure (sexual) of all happy and sad people by their beautiful forest places full of new sprouts completely wet

1. The instance of post-structuralism as being an evidence in some great Indian poetry is logically tenable because of the fact that conduct of language and experience is meant to be always infinite in nature. Hence there is a great digression of the coordinates which create a method for universality of an artistic form.
2. Bhartṛhari's *Niti-Śṛṅgāra-Vairāgya Śatakatrayam*, Sanskrit *ṭīkā*, Bhāṣāṭīkā sameta, Sri Venkateshawar Steam Press, Mumbai, 1961, p. 77.

with dew, new trees and air filled with fragrance of group of lotus flowers, sweet voice of the group of peacocks.

The form of observation expresses condition of orientation of the observer, and therefore, the received situation and the realised situation are at great distance from each other. The observer feels the love and in that way does not proceed to recognise the contents of fulfilment through what he could feel within, rather the observation is commuted in accordance with the rise of the relative functionalities of extended perception. What is now happening is happening at a great distance, for example, "in the sky", "on the earth", "in the forest" yet nothing logically is finding any worth whatsoever in the inward sensibility of the observer. The point is proved that observer upholds his assortment in the conduct of exposition never in the manner of realisation, accordingly, the language has a declension inasmuch as he could only say "भूमयः (*bhūmayaḥ*)", "वनान्ताः (*vanāntāḥ*)" and the like, meaning thereby that external evidences are casual and illusory at once and simultaneously, and therefore, leads to the prosperity of binary opposition within the formulated contents of the language. Even otherwise by the standards of experience the conscious motives (fulfilment of love through beloved) and unconscious intention of gratification of instinctual forms by overt realisation, effectively presupposes a difference between the observer, who tends to be the lover and the lover, who should have been a truthful interpreter of the perfect feelings. It is for this reason the situated forms are deeply distanced through each other and the preposition is equated in the variety of measure and manner. In fact, the moment the lover could say "सर्वमुत्कण्ठयन्ति (*sarvamutkaṇṭhayanti*)" he is only exploring how the curiosity of instinct could aberrate the suggestion of desire through an abstract motive and abstract judgement.

The predominance of the multiples of variation encoded

as stylistic feature forms an important part of post-structuralist exposition and on that account it would mean that conjunctive situation doesn't have much of a deliberate affect on the localised version of experience, consequently the presentation of a fact and the reception of the fact both are distinguished from each other. In *Mṛcchakaṭikā* of Śūdraka the concept of presentation inadvertently disunites the recognition through momentary as well as idealised displacement of the contents. Look at the following for example:

अधिकरणिकः – पश्य श्रेष्ठिन् !
वस्त्वन्तराणि सदृशनि भवन्ति नूनं,
रूपस्य भूषणगुणस्य च कृत्रिमस्य ।
दृष्ट्वा क्रियामनुकरोति हि शिल्पिवर्गः,
सादृश्यमेव कृतहस्ततया च दृष्टम्।।34।।[3]

— *Sanskrit Kāvyadhārā*, p. 406

Look, distinguished man! (head);
Different things too happen to be similar,
Beautiful, ornamental and artificial things
Which the artists and craftsman imitate
Due to dexterity or skillfulness look alike (abide similarity).

In this the constitutive elements are compulsorily displaced through exact correlation, and therefore, the determinants of factual interception like taste generated through universal objects (artist's presentation) and the material annihilation like the putting on of jewellery both have an advancement, of course, in a de-rationalised and de-institutionalised sense of the terms. In the manifestation of the excellence of artistry the motivation of content has an equivalent of truthful position while the imperfect material forms reduce the conjunctive manifestation. The generation of aberration becomes so disjointed that at every logical term the reduced form is visible,

3. Rahul Sankrityayan, *Sanskrit Kāvyadhārā*, Kitab Mahal, Sammelan Mudralaya, Prayag, Allahabad,1957, p. 406.

it is because of this the dramatist would like to say "वस्त्वन्तराणि सदृशानि भवन्ति नूनं (*vastvantarāṇi sadṛśāni bhavanti nūnaṁ*)" the application of terminal distinction has a practical disorientation while opting for a transition from unity of one institutionalised situation to the other. In fact, the progress of "रूपस्य (*rūpasya*)" and "दृष्ट्वा (*dṛṣṭvā*)" along with "सादृश्य (*sādṛśya*)" confirms the progressive version of antithesis which is primarily because the imbalance in the situation has been substantiated. We can understand that the conformity of content to the effective forms of active rationalisation and commitment for derationalisation obstructs or hampers the advancement of thought in consecutive conceptual term and therefore leads to reduction of categories and further to devolution of the entire situation as a whole.

The composition of language as emersion of the subscribed and substantiated units forms a principle of digression in post-structuralist conditions and therefore the behaviour of language in any artistic form is methodically never committed to the exact function of the units of the categories. It would mean that every unit has a de-institutionalised function to perform. In *Mudrārākṣasa* of Viśākhadatta the progress of attitude does not dislocate the presentation of an evolution either as a fact or a circumstance of the units involved in the whole process; for example, consider the following situation:

> (विलोक्य समयम्) तदयम् आर्यचाणक्यस्तिष्ठति-
> यो नन्दमौर्यनृपयोः परिभूय लोकं,
> अस्तोदयौ प्रतिदिशन्नविभिन्नकालम् ।
> पर्यायपालितहिमोश्णिम सर्वगामि
> धाम्नाऽतिशाययति धाम सहस्रधाम्नः ।।17।।[4]
>
> — *Mudrārākṣasa* of Viśākhadatta, p. 161

4. *Mudrārākṣasa* of Viśākhadatta with the commentary of Dhundhiraj, ed. with critical and explanatory notes by Kashinath Trimbak Telang, revised by V.S. Ghote, Nag Publishers, Delhi, 1985, p. 161.

(Seeing; nervously) Ha! Here is the honourable Cāṇakya.
Whilst in this world he triumphed,
The setting and the rising of the two kings
The Nanda and the Maurya
Were not disparate in time;
Thus he, by his splendour, excels
The lustre of the thousand-rayed sun,
Which failing in omnipresence,
Sheds warmth on half the globe
And leaves it cold by turns!

In this situation, the position of language doesn't obtain exact equivalents because of an interruption motivated by the medium and the content inasmuch as language functions through projective motives, and on that authority, the poet would like to say "नन्दमौर्यनृपयोः परिभूय लोकं (*nandamauryanr̥payoḥ paribhūya lokam*)" meaning thereby that the generative capability of assertive contents would always obtain a diverse enrichment and for that matter in the succeeding verse "अस्तोदयौ (*astodayau*)" brings about an abruption of synthesis by discarding the advancement of the motion. The principle and the fact, both are suitably inherited through differential evolutionary co-ordinates, and to an extent, the factual position built around the similarity of value does not re-open the possibility of association. The effect of antithesis is so wide and pervasive that the advancing categories immediately cancel the raged inversion and for that matter we are introduced to "पर्यायपालितहिमोष्णिम सर्वगामि धाम्नाऽतिशाययति धाम सहस्रधाम्नः (*paryāyapālitahimoṣṇima sarvagāmi dhāmnā'tiśāyayati dhāma sahasra-dhāmnaḥ*)" the appearance of inexact resolution in an event is tended to be a feature of post-supposition inasmuch as the activity and disturbance of the preliminary concepts (reward for virtue and punishment for evil) is deviated through substituted margins inasmuch as "धाम्ना (*dhāmnā*)" and "धाम्नः (*dhāmnaḥ*)" both necessarily prolong the period of inter-substitution.

The idea of critical antithesis in post-structuralism appears to be one of the facts brought about through the loss of a systematic groundwork for mature experiential linguistic realisation. There is no possibility to interpret the situation by holding the comprehension of fact as being suspended in relation to the diversification of figure. This becomes more advanced and prolific when we consider the fact that the margins are not associated through the consequence of substitution, rather the function of presentation displaces the motivated categories to their predated positions, and in the verses quoted above, we have the opportunity to find out an arrangement and sequence for the whole manner of comprehension of the situation and the another important condition that is obtained within the linguistic form is that it has an upward flow of the contents which obviously interpret themselves in the inconsequential positions. In *Harṣacarita* of Bāṇabhaṭṭa, we can examine the resolution of the whole form:

> ग्रीष्मसमये कदाचिदस्य स्वगृहावस्थितस्य भुक्तवतोऽ
> पराह्नसमये भ्राता पारशवश्चन्द्रसेननामा प्रविष्याकथयत्
> "एष खलु देवस्य चतुःसमुद्राधिपतेः सकलराजचक्र,
> चूड़ामणिश्रेणीषाणकोणधषणनिर्मलीकृतचरणनखमणेः
> सर्वचक्रवर्तिनां धौरेयस्य महाराजाधिराजपरमेश्वरश्री-
> हर्षदेवस्य भ्रात्रा कृष्णनाम्ना भवतामन्तिकं प्रज्ञाततमो
> दीर्घाध्वगः प्रहितो द्वारमध्यास्त" इति । सोऽब्रवीत्-
> "आयुष्मन्, अविलंबं प्रवेशय एनम्" इति।[5]
>
> — *Sanskrit Kāvyadhārā*, p. 568

Once in summer time while staying at home after having lunch in the afternoon the cousin brother of Chandrasen

---

5. *Mudrārākṣasa* of Viśākhadatta with the commentary of Dhundhiraj, ed. with critical and explanatory notes by Kashinath Trimbak Telang, revised by V.S. Ghote, Nag Publishers, Delhi, 1985, p. 568.

> entered and said: "King of four oceans, owner of the pearl like soft and pure nails of feets measured by the parameter of rubbing of the corners of the crest-jewels of all the kings, valorous in all kings, god king lord; the messenger, who has travelled a very long distance, sent by Śrī Harṣadeva's brother Kṛṣṇa is standing at the door. Live long; get him inside without any delay."

The exposition and explication of the events in this narrative situation clearly demonstrates the fact that truth as a principal condition of the generation of contents in the medium doesn't have any fixation whatsoever in the rationalised and logical models and for this reason the conscious experience (glories of the universal king) becomes an imperceptible situation in which the ideas could not be either withheld or contained; accordingly, the immediate correlative (ambassador) is absolved and disjointed inasmuch as he could only explain the visual part of the situation and could never come out with non-visual perceptions. This leads to a crisis in horizontal dispersion of the formative part of the content and the king has to say — "आयुष्मन्, अविलंबं प्रवेशय एनम् (*āyuṣman, avilaṁbaṁ praveśaya enam*)". It must be accepted that the conduct of the denotative form is unreasonably marginalised through the explication of the condition of truth beyond its prescribed limit. On the one hand we have the formal codes and on the other we have indeterminate index (figural comprehension of the largeness of the authority of the king beyond seas, mountains and the line). The basic term that invalidates the process of evolution is the display of non-additive multiplicatory signs, for example, the terms are expanded by implicative urgency (time of summer, time of lunch and amazing universality of kingship in a state of drowsiness) to only bring about inexact signified models (king becoming the god, king becoming the sea, king becoming the omnipotent and so on and so forth). The presentation of such a compulsive situation does not create a sense of equality between conscious motive and unconscious meaning and consequently the movement of the content is once again retracted and reverted, leading to concentration of language in its pre-existent models rather than post-conceptualisational forms.

The idea of inter-separation and intra-separation of the contents could presuppose the beginning of any situation through peripheral terms and Derrida could suggest that comprehension of such a situation is only an impossibility for the reason that the reader isn't capable of focusing principally and primarily on shifting terms.

In *Śiśupālavadha* of Māgha we can build up a concomitance for the whole observation; for example look at the following:

> छलयन्प्रजास्त्वमनृतेन कपटपटुरैन्द्रजालिकाः ।
> प्रीतिमनुभवसि नग्नजितः सुतयेष्टसत्य इति संप्रतीयसे ।।25।।[6]
>
> — *Sanskrit Kāvyadhārā*, p. 730

> Magician, skilled in deception (artifice), deceiving people by fraud; becoming Nagnajita's daughter's (Satyabhāmā) truth-lover, you seem to be delighted.

In this situation the position of an object in relation to the subject is unequal and therefore the examination of content and the medium both are degenerated through isolated figural association. In the capacity of affected intention Śiśupāla speaks and what he speaks is revived and reduced to his own primitive form. It would mean that the conscious assertion is relegated to unconscious models and the other side of disposition never really takes place. The reason that we are in a position to understand this is that the signifiers are constantly being displaced by debiting the terms through the forthcoming consequential losses, accordingly, Śiśupāla has to say

6. *Mudrārākṣasa* of Viśākhadatta with the commentary of Dhundhiraj, ed. with critical and explanatory notes by Kashinath Trimbak Telang, revised by V.S. Ghote, Nag Publishers, Delhi, 1985, p. 730.

"कपटवटुरैन्द्रजालिका: (*kapaṭavaṭuraindrajālikāḥ*)" and destabilise the sequence of the concept inasmuch as symmetry of orthodox terms (god, shall for ever be the god and cannot be a liar). Śiśupāla makes him a liar and deviates the contents from their inter-position in the perceptible sequence of the terms. It may be because of this that the term ends with situational displacement inasmuch as Śiśupāla could say "सुतयेष्टसत्य इति संप्रतीयसे (*sutayeṣtasatya iti saṁpratīyase*)". The largeness of imperceptibility and expansion of deviant codes have the power and strength to turn the conceptual construction through pre-disposed formations and exactly in the above-cited utterance of Śiśupāla we could comprehend the situation in a significant detail.

In Foucault, the role of contents as the units of dispersion and position of medium as an invention of present model to contain the discourse is having a full-scale applicational relevance. In *Mālatīmādhava* of Bhavabhūti, the excellence of displacement is obviously inherent. He could say, for example:

आपूर्णश्च कलाभिरिन्दुरमलो यातश्च राहोर्मुखं,
संजातश्च घनाघनो जलधार: शीर्णश्च वायोर्जवात्।
निर्वृत्तश्च फलेग्रहिर्द्रुमवरो दग्धश्च दावाग्निना,
त्वं चूडामणितां गतश्च जगत: प्राप्तश्च मृत्योर्वशम् ।।39।।[7]

— *Sanskrit Kāvyadhārā*, p. 760

Dexterous and skilled pure Indu went into Rāhu's mouth,
And dense cloud broke due to force of wind
Fruitful great tree got burnt due to forest fire
Crest-jewel of the world you went into the custody of death.

Bhavabhūti in this situation is presenting a possibility of reversibility of infinity through infinity and beginning through beginning, accordingly he could invent the independence of

7. *Mudrārākṣasa* of Viśākhadatta with the commentary of Dhundhiraj, ed. with critical and explanatory notes by Kashinath Trimbak Telang, revised by V.S. Ghote, Nag Publishers, Delhi, 1985, p. 760.

assortment by making the terms inverted and regressive. The terms of comprehension have been built around the employment of urgent communicative codes and for this reason the larger figure demotivates the fact of association by assimilating the minor figure and for the same reason "the moon is being swallowed by a moving planet", "clouds, being dispersed by ferocious wind" and "a ripened tree has been withered by the painful fire". It would mean in the next place that the act of comprehension couldn't be completed just for the reason that the sign and signifier are invariably opposed to one another and hence the poet say: कलाभिरिन्दुरमलो यातश्च राहोर्मुखं । संजातश्च घनाघनो जलधारः शीर्णश्च वायोर्जवात् । निर्वृत्तश्च फलेग्रहिर्द्रुमवरो दग्धश्च दावाग्निना *kalābhirinduramalo yātaśca raharmukhaṁ* । *saṁjātaśca ghanāghano jaladhāraḥ śīrṇaśca vāyorjavāt* ।। *nivṛttaśca phalegrahirdrumavaro dagdhaśca dāvāgnina* and thus identifies the distributive content in relation to their post-generative devolving attitude. In Foucault's terms of understanding, unity of content is always violated through an ordinate and upright context of dispersion and the fact of comprehension could not be generated by exempting or excluding any substance of corollary through any term of opposition. Bhavabhūti in these verses suggests how the actual signifier (the ruling god of the universe) has now been engulfed by the death. This opposition, this violation of reality leads to degeneration and deformation in both language and experience and when Bhavabhūti further says that, "त्वं चूडामणितां गतश्च जगतः प्राप्तश्च मृत्योर्वशम् (*tvaṁ cūḍāmaṇitām gataśca jagataḥ prāptaśca mṛtyorvaśam*)" the position of central unit of organisation seams to be lost in putting up a figurative cleavage of the terms and accordingly exceptional divergence of language as language and experience as experience becomes a principal mode of expression in these verses.

In post-structuralism the cognitive model doesn't authorise recognition through stationary explication and for that matter Derrida, Lacan and Foucault believe that the immensity and infinity of temporal unit could beget no identical situation inasmuch as the possibility of assertion is never authenticated in coherent and exact medium. The importance of this view would naturally lead to the idea that; within language or experience, no two terms could be identical and in that each has its own ability to presuppose a form for itself. In *Harṣacarita* of Bāṇabhaṭṭa, the artistic situation completes the assertion of the fact when Bāṇabhaṭṭa says:

> स्वयमपि विसिस्मिये भूपालः । सर्वतो विक्षिप्तचक्षु-
> श्चाद्राक्षीदावासस्थानसकाशात्प्रतिष्ठमानं स्कन्धावारं,
> अधोक्षजकुक्षेरिव युगादौ निष्पतन्तं जीवलोकं, अम्भो-
> निधिमव कुम्भभुवो वदनात्प्लावितभुवनमुद्भवन्तं,
> अर्जुनवाहुदण्डसहस्रसंपिण्डितोन्मुक्तमिव सहस्रधा-
> प्रवर्तमानं प्रवाहं नर्मदायाः।[8]
>
> — *Sanskrit Kāvyadhārā*, p. 580

> The king himself is led to wonder (unbelievable *realisation*). While passing from near his house (Bāṇa) looked at the camp; which looked like — let us believe — the earth (land of life) coming out of the naval of Viṣṇu, ocean like flooded Bhuvan, born out of the mouth of Agastya, like the free flow of Narmadā covered by the thousands of arrows of Arjuna.

The constitutive elements of curiosity presuppose an infinite expansion and the king could see the whole universe at his feet inasmuch as the world of beings, the life of the sea and the whole universe at large being compounded in an urgent comprehensible variety, for the matter that, Śrī Viṣṇu, Agastya and Arjuna, the god, the saint and the warrior have become

8. *Mudrārākṣasa* of Viśākhadatta with the commentary of Dhundhiraj, ed. with critical and explanatory notes by Kashinath Trimbak Telang, revised by V.S. Ghote, Nag Publishers, Delhi, 1985, p. 580.

the one and all. This is once again the suggestive position of coherence purported and perpetuated through infinite oppositional signifiers (Śrī Viṣṇu, the god and Arjuna, the warrior are distinctly contradicted) and therefore, the possibility of realisation of a divisive experience rather than adding, subtracts and therefore, instead of addition of the terms we can understand that there is a reduction in the contents of the formation. Similarly, the object's position is also uncertain inasmuch as the sight before him and the local terms of comprehension are inadequately stretched, and once again, a reverted opposition of the conceptual forms takes place; for example at the very beginning the king is led to unbelievable *realisation* "स्वयमपि विसिस्मिये भूपालः (*svayamapi visismiye bhūpālaḥ*)" continuity of the situation is obtained in distinct contradistinction inasmuch as could say and suggest "युगादौ निष्पतन्तं जीवलोकं, अम्भो-निधिमिव कुम्भभुवो (*yugadau niṣpatantaṁ jīvalokaṁ, ambho-nidhimiva kumbhabhuvo*)"and "अर्जुनवाहुदण्डसहस्रस-पिण्डितोन्मुक्तमिव (*arjunavāhudaṇḍasahasrasaṁpiṇḍitonmuktamiva*)" — thus the form of content and the manner of progression both suggest how the universal form always attaches itself to infinity and the realisable version of experience finds its way in the ordinary strength of perception and accordingly as Derrida suggests, there cannot be any signification as such, however total the situation may be.

The effect of coherence in artistic situation has also uncertain pursuits and motives because of the fact that it always falls beyond the principle of conjunction; in fact the evidence of implication doesn't specifically allow a synthesis beyond the first phase of appearance, and accordingly, the strength of presentation and power of reception accumulated in the text and the reader both are displaced consistently till the time and event, each is returned and reversed, to its place of beginning. Foucault and Lacan would insist that method of construction of language or experience in an event would obviously facilitate the process of disintegration, primarily because the formal manner of the activity of the contents doesn't have any conscious appearance in the structural scheme because of the fact that inventory and participatory units within the language and experience are by nature random. Derrida could extend the point by questioning the ethical propriety of the following units of language and experience and there is always a suspicion and doubt about how a unit within the language could associate and correlate itself with a succeeding formation. Eventually, the realisable part of association is never made evident; for example, in *Daśakumāracarita* of Daṇḍin, the attention is fixed and situated on the continuous lapse of the recognisable situation:

(2) अवन्तिसुन्दरी-प्रेम-
अथ . . . मधुकरकलकण्ठानां काकलीकलकलेन दिक्चक्रं वाचालयन्, मानिनीमानसोत्कलिकामुपनयन्, माकन्द-सिन्दुवाररक्ताशोककिंशुकतिलकेषु कलिकामुपपादयन् मदनमहोत्सवाय रसिकमनांसि समुल्लासयन् वसन्तसमयः समाजगाम।[9]

— *Sanskrit Kāvyadhārā*, p. 508.

Spring season has come. . . . the sound of flute of the sweet humming of the wandering bees from all the directions was filling the hearts of the wives with desire. It was making happy the lovers of the Kāmadeva's (god of love) journey by growing flowers on the trees of Mākanda, Sinduwār, Red-Aśoka, Palāśa and Tilaka.

The meaning and significance of inversion is obviously the technical principle that Daṇḍin has introduced and evolved and accordingly time becomes an instrument of infinite correlation through which every creature of the world could be seen to be having meaning for it. To this extent the situation

9. *Mudrārākṣasa* of Viśākhadatta with the commentary of Dhundhiraj, ed. with critical and explanatory notes by Kashinath Trimbak Telang, revised by V.S. Ghote, Nag Publishers, Delhi, 1985, p. 508.

appears to be in conformity with the theory advanced by Lacan and Foucault, in which it is stated that the formal method purporting coherence and figural variants suggesting the conjunction of coherence are supposedly brought in the manner of oppositional systematisation and here in the present context the time of autumn associates itself with multiplicative conjunctions in such a way that the length and the extent of variation becomes really infinite in its suggestions. Moreover, Daṇḍin could enlist the fact that language as a content is standardised yet the underlying intensity of multiplication is obviously an accidental feature; for this reason he could say — अथ...मधुकरकलकण्ठानां काकलीकलकलेन दिक्चक्रं वाचालयन्, मानिनीमानसोत्कलिकामुपनयन्, माकन्दसिन्दुवाररक्ताशोककिंशुकतिलकेषु कलिकामुपपादयन् मदनमहोत्सवाय रसिकमनांसि समुल्लासयन् वसन्तसमयः समाजगाम। — The attitudes inherent upon an experience are deviated appreciably through the resultant margins, accordingly every movement is specific to the reception of the effect that it generates and the perspective of post-structuralism is thus established absolutely.[10]

The presentation of the strength and the worth of theoretical models in *rasa* and post-structuralist ideas invent a committed framework for the sake of a comprehension of the artistic situation although the merits involved in such a comprehension would be assuredly very different in accordance with the nature of transformation that *rasa* and post-structuralism envisage. In *rasa,* the distribution of the categories is absolute and the resolution of an object into event is always complete and total while in post-structuralism the construction of language and experience as primary tools of

10. To be able to say that in some canonical Sanskrit poetry/text the position of language and experience tends to be infinitely reduced is also to be able to state with conviction that stretch of enrichment and precision is so high and great that these categories in themselves become logically the marks of illusion.

conceptualisation undergoes extensive abortion through a constantly and abruptly interposed configuration. Looking at the situation we could only suggest that methods of comprehension and evaluation and organisation of the categories for the sake of artistic situation proposes different manner of ratiocination and in respect of *rasa,* the situation is definitely assertive while in post-structuralism it is indefinite and lacks a clarity about the basic constitution of the units of the categories.

Conclusion

THE creation of genuine artistic environment is suggested by the internal necessity of change of an object into an event, therefore, the meaning and significance of form are primarily determined in accordance with the intensity of such a formation. In *rasa,* the entire structure and transformation are evident in the formation of wholesome categories in the form of *bhāva, sthāyī bhāva, vibhāva, anubhāva, sañcārī bhāva, śabda, pada* and *vākya*. In each, it is important to understand that the composition of content and distribution of the content, both are directly proportional to each other, and for this reason the initiation of the creation of an artistic situation intends a specific motion and movement through a vertical disposition. *Bhāva,* in that context, becomes a chief instrument of diversifying and rearranging the contents. Accordingly, nine different states of distributive and synthesised situations are observed and in each the functional part and the conceptual part, both are inter-mutational and inter-substitutional. As a factor in the growth of the process of value-generation, *bhāva* procures a habit in the concretisation of the necessary figural length of the artistic formation. There cannot be any meaning in extending the credit of an observation that the deviance of the contents occasion in *bhāva* are re-asserted and re-invented only through the formation of a variety of attitudes, instincts, acts and intentions in the human consciousness, rather every generative part of *bhāva,* in itself, an assertive term of comprehension, cognition, synthesis, correlation, modelisation and the like.

II

The construction of the empirical categories in *rasa* determines the mode and manner of presentative and communicative discourses inasmuch as every category presupposes a largest possible structure for the functional universality, for example, in *sthāyī bhāva* the assessment of the content and resolution of the context both are so well transmuted into each other that the compulsory ratiocination begins right at the beginning. Primarily, the exceptional requirement due upon the process of change has an option of variety, hence, in *sthāyī bhāva* every attributive excellence, for example, *rati, hāsa, śoka, krodha, utsāha, bhaya, jugupsā, vismaya, nirveda* enters into a combination with the intensive and extensive universal that could be found within the situation and the shape of artistic form that emerges is a factual absolute of the given form. This assertion of similarity is achieved in other wholesome instances of category construction, and, to this extent, *vibhāvas — ālambana* and *uddīpana* are always conceived at the instance of a large-scale necessity to validate the process of inquisition brought about by changing structures within the categories. This is itself a point to prove that the coordinate occupied by the content in *vibhāva* is reciprocated to formal and figurative situation occurring in *anubhāva*. The comprehension and examination of the manner of assertion brought about by the situation attends the gradual evolution of *bhāva* into *sthāyī bhāva* and *sthāyī bhāva* into *vibhāva* and *vibhāva* into *anubhāva* and *anubhāva* into *sañcārī bhāva*, and, once, when the process is completed, the reverse of the situation, to intensify the enriched contents, begins. This reversibility of transformation is one of the unique events in the resolution part of an object into event and it keeps taking place till the concrete universal is indexed as a major form. This is actually what distinguishes *rasa* from other theories claiming similarity and correspondence. The exact methodology of the event of resolution could be determined in that the progress of a category towards concentration, rationalisation and ratiocination is validated through independent assortment in the first place and collective assertion in second place inasmuch as *bhāva, sthāyī bhāva, vibhāva* have an artistic environment exclusive to them, therefore, they conduct and explicate the contents, contexts and the mediums through their own assertive intentions and as a necessary corollary to this the synthesis is functionalised at the behest of immediate situation occurring within themselves. It must be understood that the role of content within *vibhāva* or *anubhāva* is to present the significance of reception and communication and remarkably the extent of reception is always equal to the magnitude of communication. It is invariably the situation that has its fundamental merits in assertion that situates *rasa* as a principle of transformation in which the intensity of concrete universals is realistically, practically, positionally and cognitively understood.

III

In post-structuralist situation advanced and supported by the ideational and ideological intentions of Derrida, Lacan and Foucault, the form of concept has a merit in the strength occupied by the diversification, deviance and divergence of the principal categories like language and experience. It is one of the best evidences of the idea that dissociative and disintegrative injunctions are always disoriented by a compulsory movement of spatial contents towards non-spatial medium. Post-structuralism, for this reason, is essentially a logical aspect of non-reception and non-communication of language through experience and language in experience inasmuch as each of these is having a specified universal and the creation of universal is very exclusive and specific to the legitimate environment of the immediate content participating in the process of movement from one direction to the other direction having more or less a similar configuration. This might be one of the reasons why the categories are denatured inasmuch as the cleavage principle approves the intra-polar movement of the whole formation. The effect and consequence of the situation is felt in the participating strength of the language and experience. The unit of language, is, by and large, not in accord with the posterior and exterior margins, and, because of this, a complete advancement in the scale of graduation of content does not take place, consequently, the intentional identity of the primitive from is retained and the direction of the movement is aberrated and lost by the virtue of an insignificant temperance of the inducted contents. Such a situation begets disproportionate and inconclusive scheme of communication and presentation. It is important to remember that Derrida, Foucault and Lacan have divested the linguistic and emotive forms of the necessary roles that they have for communication and for the same reason one cannot have any possibility of conjunction or injunction or even correlation at any point of time in the progress of an artistic event. The concentration of the contents in the medium and the context consumes the function of location and thus the situation evokes non-spatial inter-position through multiple association in multiple absolutes. To an extent, the corollary or assertive absolutes dispersed with such a great inter-spatial movement, strength is practically invalidated to reclaim the dimension of the situation. This problem has come to be effectively fixed as a principle in post-structuralism. The necessity of institutionalisation of the categories (language and experience) doesn't have a motive and perception, therefore, no expansion is either committed or manifested or evolved in the event in which the change of language and experience seem to be becoming an imminent possibility. Each of the theorists in post-structuralist tradition insists that only de-institutionalised version of formative principle in language and experience could come up for an assertion of a disintegrated and disassociated value and the emphasis to conjunct a primitive form with a primitive principle is really an event in the reorganisation of the whole apparatus of formation of the content. The manner in which the content, context, medium, object and the subject are reduced in an unassorted sequence is also noteworthy and recognisable. The progress of language as both cause and effect of resolution is deviated by an intended deformation of the necessary primordial forms, and therefore, the letter or the syllable that tends to unite become absolutely non-recognisable in themselves and the process that is generated in consequence is to be called relative or post-supposition of inversion.

In post-structuralism there cannot by any meaning that could be attached to the relevance of the object and the event, to say in other words, there cannot be any systematic object leading to homogeneous consequences hence to stable interrelationship in object and consequence rather the imminence of a category is justifiable only through an interpolation of unequal margins developed within the reality of object and event. We can think of certain advancement in this regard when and only when an institution or form like a complete thought and stable experience could operate within the limits of determinate content. Yet, however, the essential enrichment organised through regular disappearance denies the possibility of such an association. It appears to be quite convincing to state that development of enrichment as a thought motive does not take into consideration the constantly reducing contents, and therefore, a disassociation becomes evident as a rule in the whole situation.

The configuration of the categories brought about for the sake of the creation of an ideal artistic formation has its relevance and distinction in *rasa* and post-structuralist formations. In *rasa*, for example, every category (*bhāva*, *sthāyī bhāva, vibhāva, anubhāva, sañcārī bhāva, śabda, pada* and *vākya*) has a definite presentation in the form of geometrical figuration, therefore *bhāva* or *vibhāva* or *anubhāva,* becomes expressive and assertive even beyond the time they become engaged in an induction or deduction of comprehensible varieties of artistic situation. The advancement of structure as a necessary injunction in the evolution of both form and content has its beginning in the method oriented and scaled interaction between the strength of a category say *bhāva* and the projected perception of external manifestation. Therefore in *bhāva,* the pursuit of structure is definitely a relevance that one can attach to the growth of both conscious and unconscious facts within it. It is the primacy of the formative content that lends an extreme idealisation of the actual form that emerges shortly afterwards the progress of the situation. At the behest of the discharge of regular external association in synthesised and figural attributes, while figurative attributes are adequately refined and produced through perfect and quite appropriate role-models developed for such an enterprise. The effect of such a situation is felt in the creation of stable, authentic, total, pure, complete, assertive, denotative absolutes within each of the categories. In *bhāva, sthāyī bhāva, vibhāva, anubhāva, sañcārī bhāva, śabda, pada* and *vākya* we can understand that the form of category is essentially to beget an inventory of additive and multiplicative coordinates through which relative addition and relative multiplication could be genuinely conceived and created. In this regard we can state a principle to the effect that the structure of *bhāva,* of for that matter any other form, presupposes an intention to develop cumulative and relative inter-forms and the progression mutates through the forthcoming generation of significant contents.

In post-structuralism, on the other hand, the essential configuration of language and experience has a version of devolved generation of the structure; accordingly the effect, consequence, relation and generation of proposition that is likely to form an index of artistic habit is projected at the arithmetic centres in such a way that the projection itself becomes an event of non-reversion and linear accentuation. In language, for example, syllable or a letter or a word or even a sentence is not marked by expansion alone upward and downward, or, for that matter, horizontal and vertical situation rather both of these are so suppressed that an inter-function of excessive rationalisation comes up causing a deviance in the structural formation. In fact, synthesis isn't much the proposition that could be obtained through evolution of a situation in language and experience inasmuch as every situation is deduced only with regard to its immediate utility within the system and supposedly no significance whatsoever is obtained by conducting a movement of the generated content. Even, in experience, the logical aberration of evolution is so disengaged and non-interpretative that effect of consequence is not equal to the result of association obtained by a series of causal and supra-causal inter-functions. For this reason, Lacan tends to state time and again that signification of value is only an unrealistic motive until the time the conjunction of conscious and unconscious is not concretised the authority of value would be quite appropriately a contribution to division and inter-division within the form. The possibility of an injunction in interpreting the effect of a category on the suitability of result is one of the functions of the content models appropriately engaged in the formative codes. To suggest the point, we can state with conviction that index of experience through an instinct generated in perception and judgement of both cause and effect is heterogeneously deformed at the prospective phases of absolute formation, and therefore, their cannot be any structure that could be worked out to fully examine the possibility of coherence of the contents in the artistry. This insufficiency of the realisation of an interrelationship between object and subject may be the reason why introduction of language and experience doesn't really intend the beginning of artistic manner with a rationalisation of an action. Even while a purpose is indicated for the sake of a change in the process and procedure of remodelling the structure of beginning with an assurance of no primitive function, the decay of a category is casually concretised. This is what, in modernist vocabulary, is considered as a lack of movement on the part of value-generating units. To account for post-structuralism in that way will be only to find out how greater is the length of reduction of the contents when significance is proposed to be obtained by the virtue of language-experience or experience-language correlation. In either of the cases, there cannot be a definite manner to find out how and why language initiated its contents (syllable, letter, word, sentence) or experience reinvented itself appropriately or inappropriately through conducted models. It is, perhaps, not possible to find out any answer to these problems.

IV

Generation of value quite realistically is one of the goals of *rasa* and post-structuralist theories. In *rasa*, the values are generated through an exact and pure correlation and interrelationship between object, subject, medium and the context and therefore the *rasa* as an effective theory builds up a rather strong synthesis of *bhāva* in *sthāyī bhāva*, *sthāyī bhāva* in *vibhāva*, *vibhāva* in *anubhāva*, *anubhāva* in *sañcārī bhāva*. The process of invention and re-invention in relative and cumulative manner is always characterised by reversibility and for this reason it would be possible to suggest a term in *bhāva* through *sthāyī bhāva* or for that matter *anubhāva* through *vibhāva*. This idea of cumulative correspondence originating in the first term and culminating in the last term is, in fact, continuity of categorical perfection intended and explicated as a concrete scheme of presentation. This is eventually an event that leads to the creation of structure of knowledge in the form of pure, indivisible, trans-impersonal, wonder-giving forms. The function of these structures of knowledge is supposedly the best contribution of *rasa* as a theory of artistic creation. In an artistic event, the comprehensibility of object and subject manifested through the structure and form, becomes one of the conditions through which the excellence and enrichment of an artistic situation is determined and *rasa* really comes to fulfil this conditionality by the virtue of synthesis, cognition, correlation, comprehension of the contents that it tends to introduce even as a structure, the purity of presented and exposed contents could be very well obtained inasmuch as the very beginning of *rasa* marks a corresponding initiation of the evolutionary principle in *bhāva* and *śabda, pada* and *vākya* and it continues till we arrive at the successful comprehension, of the textual interrelationship that has been built around the artistic form. It would mean that significance of *rasa* is appropriately examined even beyond completion of a rational event and for this purpose we will have to concede the purity of native forms obtained within the structure of *rasa*.

In post-structuralism the intention of generation of value within the limit prescribed and fixed by observed, introduced and explicated units, is a matter, just of homogeneous succession. To this extent we can build up an idea as to how and why a unit of language, say, letter or word or a syllable and a construct of experience, say, feeling could absolve itself and divest itself through empirical conditions found within the total category. The position of language is such that it cannot either conduct or regulate spatial motion since the external space is not observed or fixed as a frame of reference in categorically specifying the nature of medium. For this reason form of letter, or syllable or word or even feeling would continue to be spread upon diversified asymmetrical, arithmetical coordinates; accordingly, there cannot be any visible correspondence between the formal methods and the figural forms. This brings forth the imbalance in presentation of the content and reception of the presented context, accordingly, when a syllable with an intention to find out an equivalent value for itself makes the movement, the associative injunctions in feeling or emotion do not really beget an event of resolution. This ground is justified inasmuch as the value, in itself, is only a probability built around a supposed conjunction between sign and signifier, yet no such possibility could be made to be evident.

V

The universality of structures of knowledge obtains methodical evidence through substantial recognition of enriched, comprehensible, meaningful and purer categorisation of participating categories and the models. To this end, in *rasa*, the generative principle is so effective that it could randomly or concretely devise an accurate configuration of meaning and knowledge-oriented functions. For example, the effective realisation would make the experience so canonical and so idealised that it would distribute the aspects of indivisibility in the first place, through the functional and non-functional segments of the creativity in that every content is resumed as a principle of formation, and therefore, between the text and the reader or even in the text and in the reader, there would be no inter-functional gap of division as such. The presentation and reception of *bhāva* is such that it would credit the terms of perception in a thorough-going communicative situation. It would mean that the effect of presentation of *bhāva* on an intense situation occurring on behalf of an artistic situation would immediately receive and communicate the content without either displacing or marginalising the terms of the situation. The chain of correlation so established will have a bearing on synthesis and exposition. On the other hand, besides indivisibility, the predominance of inter-modellised refinement of the categories brings forth the situation of trans-impersonality in such a way that the absolute purity of received form is made more expressive in the communicative aspect in such a way that the separation of object as object and an object as subject is not distinct, rather only the concentrated form of refined object is at once perceptible. This event is also situated homogeneously in other suitable evidences of comprehension and realisation like the creation of the effect of wonder, self-illumination, surprise and the like. In each of these the intensity of resolution is so high and so appropriate that the expressive forms are immediately recognised and suitably idealised. The principle of knowledge in relation to *rasa*, is, in fact, an idea that suggests how the beginning of refinement in a category could be continued till the end and without any recognisable lapse of function suitably revived in the beginning. Such a concomitance and perpetuation of heterogeneous and homogeneous experience establishes *rasa* as a theory of infinite comprehension of knowledge form precisely because cognition, perception, intention, denotation and suggestion are manifest in the entire scheme of presentation.

In post-structuralist theories, the manner of comprehension brings about the construction of an aberration between reception, presentation and communication of language and experience; hence the necessity of forming an interpretation through judgement, cognition and comprehension is obviously deviated. In language, for example, the stationary motives of the term finds an invalid distribution in the units, and, on that account, the recognition of evidence and realisation of evidence, both are at variance with each other. Similarly, in experience, the interception of unconscious sensation and its prolonged rarefaction through sub-conscious and conscious ultimately disposes experience through distinct division and does not leave even a fraction of quotient for realisation inasmuch as divisions are so abrupt, immediate and forthwith that retention of value is not exactly possible. Lacan understands this and Foucault and Derrida support the conviction.

VI

The idea of communication is invariably one of the important principles of the conceptualisation of form and structure of *rasa*. Such a situation is brought about by the availability of comprehensible form at every juncture of transformation. The method of organisation of the categories is such that it is open to complete reception on the part of the reader and inadvertently the situation is concretised as immediately as it is refined and presented for the purview of the reader. It must be stated with conviction that length of concretisation in *bhāva, sthāyī bhāva, vibhāva, anubhāva, sañcārī bhāva, śabda, pada* and *vākya* is so harmonious and so excellent that the reader has an option to respond to both verbal and non-verbal forms hidden in the denotative and suggestive figuration of the categories. The authority of perception brought about by the advancement of effective judgement is proportionately and constitutively so evolved that the reader himself finds an opportunity to substantiate a condition of judgement through the necessary conditions open for the sake of his presentation. It is, for this reason, that the interpretation of *rasa* is realised in immediate as well as permanent forms of universal knowledge and such theoretical and practical instances of concentrated and composite cognition are rare in the Eastern and the Western theoretical models.

In post-structuralism the act of communication isn't evolved to an extent that it could invite the merit of attention simply for the reason that the language units like letters, syllables, words and experiential factors like sensation and perception are suppressed and denoted at the random as figures and the instances, for example, the valuation of any unit of language through additive signifiers or multiplicative signs does not bring about any suitable fact of value since each originates with either an apostrophe or an inversion or a question. This further implicates the necessity of disintegration that begins at the beginning and does not end at the end rather it is bound upon the question of value pre-fixed in each circumstance of inversion and apostrophe, therefore, the act of communication doesn't call for a favour of presentation through noteworthy circumstances obtained in human perception and human consciousness.

VII

Theoretical models purported for examination, evaluation and interpretation in *rasa* and principles of post-structuralism consciously motivate the choice for favour, preference, selection and determination of the inherent conceptual models. In *rasa*, we can understand that cognition, comprehension, conjunction, correlation and preposition of the categories and the contents of knowledge, is, at once realisable and could be expressed in both local and universal circumstances of perception while, on the other hand, in post-structuralism the indifference of selection of a content for the sake of its interpretative, presentative and communicative figuration is both logically and rationally an invalid situation and leads to comprehensible indetermination of both language and experience. Even beyond this the resolution of categories in *rasa* in the manner of change of an object into event is so pure, so absolute, so synthesised and so cognised that difference between object and subject is not maintained while in post-structuralism the resolution is always deviated inasmuch as contents are stationary and the displacement of content of language via construct obtained in experience is generated only in infinite division leading to an aberration. While we look at the situations at work, we will have to concede that *rasa* is the best theoretical principle for the creation, comprehension, realisation of an ideal artistic situation while post-structuralist theories of Derrida, Lacan and Foucault propose unasserted and incoherent models of change which till now, are only unconsciously felt and understood.

Glossary

ālasya	indolence
āścarya	wonder, astonishment, marvel
āvega	agitation
adbhuta	wonder as sentiment
ālambana vibhāva	stimulus
amarṣa	indignation
anubhāva	emotional reaction
apasmāra	epilepsy
aśru	tears
asūyā	envy
autsukya	inquisitiveness
avahita	concealment
bhāva	emotion
bhaya	dread, alarm, fear, anxiety
bhayānaka	fear, terror as sentiment
bībhatsa	disgust as a sentiment
capalatā	waywardness
cintā	sorrow
dainya	piteousness
dhṛti	courage
garva	arrogance
glāni	depression
harṣa	joy
hāsa	laughing, laughter, merriment
hāsya	laughed at; laughable, ridiculous, jest, joke,fun
jaḍatā	stupor
jugupsā	disgust, aversion

karuṇa	the pathetic sentiment, pathos
krodha	anger
mada	intoxication
mahāpralaya	deluge, great dissolution of the universe
maraṇa	death
mati	knowledge
moha	passion
nidrā	sleep
nirveda	indifference
pada	quarter-verse
pralaya	swoon
rasa	sentiment, relish
rasa-niṣpattiḥ	*rasa* realisation
rati	pleasure, enjoyment, satisfaction
raudra	the terrible, anger as a sentiment
romāñca	horripilation
śabda	sound, word, language
śama	peace
saṁyoga	union
Saṁyogaśr̥ṅgāra	love in union
sahyogā	union of
*sañcārī bhāva*s	transitory emotion
saṅkā	doubt
śānta	bliss, calm or compose as sentiment
*sāttvika bhāva*s	emotion indicating an inward feeling or sentiment
smr̥ti	recollection
śoka	anguish, sorrow, grief
spuṭa	dream
śrama	weariness
śr̥ṅgāra	the erotic sentiment
stambha	torpidity
sthāyībhāva	abiding emotion
svarabhaṅga	change in tone
sveda	perspiration
trāsa	fright

uddīpana vibhāva	stimulant
ugratā	ferocity
unmāda	insanity
utsāha	high spiritedness
vaivarṇya	discolouration
vākya	utterance, speech of words
vepathu	trembling
vibhāva	stimulus provided by characters and excitants
vibodha	awakening
vīra	valour as sentiment
viṣāda	despair
vismaya	surprise, wonder, amazement, pride
vitarka	deliberation
viyogaśṛṅgāra	love-in-separation
vrīḍa	shame
vyādhi	sickness
Vyabhicārī	transitory emotion

Bibliography

Western Poetry and Criticism

Alighieri, Dante, 1910, *The Divine Comedy,* translated by Henry Francis Cary with 109 illustrations by John Flaxman, Geoffrey Cumberlege, Oxford University Press, Amen House, London E.C.4.

Alonso, Carlos J., 2002, *Editor's Column: Position Paper,* PMLA: Publications of the Modern Language Association of America, 117, 201-06.

Arnold, Matthew, 1964, *Essays in Criticism: First and Second Series.* London: J M Dent.

Bach, Richard, 1970, *Jonathan Livingston Seagull,* New York: Avon Books.

Beran, David, 2001, *Early British Romanticism, the Frankfurt School, and French Post-Structuralism: In the Wake of Failed Revolution,* Studies on Themes and Motifs in Literature, 53 (New York: Peter Lang.)

Bosnaquet, Bernard, 1911, *Logic or the Morphology of Knowledge* in 2 vols. Oxford: Clarendon Press.

Bradley, F.H., 1927, *Ethical Studies,* Oxford: Clarendon Press.

———, 1914, *Essays on Truth and Reality,* Oxford: Clarendon Press.

———, 1922, *Principles of Logic* in 2 vols., Oxford: Clarendon Press.

———, 1930, *Appearance and Reality,* Oxford: Clarendon Press.

Butcher, S.H., (tr. & ed.), 1981, *Aristotle's Theory of Poetry and Fine Art,* —— Delhi: Kalyani Publications.

Calvino, Italo, 1983, *Difficult Loves,* Minerva.

Camus, Albert, 1975, *"The Myth of Sysiphus",* in *The Myth of Sysiphus,* tr. Justin O'Brien, London: Penguin.

Culler, J., 1981, *The Pursuit of Signs: Semiotics, Literature & Deconstruction,* London: Faber & Faber.

———, 1983, *On Deconstruction: Theory and Criticism after Structuralism,* London: Routledge.

Culler, Jonathan, 2001, *The Pursuit of Signs,* Routledge Classics, London EC_4p_4EE.

———, 2001, *The Pursuit of Signs: Semiotics, Literature, Deconstruction, Augmented*, ed. with a new Preface by the author, Ithaca, NY: Cornell University Press.

Daiches, D., 1982, *Critical Approaches to Literature*, Longmans: London.

Das, Vihar Kumar, 1996, *Twentieth Century Literary Criticism*, New Delhi: Atalantic Publishers and Distributers.

De Saussure, Ferdinand, 1916, *Course in General Linguistics*, London: Fontana.

Derrida, Jacques, 1976, *Of Grammatology*, tr. Gayatri Chakravorty, Spivak, Baltimore and London: The John Hopkins University Press.

———, 2001, *Writing and Difference*, tr. Alan Bass, 'L'écriture et la différence'. Paris : Éditions du Seuil, 1967, Routledge Classics, London EC_4p_4EE.

Donne, John, 2000, *Elegies and The Songs and Sonnets*, ed. Helen Gardner, Oxford University Press.

———, 1896, *Poems of John Donne*, vol. II, E.K. Chambers, ed., London: Lawrence and Bullien.

Eagleton, T., 1983, *Literary Theory: An Introduction*, London, Basil Blackwell.

Eliot, T.S., 1933, *Use of Poetry and Use of Criticism*, London: Faber & Faber.

———, 1952, *Selected Essays*, London: Faber & Faber.

———, 1952, *The Complete Poems and the Plays*, New York: Harcourt, Brace and Co.

———, 1978, *To Criticize The Critic*, London: Faber & Faber.

Fitz, Earl E., 2001, *Sexuality and Being in the Poststructuralist Universe of Clarice Lispector: The Differance of Desire*, Austin, TX: University of Texas Press.

Foucault, Michel, 1972, *The Archaeology of Knowledge*, tr. from French by A.M. Sheridan Smith, Tavistock Publications, London EC_4p_4EE.

Ginesberg's Allen, 1974, *Howl' in Ronald Gottesman's The Norton Anthology of American Literature*, vol. 2, *1865 to Present*, Yeats, William Butler: Selected Poetry, London: Pan Books.

George, Luis Borges, 1971,*The Book of Sand*, tr. Norman Thomas di, Giovanni, London: Penguin.

Groden, M. and Kreiswirth, M. 1994 (eds.), *The Johns Hopkins Guide to Literary Theory and Criticism*, Baltimore.

Guerin, Wilfred L., 1992, et al. *A Handbook of Critical Approaches to Literature*, Oxford: Oxford University Press.

Han-Shan, 1992, *Cold Mountain*, translated by Burton Watson, Boston: Shambhala.

Hänninen, Ukko, 1999."Poststructuralism and the Rebirth of the Author", in *Proceedings from the 7th Nordic Conference on English Studies*, ed. Sanna-Kaisa Tanskanen & Brita Warvik, Turku, Finland: University of Turku.

Harland, R., 1987, *The Philosophy of Structuralism and Post-Structuralism.* Methuen: London.

Hemingway, Ernest, 1970, *The Old Man and the Sea*, Delhi: Surjeet Publishers.

Hennelly, Mark M., Jr., 2001, *"Framing the Gothic: From Pillar to Post-Structuralism"*, *College Literature*, 28 68-87.

Hornby, A.S., 2000, *Oxford Advanced Learner's Dictionary of Current English*, 6th edn. Sally Wehmeler, Phonetics ed. Michael Ashby, Oxford: Oxford University Press.

Jameson, F., 1972, *The Prison-House of Language*, New Jersey: Princeton University Press.

Juvan, Marko, 2003, "On Literariness: From Post-Structuralism to Systems Theory", in *Comparative Literature and Comparative Cultural Studies*, ed. Steven Totosy de Zepetnek West Lafayette: Purdue University Press, pp. 76-96.

Kafka, Franz, 1904-1924, *Franz Kafka: Stories* tr. Eloise Roach, Nobel Prize Books.

Kurzweil, E., 1980, *The Age of Structuralism: Lévi-Strauss to Foucault*, New York: Columbia University Press.

Lacan, Jacques, 1989, *ò critis: A Selection*, trs. Alan Sheridan, Routledge Classics, London EC_4p_4EE.

Lawrence, Karen R., 2000, *Postpoststructuralist Administration: A User's Manual, ADE Bulletin*, 126, 18-21.

Lennard, J., 1996, *The Poetry Handbook: A Guide to Reading Poetry for Pleasure and Practical Criticism*, Oxford, Oxford University Press.

Lentricchia, F. and McLaughlin, T., 1995, *Critical Terms for Literary Study*, University of Chicago Press.

Levin, H., 1966, *What Was Modernism? in Refractions: Essays in Comparative Literature*, New York: Oxford University Press.

Lodge, D., 1966, *Language of Fiction: Essays in Criticism and Verbal Analysis of the English Novel*, New York: Columbia University Press.

Longenbach, J., 1997, *Modern Poetry after Modernism*, Oxford University Press.

Lurie, Susan et al. 2001, *"Restoring Feminist Politics to Poststructuralist Critique"*, *Feminist Studies*, 27, 679-707.

Herbert J.C. Griersonp, 1921, *Metaphysical Lyrics & Poems of the 17th Century* vol. VII.

Miall, David S., and Don Kuiken, 1998, *"The Form of Reading: Empirical Studies of Literariness"*, *Poetics*, 25, 327-41.

Milton John, 1968, *The Poems of John Milton*, ed. John Carey and Alastair Fowler, New York: Longman Group Limited.

Moulthrop, Stuart, 2002, "Testing the Wires", *in Reimagining Textuality: Textual Studies in the Late Age of Print*, ed. Elizabeth Bergmann Loizezux and Neil Fraistat Madison, WI: University of Wisconsin Press, pp. 225-40.

Newman, Saul, 2000, *"Universalism/Particularism: Towards a Poststructuralist Politics of Universality"*, *New Formations*, 41, 95-108.

Norman, Renee, 2001, *House of Mirrors: Performing Autobiograph(icall)y in Language/Education, Counterpoints*, Studies in the Postmodern Theory of Education, 146, New York: Peter Lang.

Norris, C., 1982, *Deconstruction: Theory and Practice*, London: Methuen.

Poetical Works of John Keats, 1895, ed. Buxton Forman, Crowell Publication.

Pope Alexander and Tillotson Geoffrey, 2004, *The Rape of the Lock*, 3rd edn., revised, Routledge.

Regard, Frederic, 2000, *"The Ethics of Biographical Reading: A Pragmatic Approach"*, *Cambridge Quarterly*, 29, 394-408.

Shakespeare William, 1821, *The Plays and Poems of William Shakespeare*, by James Boswell, Edmond Malone, Alexander Pope, Samuel Johnson, William Warburton, Edward Capell, Theobald (Lewis), George Steevens, Richard Farmer, Thomas Hanmer, Nicholas Rowe, Isaac Reed, Arthur Brooke, George Chalmers, Pub. R.C. and J. Rivington.

Spolsky, Ellen, 2002, *"Darwin and Derrida: Cognitive Literary Theory as a Species of Post-Structuralism"*, *Poetics Today*, 23, 43-62.

The Complete Works of William Shakespeare 1961, (The Oxford Shakespeare), ed. with a glossary by W.J. Craig, Oxford University Press, Scene VI — The same: Before the Castle (Act I Macbeth).

Victor E. Taylor, Charles E. Winquist, 1998, *Post-Modernism: Critical Concepts*, Taylor & Francis Publication.

William, Blake, 1966, *Complete Writings*, ed. Geoffrey Keynes, Oxford University Press.

Sanskrit Poetics and Criticism

A Monograph on Bharata's Nāṭyaśāstra, 1967, (*Indian Dramatology*), tr. in English by P.S.R. Appa Rao and P. Śrī Rama Sastry, Naatya Maalaa Publishers, Hyderabad.

Abhinavagupta (10th century BCE) *Abhinavabhāratī*, (tr. and ed.) Delhi: University of Delhi Press.

Abhinavagupta, 1965, *Locana with Prakāśa, Hindi Translation of Dhvanyāloka by Ācārya Jagannātha Pathak,* Varanasi: Chowkhamba Vidya Bhavan.

Ānandavardhana, 1971, *Dhavnyāloka,* New Delhi: Motilal Banarsidass.

Appayya Dixita, 1976, (16th century BCE) *Kuvalayānanda,* tr. Dr. Bhola Shankar Vyas with Alamkarsurabhi Hindi Vyākhyā, Varanasi: Chowkhamba Vidya Bhavan.

———, Citramīmāṁsā, (ed.) Jagdish Chandra Mishra with the Sudha Sanskrit Commentary of Dharanananda, 1971, Varanasi: Chowkhamba Sanskrit Sansthan.

Aśvaghoṣa: 1970, *The Buddhacarita, The Bible of the World,* ed. Robert O Ballow, et. al., New York: Avon Books.

Bāna's *Kādambarī* 1968, [Pūrvabhāga complete] ed. Late M.R. Kāle, Delhi: Motilal Banarsidass.

Bhāmah, *Kāvyālaṁkāra,* tr. Davendra Nath Sharma, 1962, Patna: Bihar Rashtra Bhasa Parishad.

Bharatamuni, *Nāṭyāśāstra,* ed. Madhusudan Shastri, vol. 1 and vol. 2, Banaras: Kashi Hindu Vishwavidyalaya.

Bhartṛhari's 1961, *Niti-Śṛṅgāra-Vairāgya Śatkatrayam,* Sanskrit ṭīkā, Bhāsaṭīkā sameta, Mumbai: Sri Venkateshawar Steam Press.

———, 1980, *Vākyapadīyam, Part I and II with commentary of Pūṇyarāja and Ambakartrī by Pt. Raghunath Sharma,* Varanasi: Sampurnanand Sanskrit Vishwavidyalaya.

Bhoja, 1979, *Sarasvatīkaṇṭhabharaṇa,* ed. Vishwanatha Bhattacharya, Varanasi: Banaras Hindu University Sanskrit Series.

Bucknell, R.S., 1991, *Sanskrit Manual: A Quick-Reference Guide to the Phonology and Grammar of Classical Sanskrit,* Delhi: Motilal Banarsidass.

Chaturvedi, B.M., 1996, *Some Unexplored Aspects of the Rasa Theory,* tr. P. Sri Ramachandrudu, Delhi: Vidyanidhi Prakashan.

Daśarūpaka of Dhanañjaya, by George C.O. Haas, 1962, Varanasi: Motilal Banarsidass.

Daśarūpaka of Dhanañjaya with *Avaloka* of Dhanika, ed. R.S. Tripathi, Varanasi: Vishwavidyalaya Prakashan.

De, S.K. 1959, *Some Problems of Sanskrit Poetics,* Calcutta: Firma KLM.

———, 1960, *History of Sanskrit Poetics,* Calcutta: Firma KLM.

De, S.K. and Gerow, E., 1963, *Sanskrit Poetics as a Study of Aesthetic,* University of California Press.

Dhanañjaya, (11th century BCE) 1955, *Daśarūpaka* with Candrakala Hindi Vyākhyā, ed. Bhola Shankar Vyas, Varanasi: Chowkhamba Sanskrit Series,

Gajendragadkar, A.B., 1962, *The Abhijñānaśākuntala of Kālidāsa*, 7th edn. Surat: The Popular Book Store.

Gaṅgānāthajhā-Granthamālā (vol. 14), *Nāṭyaśāstra of Bharatamuni* (Part Two) with *Abhinavabhāratī* by Abhinavaguptācārya & *Manoramā* (Hindi Commentary) by Pārasanātha Dvivedī, 1996, ed. Pārasanātha Dvivedī, Varanasi: Sampurnanand Sanskrit University. p. 131.

Gnoli, Piers, 1950, *The Aesthetic Experience according to Abhinavgupta*, Varanasi: Chowkhamba Sanskrit Series.

Gupta, Rakesh, 1950, *Psychological Studies in Rasa*, Aligarh: Laxmi Narayan Agrawal.

Iyer, Soubramania, K.A. Bhartṛhari, 1997, *A Study of Vākyapadīya in the Light of Ancient Commentaries*, Poona: Deccan College Postgraduate Research Institute.

Jha, Bechan, 1956, *Concept of Poetic Blemishes in Sanskrit Poetics*, Varanasi: Chowkhamba Sanskrit Series.

Kapoor, K. 1990, *"Some Reflections on the Interpretation of Texts in the Indian Tradition"*, in H.S. Gill (ed.) *Journal of School of Languages/ Structures of Signification*, vol. I pp. 208-86, New Delhi: Jawaharlal Nehru University; Willey Eastern Ltd.

Krishnamoorthy, K. (tr.), *Dhvanyāloka of Ānandavardhana*, Delhi: Motilal Banarsidass.

———, 1964, *Essays in Sanskrit Criticism*, Dharwar: Karnataka University Press.

Kuntak (10th century BCE), 1961, *The Vakroktijīvita of Kuntaka*, ed. S.K. De, Calcuta: Firma KLM.

Kuppuswamisastri S., *Highways and Byways of Literary Criticism in Sanskrit* (K.S.R.Institute) — rpt. 1993, Madras: Paprinpack (Printers), Kuppuswami Sastri Research Institute, (1st edn. 1988).

Macdonell, Arthur A., 1893, *Sanskrit English Dictionary*, London: Longmans, Green, and Co.

Mahāmahopādhyāya Sir Ganganatha Jha, 1996, *Kāvyaprakāśa of Mammaṭa* with English Translation (revised), Varanasi: Bharatiya Vidya Prakashan, pp. 63-64.

Mahimbhaṭṭa, *Vyakti Viveka*, Varanasi: Chowkhamba Sanskrit Series.

Mammaṭa, (11th century BCE), 1985, *Kāvyaprakāśa*, tr. & ed. Sir G.N. Jha, New Delhi: Bharatiya Vidya Bhavan.

Masson J.L. and M.V. Patwardhan, 1970, *Aesthetic Rapture*, 2 vols., Poona: Deccan College, vol. 1.

———, *Śānta Rasa and Abhinavagupta's Philosophy of Aesthetics*, 1969, Bhandarkar Oriental Series no. 9, Poona: Bhandarkar Oriental Research Institute.

Mukherjee, Subdhachandra, 1926, *Rasādhyāya*, On the Sentiments, with Abhinavabharati Calcutta: Sri Satguru Publications.

Mukhopadhyaya, K.L., 1959, *Some Problems of Sanskrit Poetics*, Calcutta: Contains many important articles, Enright D.J. and Chickera De Ernest.

Pandey, Kanti Chandra, 1972, *Comparative Aesthetics, vol. II*: Western Aesthetics, The Chowkhamba Sanskrit Series Office (Publishers and Oriental & Foreign Booksellers), Varanasi.

Pandey, K.C., 1972, *Comparative Aesthetics, vol. II*: Indian Aesthetics, The Chowkhamba Sanskrit Studies vol. IV, Varanasi.

Panditraj Jagannatha (17th century BCE), *Rasagaṅgādhara*, ed. Madhusudan Shastri with Marmaprakash of Nagesha Bhatta, Varanasi: B.H.U. Press.

Ranade, R.D., 1968, *A Constructive Survey of Upanisadic Philosophy*, Bombay: Bhartiya Vidya Bhavan.

Ruyyaka, Rajanaka, 1971 *Alaṁkārasarvasva & Maṅkha with the Vimarśinī of Jayarath*, tr. Rewa Prasad Dwivedi, Varanasi: Chowkhamba Sanskrit Series.

Rajaśekhar (9th century BCE) 1965, *Kāvyamīmāṁsā*, ed. Pt. Kedarnath Sharma, Patna: Bihar Rashtra Bhasa Parishad.

Sāhityadarpaṇa of Viśvanāth Kavirāja with Vimalā 1956, (Hindi commentary) by Śrī Śalgramshastri, Varanasi: Motilal Banarsidass.

Śakuntalā or the Recovered Ring, Six Sanskrit Plays in English tr. ed. Henry W. Wells, 1964, New York: Asia Publishing House, p. 201.

Sankrityayan, Rahul, 1957, *Sanskrit Kāvyadhārā*, Allahabad: Kitab Mahal, Sammelan Mudralaya, Prayag.

The Aesthetic Experience according to Abhinavagupta, Chowkhamba Sanskrit Studies vol. LXIII, Varanasi, 1968. (Second Edition revised Enlarged of the original, 1956, ISMEO Edition).

Tiwari, R. S., 1984, *A Critical Approach to Classical Indian Poetics*, Delhi: Chowkhamba Sanskrit Series.

Vāmana (8th century BCE) 1954, *Kāvyālaṁkāra Sūtra Vṛtti*, ed. Nagendra, Delhi: Atmaram & Sons.

Electronic Sources

Aeschylus, Agamemnon 2, Agamemnon Cont., tr. H.W. Smyth, Lines 1551 to 1559, www.theoi.com/Text AeschylusAgamemnon2.html.

Alcoholic poet dark blog in prose poetry, http://www.alcoholicpoet.com/2006/10/poverty.html

An Introduction by Sean Homer Routledge, 2004, *Metapsychology Online*

Reviews: Review by Sam Brown, Ph.D. 20 June 2006 (vol. 10, Issue 25), Review.

Beckett, Samuel, *Waiting for Godot - Act 3 - Waiting for . . . Mustadio* by Mark Matarazzo, http://raptox.us/fanfic/wfg3/wfg3.html

Beggar to Beggar Cried by William Butler Yeats, http://www.poemhunter.com/poem/beggar-to-beggar-cried/

Blake William (1757-1827) p. 1793, *Portable Poetry. . . .* poems from your pocket, The Portable poetry company, http://www.portablepoetry.com/poems/william_blake/ah_sunflower.html

Charles Baudlaire's Flowers of Evil, translated by William Aggeler, The Flowers of Evil (Fresno, CA: Academy Library Guild, 1954) http://www.fleursdumal.org/poem/119.

Coleridge, Samuel Taylor, *The Rime of the Ancient Mariner*, Electronic Text Center, University of Virginia Library, http://etext.virginia.edu/toc/modeng/public/Col2Mar.html, p. 25-26.

D.H. Lawrence, *Full Text of Love Poems and Others*, Duckworth and Co. Covent Garden, London MCMXIII Love in the Farm: 'Cruelty and Love', http://www.archive.org/stream lovepoemsothers 00lawrrich/lovepoemsothers00lawrrich_ djvu.txt

Eliot, T.S. *The Hollow Men*, American Poems, http://www.americanpoems.com/poets/tseliot/1076.

Gilbert, W.S., *When I, Good friends, was called to Bar*, Full Text of W.S. Gilbert, http://www.archive.org/stream wsgilbert00049 1mbp/wsgilbert000491mbp_djvu.txt

Jacques Lacan, *Philosophy*, http://metapsychology.mentalhelp.net/poc/view_doc.php?type=book&id=3154&cn=394

Jones, Roger, "Post Structuralism", in *Philosophy since the Enlightenment*, <http://www.philosopher.org.uk> [accessed 18 December 2003]

Mayakovsky, Vladimir, *The Cloud in Pants*, Adapted from the Russian by Augustus Young, ARS Interpres, An International Journal of Poetry Translation & Art, http://www.arsint.com/2006/v_m_6.html

Owen Wilfred, (1893-1918): *Futility*, http://users.fulladsl.be/spb1667/cultural/owen/futility.html

———, (1893-1918), *Strange Meeting, deviantART*: geaannunziata journal, http://geaannunziata.deviantart.com /journal/22625525/

Pablo Neruda's *'Adonic Angela', 1904-1973*, http://www.pierdelune.com/neruda9.htm

Rainer Maria Rilke, *"The Beggar's Song"*, *Poetry Connection*, http://www.poetryconnection.net/poets/Rainer_Maria_Rilke/3230

Rimbaud, *Selected Poems, "The Sly Girl"* A. S. Kline © 2002, 2008 http://www.poetryintranslation.com/PITBR/French/Rimbaud1.htm

———, *Selected Poems, "The Song of the Highest Tower"* A. S. Kline ©2002,2008 http://www.poetryintranslation.com/PITBR/French/Rimbaud1.htm#_Toc196916307

Roland Barthes Mythologies, translated by Annette Lavers, Hill and Wang, New York, 1984 MYTH TODAY, The Athenaeum Library, Athenaeum Reading Room http://evans-experientialism.freewebspace.com/barthes04.htm

Rumi's Divan of Shems of Tabriz: Selected Odes (*Element Classics of World Spirituality*) by Jalal Al-Din Rumi (author), Maulana Jalaluddin Rumi (author), James Cowan (author, translator) *Love Poems of Rumi*, http://www.khamush.com/love_poems.html

Silverstein,Shel, *Poems and Drawings*; http://www.poets.org/viewmedia.php/prmMID/16480

Tamilrorrents, *Poems Love & Friendship, Love, She Couldn't Stand the Silence*, http://www.tamiltorrents.net/forums/archive/index.php/t-8656.html

The Victorian Web, http://www.victorianweb.org/authors/tennyson/ulyssestext.html

Index